『谨以此书纪念博士毕业十周年及云览信通成立五周年』

THIS BOOK IS DEDICATED TO
MY 10TH ANNIVERSARY OF RECEIVING THE DOCTOR DEGREE OF MANAGEMENT
AND THE 5TH ANNIVERSARY OF inforLane TECHNOLOGY

信誉的成本

——源于服务失误的管理策略工程研究

THE COST OF CREDIBILITY

— A STUDY OF MANAGEMENT STRATEGIES DERIVED FROM SERVICE FAILURES

李瑾　著

图书在版编目（CIP）数据

信誉的成本：源于服务失误的管理策略工程研究 / 李瑾著．—天津：天津大学出版社，2017.6

ISBN 978-7-5618-5857-8

Ⅰ．①信… Ⅱ．①李… Ⅲ．①移动通信－运营管理－研究－中国 Ⅳ．①F632

中国版本图书馆 CIP 数据核字 (2017) 第 119063 号

策划编辑 金　磊 韩振平

责任编辑 郭　颖

装帧设计 陈凤美

版式设计 A.N.D.Y. 工作室

出版发行 天津大学出版社

地　　址 天津市卫津路 92 号天津大学内（邮编：300072）

电　　话 发行部：022-27403647

网　　址 publish.tju.edu.cn

印　　刷 北京信彩瑞禾印刷厂

经　　销 全国各地新华书店

开　　本 169mm × 229mm

印　　张 14.75

字　　数 210 千

版　　次 2017 年 6 月第 1 版

印　　次 2017 年 6 月第 1 次

定　　价 66.00 元

目录 CONTENTS

写在前面

时间回到了 10 年前。

2007 年 12 月 1 日，香港红磡体育馆。

从香港理工大学校长潘宗光（Poon Chung-kwong）教授手中接过毕业证书，随着校长把博士帽的流苏缓缓地从博士帽的右前方捋到左前方，预示着在历经了从 2004 年 11 月 18 日开始的 1108 个日日夜夜之后，我终于获得了由香港理工大学与中国人民大学联合颁发的“管理学博士（Doctor of Management）”学位。看着台下众多的校友、同学，还有亲人，我异常兴奋，同时伴随着莫大的激动，百感交集。回顾三年多的学习历程，真是人生中的又一次极限挑战。

尽管了解香港理工大学严谨的治学口碑并做了充分的心理准备，但治学道路上遇到的困难和压力依然远远超出了我的预料。当我身着博士华服沉浸在庄严的国歌声中时，付出和收获，使我终生无憾。

正如香港理工大学时任校长潘宗光教授在毕业典礼祝词中所说的："香港理工大学工商管理研究院自2003年成立以来，提供的课程品质不断提升，成绩屡攀高峰，现已成为亚太区一所优秀的工商管理研究院。研究院声誉日隆，除了学术水平屡获国际肯定外，其香港和内地毕业生在各自工作岗位均有出色的表现，亦是口碑载道的重要因素。毕业生不但具备丰富的专业知识，在工作上也充分显示出敏锐的商业触觉。"

由香港理工大学与中国人民大学合办的管理学博士（Doctor of Management）的目标是培养"学者型领袖"。香港理工大学工商管理博士及管理学博士课程总监费迪南德（Ferdinand A. Gul）教授如此说道："透过课程，学员都能以严谨的科学态度，结合最新的商业管理理论及思维，解决企业或社会面临的实际问题。日后，他们就能以高瞻远瞩的视野，为企业创造成功。因此，课程非常受高层管理人员欢迎，学员包括上市公司主席、跨国企业董事、执业会计师甚至政府的高级管理人员。"

项目结合知识，科研结合实践，通过培养高管人员发挥管理与应用的能力，从而推动企业的创新与发展，是我们每个管理学博士课程学员深刻的体会。参加到本课程的学员必须具有硕士学位，同时具备八年或以上高层管理经验者才有资格参与笔试和面试，这也是唯一获得国家教育部正式认证的中港合作管理学博士项目，同时，学位也得到了国家教育部的认证。

笔者在香港红磡体育馆参加香港理工大学第十三届毕业典礼，2007 年 12 月 1 日

"恭喜你，正式获得香港理工大学管理学博士学位！"伴随着潘校长深邃睿智

笔者与香港理工大学时任校长潘宗光教授在毕业典礼上亲切握手，2007 年 12 月 1 日

的目光，我们的手紧紧地握在一起，我的思绪也随之飘向远方。

2004 年 9 月 27 日，北京，西单某电信大楼。

怀着忐忑不安的心情来到了位于北京西单附近的一个电信运营商大楼。来这里是为了参加管理学博士入学电视电话面试。于面试前一天深夜才返回北京的我，是因为要在福建参加一个重要的客户会议。此时正值国内运营商大力发展移动通信以及相关的数字业务的关键阶段，巨大的市场及销售任务压得我们喘不过气来。在这期间，我在摩托罗拉担任销售总监职务。我作为摩托罗拉的高管，同时又具备良好的销售业绩，于是被公司推荐，赶回来参加这个管理学博士班项目的面试和笔试。

在一番自我介绍以及轻松回答了几位来自香港理工大学教授的提问之后，Ferdinand A. Gul 教授问道：“Jeff（我的英文名字），你的 EMBA（工商管理硕士）

论文的题目、导师还有相关内容，请你向我们介绍一下吧。”

接下来就是快速的回忆。时间又闪回到了两年前，2002 年的 4 月。当时，我在美国纽约州立大学布法罗管理学院攻读在职 EMBA 学位。我的报告是有关“组织行为学”的课题。因为当时对这门课程非常感兴趣，与老师詹姆斯·梅林德（James Meindl）沟通得非常融洽与充分，于是，课题报告也就脱口而出——《组织过程与行为——个人案例的实例分析》（*Organizational Processes and Behavior — Personal Case Analysis*）。由于是有关自己部门组织架构以及人员职责变更方面的实例分析，因此表述得非常完整与详细。听完我的表述，Gul 教授非常满意地点了点头。

对于没有多余时间做充分准备的我来说，面试应该算是很顺利了。

接下来就是要进行开课前的预习工作。在当时一边应对繁重的市场和销售任务，面临几乎天天出差的“飞人”生活的同时，我还要预习几大本约两寸厚的英文书籍，艰难程度可想而知。但随着课程的开始，时光仿佛又回到了大学时代。与青年校园时期最大的不同，则是由于有了十几年的工作经历，可以把自己亲身体会到的点点滴滴，与理论研究有机地结合在一起，从而得到一个新的体会与升华。正如前面所言，“项目结合知识，科研结合实践”。而这种体验，只有亲自体会之后才能真切感悟到。每次在教室里，与同学、老师同堂学习、讨论、研究甚至争论到很晚，都成了繁复销售工作中的一种积极的回味与享受。

我选择的研究方向是服务市场（Service Marketing）。之所以选择这个研究方向，一个原因是我所从事的工作就是销售市场管理及服务，在比较熟悉和感兴趣的同时，我也研究了一下服务市场在国内全部 GDP 中所占的比例是 40% 左右，但是在过去的 30 年间，这个比例在中国从 24% 一路增加到了 40%，与此同时，与全球发达国家的服务市场所占的国内生产总值（GDP）比例相比较，这个比例则为 80% 左右。数据上已经明显表明，在服务市场，中国一定还会再有一次大的腾飞。我有理由坚信，在中国，在服务市场，特别是在企业级的服务市场，一定还会有一次大的突飞猛进。

提到服务，不能不提到服务的几个特性。首先是服务于“无形”（Intangibility），服务提供者的任务是使服务在一个或几个方面有形化。与产品营销人员努力在增加有形产品的无形成分正好相反，服务人员努力增加的是无形产品的有形成分。因此，服务是与提供服务的“人”密不可分的（Simultaneous Production and Consumption）。正因为如此，物质商品的消费效果和品质通常是均质的，而同一种服务的消费效果和品质往往存在着显著的差异（Heterogeneity）。与此同时，因为服务是一次“行动”或一次“表演”，而不是顾客可以保留的一件有形的物品，所以它是不能被储存的（Perishability）。当然，必要的场地、设备和劳动能够被事先准备好以创造服务，但这些仅仅代表生产能力，而不是产品本身。

我由此想到，既然服务是与“人”密不可分的，那么，是“人”就会犯错误，就会造成服务失误，从而引发顾客的抱怨。而要达到顾客的满意，唯有提高服务的品质，从而提升企业自身的竞争力。

服务失误与服务补救在西方的研究已经比较成熟，而在国内的相关实证研究还不是很多。以往的研究也主要侧重在餐饮、酒店等有限的领域。由于工作的特性，我则选取了移动通信行业作为研究对象，旨在通过对高科技行业的典型性代表来验证西方相关理论是否适用于中国，并借此拓展相关理论在中国的实用性，特别是对于企业级的客户，会产生积极的参考作用。

对企业客户来讲，服务失误则意味着所提供的服务未能达到企业所规定的要求。而对顾客来讲，服务失误意味着顾客所接收到的服务没有达到其预期的程度。企业导向的服务失误定义与顾客导向的服务失误定义的关键差别在于，后者考虑到了顾客可以对同样的服务感知到不同的质量水平，从而对是否发生服务失误有自己的评价。

有效的服务补救措施不应仅仅被看作“损失的控制”，更应该是公司的一个战略重点。通过服务补救可以与顾客有更多交流的机会，从而有机会强化并提升顾客对企业的忠诚度。

服务失误是服务业的重要事件，即使最好的公司也避免不了服务失误的发生。而服务补救即是企业用来解决顾客抱怨，并通过抱怨处理建立对企业信誉的策略。因此，服务补救措施对于顾客在衡量企业及其行为时，会产生正面影响，进而加强企业与顾客之间的关系。

当初，我的管理学博士毕业论文的题目是《服务补救与知觉公平、关系品质及行为意向的关系》（*Relationships Between Service Recovery and Perceived Justice, Relationship Quality, and Behavioral Intention*），通过研究服务补救动态与顾客知觉公平、关系品质以及顾客行为意向的关系，来指导服务补救的具体实施，从而有助于服务商评估自己的服务补救绩效。从后来的实际发展来看，这个研究在指导我后来的工作以及进一步的事业发展方面，起到了至关重要的作用。

2006 年 6 月 12 日，北京现代大厦。

这又是一个值得纪念和回忆的日子。由于行业的变化以及各方面的需要，我从工作了 12 年的摩托罗拉转战到了微软中国。而这是我去微软报道的那天。

从 CT（通信行业）到 IT（信息行业），看上去很接近，实则相去千里。从在 CT 行业的负责几个到十几个客户，到 IT 行业的负责近八百个客户；从单个合同金额可以到达 1 亿美金，到平均合同金额的 9 万美金，这里面的差异，可以想象。

最明显的变化，是我原来的同事觉得我的语速和节奏快多了，走路的步伐频率也高多了，还有就是，每天的睡眠时间也更少了。但是，这种节奏的变化也同时给我带来了非常不一样的改变：了解，并理解了更多的客户以及市场和行业的需求，更加实时、迅捷，按需、动态地分配并调整策略及行动方案的能力，以结果为导向通过有效甚至高效的方式专注并取得最终的结果，以便获得更高、更好的市场效果及客户的满意度。

工作上需要投入更多的精力，另一方面，管理学博士学业也在最后的冲刺阶段。于是我特意在我的办公室里放置了一台投影仪，只要是不出差的日子，在处理完日常工作，大约是晚上 10 点以后，再到夜里 3 点之前，便是我写论文以及准备论文答辩 PPT 的时间。这样的日子大约持续了四个月。

时间又回到了 2007 年的 12 月 1 日。

当晚，在红磡体育馆毕业典礼后与香港理工大学各位老师跟同学们举办的“博士班答谢晚宴”上，作为班长的我第一个被邀请上台做毕业感言。台下，有所有香港理工大学管理学博士班的老师，摩托罗拉亚太区总经理梁念坚（Simon Leung），以及中国区的总经理高瑞彬（Ruey Bin Kao），还有所有管理学博士班的同学们。

我走上台前，沉思了很久。

“摩托罗拉不是一家‘好’公司！”

笔者在博士班答谢晚宴上发表毕业感言，2007 年 12 月 1 日

此话一出，刚才还窸窸窣窣欢声笑语的全场突然间变得安静下来。我能体察到来自 Simon 和 Ruey Bin 那有些诧异的目光，更有来自台下所有老师、同学略显惊异的目光和表情。因为此时，全场只有我一个人来自“微软中国”。

我此时已是感慨万千。是的，作为摩托罗拉的一名“老兵”和高管加入此次管理学博士班的学习，并被选为“班长”，而毕业时，已经是微软中国电信及媒体事业部的总经理，这期间经历了多少汗水和努力，还有各种的付出和心血。作为唯一的一名“非摩托罗拉”学员，能够从这个博士班毕业并取得管理学博士学位，已经足够令我唏嘘不已。

“但是，摩托罗拉是一家伟大的公司！”

顿了几秒钟。台下爆发出经久的掌声，还有众人纷纷起立的欢呼声。大家已经完全理解了我想说什么。演讲结束后，Simon、Ruey Bin 还有各位老师、同学们纷纷举起酒杯，共同祝贺与纪念这难忘的时刻与岁月。

是的，不仅仅是摩托罗拉，同时，微软中国对我的管理学博士学业也给予了巨大的支持，从时间安排到工作协调等方方面面。如果没有微软中国的协助，我难以走到这个讲台上。就像我在答辩 PPT 中所提到的：“衷心感谢摩托罗拉还有微软中国！”

2011 年 9 月 6 日，西藏，唐古拉山口。

2011 年注定又是不平凡的一年。这一年的 9 月，我与相识 30 年的高中同学，自驾两万余公里，途经西宁、青海湖、格尔木、拉萨、拉兹、阿里、樟木、加德满都、蓝毗尼、博卡拉、成都、西安，最后返回北京。历经唐古拉雪山遐思，蓝毗尼心灵感悟，加德满都地震惊悚，青朴修行僧侣的目光，拉姆拉措的灵魂穿越，还有南迦巴瓦奇缘……这其中，改变我一生的一个感悟和决定，则是发生在唐古拉山口，也就是下面这张照片的地方。

笔者拍摄于海拔 5231 米的唐古拉山口，2011 年 9 月 6 日

当时的海拔是 5231 米。我和我的同学因为在可可西里无人区纵深徜徉，并跟随藏羚羊等野生动物亲密拍照，当开到唐古拉山口时已经是下午 4 点 35 分。当时我们意犹未尽，随着向右的一个 45 度，转到慢速四驱，我们的“大切”（大切诺基）轰鸣着离开了 G109 国道，开始爬上了一个根本就没有路的山峰。

当时的血氧，只有不到 50%。而这张照片是用 11 张照片合成后完成的，体现了唐古拉山口的宏伟和一望无垠的场景。为减少相机的抖动，在按动快门时尽量地屏住呼吸，在含氧量极低的唐古拉山口，这样连续拍照后的结果，就是整个人是一种要虚脱的感觉。

历经了千辛万苦到达了一个令人举目难忘、美若仙境之处，虚静而饱满，感受到的是静谧和能量的无处不在。恰恰是在这个地方，我明白了一件事。

那就是，一定要有机会，做自己最喜欢做的事。

于是，就是在这里，开始有了全新的想法和行动。

经历了 38 天艰苦而难忘的旅程回到北京之后，即刻开始了行动。我做了几件事。

第一件，我辞去了惠普中国区副总裁的职务。第二件，开始做一些“调研”工作。我调研了两件事情：① 调查周边的朋友对我的“想法”的“态度和反馈”；② 研究了 24 家市场主流 IT 厂商的云解决方案。

我询问了 40 位朋友，有的表示“疑虑”，有的表示“反对”，而大多数则表示“懵懂”，表示完全理解和赞赏的有一人，达 2.5%！于是，我的信心“大增”了起来。

2012 年 9 月 5 日，北京。

就在拍完唐古拉山口这张照片后的整整一年，也就是 2012 年的 9 月 5 日，云览信通（inforLane Technology）正式成立了。

我常常跟身边的小伙伴们说，如何去做一件事，这只是一个战术。而真正明白自己最想做的是什么，则是战略。战略的价值往往要高于战术的价值。至今为止，我一直非常感谢当初赞赏与支持我的那位朋友，更感谢余下的那 39 位没有明确表示支持与赞赏的朋友，正是这个结果，才更让我坚定了信心，做好与实现这个“想法”。

所以，我们不追风口，不盲从。我们选择谨慎对待。非常幸运的是我们找到了我们喜欢做也应该做的事。我们不仅仅找对了方向，也找对了合作伙伴。

我一直认为，我们并非选择创业，而是选择了做自己喜欢做的事。正因为如此，我们才不会认为我们是在高空行走，而是在脚踏实地。因为喜欢，才有激情去触摸云端。而独立思考和强大的执行能力是我们必备的素质。

开始做自己喜欢的事情之前，首先要有自己的价值观。我们以“PERFORM”作为我们的核心价值观，强调 Passion（激情）、Execution（执行）、Readiness（准备）、Fairness（公平）、Optimism（乐观）、Result（结果）、Management（掌控），进而以实际的“PERFORM（行动）”去实现我们的使命及愿景。所以，我觉得最好的状态，就是从自己发自内心喜欢的事情入手，然后从自己的身边寻找到合适的

“PERFORM | 行动”作为核心价值观的体现

人组建团队，同时满足市场的实际需求。

2017 年。正好是我的博士论文获得通过并获得管理学博士学位 10 周年，同时也是云览信通成立 5 周年的日子。

回顾这 10 年走过的历程，以及 10 年前所做的研究工作，感触颇深。

从源于市场的实际案例出发，研究由于服务失误造成的顾客不满，同时通过研究服务补救动态对顾客知觉公平、关系品质以及顾客行为意向的关系，以及有助于指导服务补救的具体实施，有助于服务商评估自己的服务补救绩效和通过更多的客户案例，进一步将研究结论与实践相结合，进而总结出一个命题：信誉的成本。

如何处理及建立对企业信誉的策略将成为一个关键。因此，在这篇研究论文获得通过之后的今天，我又重新审视了一遍，根据自己这些年的一些体会以及沉淀，在对很多篇幅进行了重新修改之后，把这篇论文的名字也修改为《信誉的成本——源于服务失误的管理策略工程研究》。

企业，与做人一样。人讲的是“人品”，在英文中称作“Personality”。

而做企业，讲的则是“信誉”，也就是“企业的人品”，于是我创造了一个新词，把“企业的人品”称为“Corpnality”。

而无论是“人”，还是“企业”，都应该像珍惜双眼一样来珍惜其“Personality”或“Corpnality”。而其本质，则是信誉。正因为如此，在成立云览信通之时，亦把“信任服务与管理”作为公司的立足之本，强调必须要给客户提供值得信任的服务以及管理体系，不惜“成本”地去投入、建设，提升自身的信誉，才能够在随后公司的发展过程中来降低“信誉的成本”。

在 2013 年，我看到了一篇慧锐公司（Verint）委托全球市场调查公司 IPSOS 进行的一项关于亚太区消费者对服务现状满意度的调查研究报告。本次调查覆盖中国（包含香港）、印度、日本、澳大利亚和印度尼西亚等五个国家和地区的 5800 多名消费者，中国大陆消费者占 1139 名，其中大多数受访者表示曾经经历糟糕的客户服务。中国受访者经历恶劣客户服务的行业包括零售（74%）、酒店和旅游（69%）、金融服务（67%）、公用事业（57%）和电信（56%）。调查结果显示：在所有参与调查的亚太区国家中，消费者经历恶劣服务的比例都很高，其中中国大陆受访者比例更达到 63%，高于受访地区平均水平。

由于曾经经历糟糕的客户服务，消费者认为服务的重要性超过价格。调查显示：45% 的消费者愿意为服务支付更高的价格，对于中国受访者来说，这一比例更是高达 56%，在所有受访国家中位列第一。

对于消费者来说，社交媒体的发展使得他们有更多渠道分享自己的服务体验。调查显示：53% 的消费者会在社交媒体、博客上分享自己的体验，并在商家官网上发表评论，其中 42% 使用社交网站，24% 在博客上分享体验。在这其中，愿意分享正面体验的消费者（41%）多于分享负面体验的消费者（32%）。中国大陆消费者更愿意在社交媒体上分享正面体验，这一比例高达63%，相当于香港地区和澳大利亚的总和。

面对以上调查结果，我们不禁要问：哪些原因导致消费者对客户服务不满意呢？导致消费者服务体验欠佳的两大因素包括解决问题的时间太长（21%）以及员工因缺乏相关知识而不能为客户提供有效帮助（20%）。

面对以上调查结果，相信每一个致力于提高客户服务满意度的商家都会感到沮丧，而因此就认为他们不重视客户体验就太过于片面了。在社交媒体如此发达的今天，任何一个细微的客户的不满可能都会被无限扩大，而伴随越来越多商家提供线上、线下结合的客户体验和服务，如何确保服务质量的标准化，如何实现跨渠道销售，都是摆在他们面前的难题。

在完成我的博士学业后的第5年看到这样的报告，感觉我的研究结论得到了更广泛的证实与验证。与此同时，我也更想将自己对服务市场更进一步的理解与心得，写出来与大家分享。这也是我出版此书的一个初衷。

最后，希望借此机会，表达我的感谢之情……

Foreword

Time goes back to 10 years ago.

December 1, 2007, Hong Kong Coliseum

I received the certificate from Professor Poon Chung-kwong, then President of the Hong Kong Polytechnic University (PolyU). As the president slowly stroked the doctoral hat's tassel from the hat's right side to its left side in the front, it meant that I eventually obtained the Doctor of Management degree jointly granted by PolyU and the Renmin University of China after 1108 days of study day and night starting from November 18, 2004. Looking at many alumni, classmates, and my loved ones under the stage, I was extremely excited and emotional, and a multitude of feelings surged up. The program of over three years was really another challenge for me to push the limits.

Although I knew the rigorous reputation of PolyU and was mentally prepared for the challenges, the difficulties and pressures encountered were still far more than what I had expected. When standing there in the doctoral gown as the solemn national anthem was played, I felt that my hard work was paid off, and I would not have any regret for the rest of my life.

"Since the PolyU Graduate School of Business was established in 2003, the quality of the courses offered has been improving, there have been new accomplishments again and again, and it now has become an excellent graduate school of business in Asia Pacific," said Professor Poon Chung-kwong, then President of PolyU, at the commencement ceremony. "The graduate school has become increasingly well-known. Besides its academic standard, which has been recognized internationally again and again, the exceptional performance of its graduates from both Hong Kong and Mainland China in their respective positions is also an important factor contributing to the great word-of-mouth. Besides being very knowledgeable, the graduates have also demonstrated a sharp acumen in business."

The goal of the joint Doctor of Management program between PolyU and Renmin University of China is to train "scholarly leaders". "Through this program, the students will be able to solve the real problems faced by their company or the society with a rigorous scientific attitude in conjunction with the latest business management theories and mindsets," said Professor Ferdinand A. Gul, head of the Doctor of Business Administration and Doctor of Management programs at PolyU. "After graduation, they'll be able to create success for their company with a broad vision. Therefore, the program is very much welcomed by senior executives, with students including chairmen of public companies, directors of multinational companies, licensed accountants, and even senior government officials."

The program is designed to develop the ability of senior executives to leverage their management and application skills to drive their company's innovation and growth by combining project with knowledge and combining research with practice. This is the profound understanding of each of us as the students of the program. You've got to have a Master's Degree to take this program. You also have to have eight or more years of management experience in a senior position to be eligible for the written examination and interview. And this is also the only joint Doctor of Management program between Hong Kong and Mainland China officially recognized by China's Ministry of Education, which accepts the degree.

"Congratulations! You've received the Doctor of Management degree from PolyU!" said President Poon. Our hands held tightly together. Following his penetrating eyes, my train of thought was wandering far away.

September 27, 2004, a telecom Building in Beijing's Xidan area

With uneasiness, I came to a telecom building near Beijing's Xidan area. I came here to attend a teleconference interview for the Doctor of Management program. I didn't come back to Beijing until one day before the interview late that night, as I had to attend an important meeting with customers in Fujian. At that time, it was a critical stage for China's carriers to step up their effort with respect to mobile communications and related digital services, and we were barely able to breathe under the tremendous sales & marketing pressure. During that period, I was the Sales Director for Motorola China. I was a senior executive of Motorola and also had a strong sales performance, and was therefore recommended by the company to come back and attend the interview and the written examination for the Doctor of Management program.

After a self-introduction, and after I answered the questions from several PolyU professors with ease, Professor Ferdinand A. Gul asked: "Jeff, please tell us the title of your EMBA paper, your tutor, and other relevant things."

After that, it was a fast recalling process. Time flashed again back to two years ago in April 2002. At that time, I was taking the EMBA program at the School of Management, the State University of New York at Buffalo (UB School of Management). My paper was about organizational behaviors. Since I was very interested in the program, and I also talked with Professor James Meindl cordially and adequately, I was able to easily speak out the title of my paper: "Organizational Processes and Behavior—Personal Case Analysis". As it's an analysis of a real case about the changes in my own BU's organizational structure and job description, my expression was very complete and detail-oriented. After listening to my elaboration, Professor Gul nodded very satisfactorily.

Although I didn't have any time to make preparations, the interview was really successful without a hitch.

What I would need to do next was to preview the stuff before class. At that time, I had to cope with the heavy sales & marketing assignments and had to fly almost every day on business trips on the one hand while previewing several English books with each being about two inches thick on the other hand, so you can imagine how difficult it was. But with the beginning of the class, it seems that I was back to my university days again. The biggest difference from the school life when I was young is that, more than ten years after graduation, I could combine my own tidbits of experience with theories effectively together, so as to take my understanding to a new level. As said above, it is to "combine project with knowledge and combine research with practice". And you can't really get such a feeling until you've personally gone through the process. Every time when I was learning, discussing, studying or even arguing with classmates and teachers in the classroom to very late, I would feel that it's a kind of positive recollection and enjoyment after the busy and meticulous sales work.

My research area was service marketing. One reason that I chose this research area was because my job was sales & marketing management and service. While being familiar with and interested in this subject, I also learned that the percentage of service marketing in China's GDP was around 40%, but the number was growing from 24% to 40% in China during the past 30 years, and in comparison it was around 80% in the developed countries of the world. The data clearly showed that China would definitely have another major jump in terms of service marketing. I had a reason to strongly believe that there would definitely be a round of dramatic growth in service marketing, especially in enterprise-class service marketing.

Talking about service, I have to mention several features of service. First of all, services are intangible (Intangibility), and the task of the service providers is to make services tangible in one or more aspects. As opposed to product marketers who are trying to increase the intangible elements of tangible products, service providers are trying to increase the tangible elements of intangible products. Therefore, services are inseparable from people who provide them. (Simultaneous Production and Consumption). It is because that the consumption result and quality of material goods are usually homogenous, whereas the consumption result and quality of the same services are often significantly heterogeneous (Heterogeneity). At the same time, because a service is an "action" or a "performance", not a tangible object that can be kept by customers, it is perishable (Perishability). Of course, necessary sites, equipment and labor can be prepared in advance to create services. But these things represent production capacity only, not products themselves.

I realize from that, since services are inseparable from people, as people can make mistakes and render service failures, it's inevitable to have complaints from customers. Only by improving the quality of your services, can you make your customers satisfied, so as to increase your company's competitiveness.

The study of service failures and service recovery is already a mature field in the west. But there aren't many empirical studies about this in China. Previous studies were mainly focused on limited areas such as the HoReCa industry. Due to my job, I chose to study the mobile communications industry, aiming to test if related western theories are applicable to China using a typical branch of the technology industry, and to expand the practicality of related theories in China, especially for enterprise customers, to which this study will be of a reference value.

For companies, service failures would mean that the services you provided have failed to meet your requirements. And for customers, service failures would mean that the services they received have failed to meet their expectations. The key difference between the enterprise-oriented definition of service failures and the customer-oriented definition of service failures is that the latter takes into consideration that the quality level of the same services perceived by customers can be different, and therefore they have their own opinions about whether there are service failures in the first place.

Effective service recovery measures shouldn't be just seen as "damage control". Instead, they should be seen as a strategic focus of your company. Through service recovery, you can have more opportunities to communicate with your customers, so as to reinforce and improve customer loyalty.

Service failures are important incidents in the service industries. Even the best companies can't avoid service failures. And service recovery is a strategy used by companies to solve customer complaints and build their corporate reputation in this process. Therefore, service recovery measures can have a positive impact on customers when they are measuring companies and their behaviors, thus helping to enhance the relations between companies and their customers.

The title of my Doctor of Management dissertation is *Relationships between Service Recovery and Perceived Justice, Relationship Quality, and Behavioral Intention*. The idea was to guide the actual implementation of service recovery measures by studying the relationships of service recovery dynamics with customer's perceived justice, relationship quality and behavioral intention, so as to help service providers evaluate their own performance in service recovery. Later practice shows that this study played a vital role in guiding my work and my career development later on.

June 12, 2006, Hyundai Motor Tower, Beijing

This was another memorable day. Due to changes in the industry as well as the needs of various parties, I left Motorola China, which I had been with for 12 years, for Microsoft China. And that was Day One for me at Microsoft China.

The distance from the CT to the IT industry seems to be very short, but they are actually poles apart. In the communications industry, I just managed several or a dozen of customers, whereas in the IT industry, I had to manage nearly 800 customers; in the communications industry, the value of a single contract could be up to $100 million, whereas in the IT industry, the average value of a contract is just around $90 thousand. Imagine the difference between them.

The most obvious change was that my former colleagues felt that I spoke much faster and my step frequency was much higher. Another thing was that I slept less every day. But such rhythmic changes also led to other very unusual changes in me: I learned and also understood a lot more needs of the customers, the markets and the industries, and I had the ability to allocate and adjust my strategies and action plans in a more timely fashion, faster, on-demand, and dynamically, and I became results-oriented, striving to become focused efficiently and effectively, to achieve better results and customer satisfaction through the final outcomes.

As I needed to spend more time on work, and my Doctor of Management program also reached the final sprint stage, I put a projector in my office. As long as I was not on a business trip, after finishing my routine—roughly after 10pm, I would work on my dissertation and prepare the PPT for dissertation defense until 3am. My days were like that for about 4 months.

Times goes back to December 1, 2007 again.

That night, at the "thank you" dinner party of the Doctor of Management class with the teachers and classmates of PolyU after the commencement ceremony at Hong Kong Coliseum, I, as the head of the class, was the first to be invited to deliver the commencement speech on stage. People under the stage included all the teachers of the PolyU Doctor of Management program, Motorola Asia Pacific GM Simon Leung, Motorola China GM Ruey Bin Kao, as well as all the classmates of the Doctor of Management program.

I took the stage. After being silent for a long while, I said:

"Motorola is not a 'good' company!"

Hearing that, the noisy audience suddenly became quiet. I could detect the somewhat puzzled impression of Simon and Ruey Bin as well as the slightly surprised eyes and impression of all the teachers and classmates under the stage, because at that point I was the only one who came from Microsoft China.

I was already very emotional at that point. Yes, I joined the Doctor of Management program as a Motorola executive and was elected the class head, but was already the GM for Microsoft Communications Sector upon graduation.

I shed a lot of blood, sweat and tears during that period. Being able to graduate from the program with a Doctor of Management degree as the only student in the class who's not from Motorola was already enough to make me extremely emotional.

"But Motorola is a great company!"

After a pause of several seconds, a long-lasting round of applause exploded under the stage with a standing ovation. They already knew exactly what I wanted to say. After my speech, Simon, Ruey Bin, and all the teachers and classmates raised their glass to toast for the unforgettable moment and the memorable days.

Yes, not just Motorola, Microsoft China also provided tremendous support for my study in the Doctor of Management program in every aspect possible from time arrangement to work coordination. It would be very hard to imagine that I could take the stage without the assistance from Microsoft China. "I would like to express my sincere thanks to Motorola and Microsoft China," I said in the PPT for my dissertation defense.

September 6, 2011, Tanglha Pass, Tibet

It was deemed to be an extraordinary year. In September of that year, a high-school classmate and I—we had known each other for 30 years—drove over 20 thousand kilometers from Beijing, via Xining, Qinghai Lake, Golmud, Lhasa, Lazi, Ali, Zhangmu, Katmandu, Lumbini, Pokhara, Chengdu, and Xi'an to return to Beijing. I would like to mention the reverie at Tanglha, the soul-provoking experience at Lumbini, the shocking aftermath of the earthquake at Katmandu, the unforgettable eyes of the mediating monks at Qingpu, the mental time tunnel at Lhamo La-tso, the strange encounter at the Namcha Barwa...And a decision that would change the rest of my life was made at the Tanglha Pass, which is the place shown on the photo below.

At that point, the elevation was 5231 meters above sea level. As my classmate and I were chasing wild animals like Tibetan antelope to take pictures deep in the uninhabited Hoh Xil, it's already 4:35pm when we arrived at the Tanglha Pass. We were still in high spirits. With a 45-degree right turn, our Grand Cherokee roared to get off G109 on 4WD and began to climb a peak that has no road at all. Our blood oxygen level was less than 50% at that time. This photo is a montage of 11 photos showing the magnificent and boundless Tanglha Pass. To reduce camera shake, when pressing the shutter button, I held my breath as long as I could. At the Tanglha Pass where the oxygen level is extremely low, and keep taking pictures like this, you will definitely feel exhausted.

We eventually came to such an unforgettable, fairyland-like place after so many ordeals, and I could feel the ubiquitous quietness and energy. But it was at that place I became clear about one thing, which is that I must have the opportunity to do things I love to do the most.

As such, I began to have a totally new idea and action plan right there at that moment.

After returning to Beijing from the 38-day arduous but unforgettable trip, I immediately began to act. I did several things.

The first thing was that I resigned from the VP position of HP China. The second thing was that I began to do some "researches". I researched two things: ① the "attitude and feedback" of my friends toward my "idea"; ② the cloud solutions of 24 mainstream IT companies.

I asked for opinions from 40 friends. Some had "misgivings", some were "against" my decision, and most of them had no idea as to whether it's a good or bad decision. There's 1 person or 2.5% of my friends who completely understood and appreciated my decision. As such, my confidence was "greatly" increased.

September, 5, 2012, Beijing

A whole year right after taking the photo at Tanglha Pass, on September 5, 2012, inforLane Technology came into being.

I often tell people around me that how to do something is just a tactic issue, whereas really understanding what you want to do the most is a strategic one. The strategic value is often higher than the tactic value. To date, I've been very thankful to the friend who appreciated and supported my decision back then. I would like to thank the remaining 39 friends who didn't express clear support and appreciation for me even more. It was because of this result that I had become more confident to do a good job and turn my "idea" into reality.

So, we don't follow the trends blindly. We choose to take a cautious attitude instead. Very luckily, we've found the things we should do and also like to do. We not just have found the right direction, but also have found the right partners.

I always believe that we didn't choose to start a business, but choose to do things we like to do. It's because of this that we think we are not walking above the ground but are down to earth. We're passionate because we like it, like to touch the cloud. And having an independent mindset and powerful execution is essential to us.

Before beginning to do things you like to do, you should have your own values first. Our core values are summarized as "PERFORM", which stands for "Passion", "Execution", "Readiness", "Fairness", "Optimism", "Result" and "Management". We want to fulfill our mission and vision by performing. So, I think it's best to start from things you really love to do and then find the right people around you to form a team while striving to meet the actual needs in the marketplace.

The year 2017 marks the 10th anniversary of my doctoral dissertation getting passed and my receiving the Doctor of Management as well as the 5th anniversary of inforLane Technology.

I really have a lot of thoughts and feelings when looking back at my experience over the past ten years as well as the study I completed ten years ago.

I studied customer dissatisfaction caused by service failures based on real-world examples, and also explored the relationships of service recovery dynamics with customer's perceived justice, relationship quality and behavioral intention, so as to help guide the actual implementation of service recovery measures and help service providers evaluate their own performance in implementing service recovery measures. Then, based on additional customer cases, I went further to come up with a topic: the cost of credibility, by combing the conclusions of my study with practice.

How to handle and establish a strategy for corporate reputation would become a key issue. Therefore, after this paper was passed, I re-examined it, revised many parts of it based on my thoughts over the years, and then changed the title of the paper into "The Cost of Credibility: A Study of Management Strategies Derived from Service Failures".

Companies are actually like people. People have their personality. I think companies should put importance on their "personality" too. Therefore, I coined a new word "corpnality".

People or companies should treasure their "personality" or "corpnality" as if they treasure their eyes. And the essence of it is reputation. It is because of this that when inforLane Technology was formed, we wanted to build the company on "trusted service and management", emphasizing that we must provide trusted services and management systems for our customers and do whatever possible at any cost to improve our reputation. Only this way, can we reduce "the cost of credibility" for the company later on.

In 2013, I read a study about consumer satisfaction for services in Asia Pacific, which was conducted by global market research firm Ipsos for Verint. The study shows that, among all the Asia Pacific countries participated in the survey, the percentage of consumers who had experienced bad services was very high, and this number was 63% for respondents in China, higher than the average level of the countries surveyed.

As having experienced bad customer services, consumers believe that services are more important than prices. The study shows that, 45% of consumers were willing to pay higher prices for the services they received, and this number was 56% for respondents in China, ranking No.1 among the countries surveyed.

For consumers, the development of social media enables them to share their service experience through more channels. The study shows that, 53% of consumers would share their experience on social media or via blogs and would also make comments on the official websites of the service providers, and among them, 42% used social media and 24% used blogs to share their experience. There were more consumers (41%) who were willing to share their positive experience than consumers (32%) who were willing to share their negative experience. Chinese consumers were willing to share their positive experience on social media more than consumers in any other place at 63%, which was equivalent to the combined percentage of Hong Kong and Australia.

Facing the results of the study mentioned above, we can't help asking: what are the causes that lead to consumer dissatisfaction for customer services? There are two factors that can cause a poor service experience for consumers: 1) it takes too long to solve a problem (21%); 2) the employees don't have the required knowledge to provide effective help for customers (20%).

Given the above results, I believe that every service provider dedicated to improving customer satisfaction would feel frustrated, but it would be too one-sided to think that they don't take customer experience seriously just because of this. In a world where social media are so developed today, any minor customer dissatisfaction might be unlimitedly enlarged. And with more and more companies providing customer experiences and services both online and offline, how to ensure the standardization of service quality and how to enable sales across channels are all challenges they have to address.

Seeing such a report 5 years after completing my Doctor of Management program, I felt that the conclusions of my study were confirmed and corroborated by more evidences. Meanwhile, I also wanted to put my understandings and thoughts for service marketing into words to share with the readers. That's also one of the reasons for me to publish this book.

Finally, I would like to take this opportunity to express my sincerely thanks...

致谢

在攻读博士学位期间我受益良多。最为幸运的是我有一位学识渊博，治学严谨，儒雅睿智的导师——徐惠群教授。我要感谢我的导师，在论文选题、整体构思、写作以及定稿的整个过程中，徐教授倾注了大量的精力和心血。徐教授渊博的学识、丰富的经验，给我留下了深刻的印象；徐教授严谨的治学态度、一丝不苟的教学作风和崇高的敬业精神，使我终身受益。

笔者与管理学博士导师徐惠群教授在香港理工大学

微软大中华区首席执行官陈永正先生对笔者的博士学业给予了全力的支持

我要感谢香港理工大学工商管理研究院许许多多老师的无私帮助。在教学中他们对我个别辅导，循循善诱，悉心赐教。在论文写作过程中，他们对论文提供了许多有意义的指导、建议；协助我搜集了大量宝贵的资料，对我遇到的有关技术性问题的解决给予了大力的支持。借此机会，我衷心地表示感谢，没有他们的辛勤教诲，成就学业必是举步维艰。

我要感谢我的同窗好友。论文的完成离不开我的各位同学。与他们的每一次交流都使我获益匪浅，他们始终激励着我克服学习中的各种困难。

我要特别感谢 David Ho(何庆源)、Ruey Bin Kao(高瑞彬)、Kerry Strong(强明远)、Yan Ling（晏翎）、Jeanette Liu(刘金花)，是摩托罗拉的领导和同事们的大力支持

笔者与摩托罗拉大中华区总裁高瑞彬（右）及管理学博士班项目经理刘金花（中）在香港理工大学合影

和悉心安排，让我拥有了一段最值得回忆的学习时光。

我也要感谢微软公司的领导和同事们，是你们的精心安排和全力支持，使我可以继续坚持我的学业。没有你们的倾心帮助，承担尽量多的工作，为我挤出尽可能多的学习时间，我的学业将非常艰难。

笔者与管理学博士答辩小组在答辩过程中

笔者在论文答辩中对摩托罗拉及微软中国表达由衷感谢

笔者在论文答辩中对香港理工大学管理学博士班的教授及导师们表达由衷感谢

管理学博士班同学与香港理工大学及中国人民大学的教授老师们的合影，2007 年 12 月 1 日

我要感谢福建移动 10086 服务中心的张科奎总经理以及服务中心的领导和参与问卷调查的 800 位呼叫中心的同事们，是你们的鼎力帮助和悉心填写，使我获得了非常宝贵和有价值的一手资料和数据，使得后续的研究得以顺利进行。

我要感谢我的父母，他们为培养我们姐弟成才辛勤劳作，可谓呕心沥血。我要感谢我的姐姐们为我所做的一切，我们用努力和奋进共同谱写着对父母深深的爱。

我要特别感谢我的夫人在此期间做出的巨大的牺牲，以及在我为论文进展缓慢而焦躁忧虑时，那句“英雄耐得住寂寞”对我所产生的巨大动力。是她始终在鼓励我前行。

当整篇论文完成的那一刻，我有一种如释重负的感觉。就像是一个经过艰辛跋涉之后刚刚抵达目的地的行者，尽管满身旅尘，但内心却洋溢着喜悦。我也要感谢自己，感谢自己这些年的坚持。

再次感谢我所有的老师、同学和朋友们！

2017 年 2 月 3 日

Acknowledgement

I benefitted a lot from the Doctor of Management program. The luckiest thing was that I had a tutor, Professor Cathy Hsu, who is knowledgeable, rigorous, graceful, and intelligent. I would like to thank Professor Hsu for her painstaking efforts during the entire process from choosing a topic for the dissertation, designing the overall structure of it and actually writing it to finalizing the draft. I was deeply impressed by Professor Hsu for the breadth of her knowledge and the depth of her experience. I would benefit from the rigorous academic attitude, meticulous teaching style and admirable professionalism of Professor Hsu for the rest of my life.

I would like to thank many teachers from the PolyU Graduate School of Business for their selfless help. In teaching, they coached me individually and patiently without reservation. When I was writing my paper, they provided a lot of meaningful guidance and advice on the paper, helped to gather a lot of valuable information for me, and gave me great support for the technical issues I encountered. Taking this opportunity, I would like to express my sincere thanks to them. It would have been extremely difficult for me to complete the program every step of the way without their hard work.

I would like to thank my classmates. The completion of the paper would not have been possible without them. I would benefit a lot from talking with them every time. And they always encouraged me to overcome various difficulties in learning throughout the process.

I would like to thank David Ho, Ruey Bin Kao, Kerry Strong, Yan Ling, Jeanette Liu from Motorola leadership team. It was because of your painstaking efforts that I was able to spend a period of time that was most memorable to me.

I would like to thank the leaders and colleagues at Microsoft. Your thoughtful arrangements and full support enabled me to keep going with my study. It would have been much more difficult for me to complete my study without your wholehearted help and effort to do as much work as possible so that I could spend as much time as possible on my study.

I would like to thank GM Kekui Zhang of Fujian Mobile's 10086 call center as well as the center's other leaders and the 800 colleagues at the center who participated in the questionnaire survey. You provided great help for me and carefully completed the questionnaires, allowing me to obtain very valuable first-hand information and data, and enabling me to carry on my subsequent work without a hitch.

I would like to thank my parents. They worked very hard and made painstaking efforts in order to raise my older sisters and me. I would like to thank my older sisters for everything they did for me. We express our deep love for our parents together by working hard and by being motivated.

Especially, I would like to thank my wife for her tremendous sacrifice during my study as well as the huge boost she gave me by saying "heroes can bear with the loneliness" when I was anxious about being slow on my paper. It is her who's been encouraging me to move forward.

At the moment when the entire book was completed, I felt a strong sense of relief. I was like someone who just arrived at his destination after an arduous trip, tired, but really happy. I would also like to thank myself for the perseverance over the years.

Thanks again to all my teachers, classmates, and friends!

February 3, 2017

第 1 章

导论

越来越多的国家已经进入“服务经济社会”。与此同时，制造业的服务化趋势也初露端倪，服务已经成为企业间竞争最重要的手段和工具。由于制造业的服务化倾向，很多企业现在所面临的不再是狭义的产品问题，而是服务问题。Janelle 在 1996 年的一份研究报告中提出，“抱怨是一份礼物”，因此如何针对顾客抱怨进行服务补救处理将是服务商们感兴趣的话题，这将有助于增加服务商对顾客忠诚度的理解和把握。毫无疑问，在已有研究的基础上，通过引入服务对象的感知，来探讨服务失误、服务补救的过程及顾客行为意向之间的作用机理，可以为企业持续改进服务和重新赢得顾客提供有价值的信息。而这些则构成了本研究的动机 。

Chapter 1

Introduction

More and more countries have become "societies of service economies". Meanwhile, "manufacturing as a service" is also becoming a trend, and services have become the most important means and tools for companies to compete with each other. Given the "manufacturing as a service" trend, what many companies face now is no longer how to provide great products in the narrow sense, but how to provide great services. Janelle Barlow said in a 1996 study, "A complaint is a gift". Therefore, how to recover customer loyalty in accordance with their complaints is a topic of interest to service providers. This will help service providers understand and measure customer loyalty. There's no doubt that exploring the mechanism that works between service failures, service recovery and customer's behavioral intention through the perception of service objects based on existing studies can provide valuable information for companies to improve their services on an ongoing basis and regain customers. And these constitute the motivation for this study.

在中国移动通信运营业大发展的同时，运营商内部结构也经历了较大的变化，突出表现在中国联通的成立发展。1994 年中国联通作为后进入者打破了中国电信的完全垄断格局，历经十年，目前已壮大为拥有 1 亿用户的世界第三大运营商，资产由 13.4 亿元增加到 2050 亿元，10 年增值 150 多倍。从明晰产权关系到资产重组，从上市融资到建立规范的法人治理结构，如今的中国联通已成为按照现代企业制度和国际规范运行的综合电信企业。中国联通移动用户市场占有率 35.7%，新增用户市场占有率 34. 6%，作为移动通信市场的后进入者，初步具备了与龙头老大中国移动博弈抗衡的实力。考察世界上一些发达国家的发展历程，我们不难发现，由垄断逐步走向竞争是电信产业组织演进的大趋势。在这种情况下，必然会有越来越多的竞争者加入运营商之列，从而带来越来越多类似中国联通的后进入者。

在经历了长达十年的高速增长期后，我国电信业目前已经从千亿级市场成长为万亿级的市场，成为国家举足轻重的产业。但随着用户渗透率提升，技术升级使得资费大幅降低，电信市场营收和利润水平增速急剧放缓。而互联网宽带业务可以说是这两年发展最快的业务，2015—2017 年期间是各家运营商最大力投入发展的业务，用户增长呈现爆发趋势。另一方面，移动用户数增长自 2010 年起低于两位数，已经进入了增速放缓期。对比发达国家用户渗透率，我国东部发达省份渗透率接近 110%，增长空间主要在西部地区，未来自然增长的用户将越来越少。而数据业务发展一枝独秀，成为未来的主要争夺点。

电信行业变迁以移动通信作为代表，从模拟电话到 2G/3G/4G，以及目前已经进入实验阶段的 5G 移动通讯技术等革命性的变化，正在引领业务形态发生重要升级。

对运营商来说，还值得欣慰的是，移动互联网的崛起带动了用户对数据流量的需求，而且是高增长并且望不到尽头的需求。2G 到 4G 乃至 5G，网络所能提供的带宽提高了约 10000 倍，手机终端支持的业务种类越来越多，网络上各种多媒体内容越来越丰富。以十年为周期来看，数据业务就是运营商们十年内的未来。

因此，电信市场已经进入存量市场，整体营收和利润水平将在较长时期内保持大体稳定，目前已经在网服务的用户成为市场主要贡献者，新增用户贡献度越来越低。这导致电信运营商将主要的经营目标从原来的发展新用户，转为争夺已经在网的服务用户群体，存量用户竞争将进一步加剧。由此可见服务质量已成为影响消费者选择和购买移动通信商品的重要因素。随着顾客消费意识的增强，他们对移动通信服务品质的要求日益增强甚至苛刻，这也使得移动通信服务运营商在当今社会比以往任何时候都更要面对紧张的客户关系的压力。服务失误影响重大，因为服务失误会造成顾客不满，不满意的顾客就可能从移动通信服务运营商那里流失。不满意的顾客还可能产生负面行为，比较极端的就是“恐怖分子”的出现，他们会到处宣扬使其不满的运营商，严重影响运营商的形象和利润。

具有高技术含量、高附加值特点的信息产业已经成为众多发达国家保持经济持续增长的重要手段。统计数据显示，顾客不满意所耗费的成本约占企业全年营业收入的 10%（Brown，2001），吸引一位新顾客所花的成本是保留现有客户的 5 倍（美国顾客服务协会，2003）。而顾客满意度持续上升的企业，其年获利提升 10% 以上（Reichheld and Sasser，1990）。因此，认识服务补救的重要性，提高处理服务失误的能力，对电信运营商与其他服务商来讲都非常迫切。

1.1 研究背景

“抱怨是一份礼物”（Janelle et al.，1996），公司应该欢迎并鼓励顾客抱怨和投诉，同时教会顾客怎样抱怨：让他们知晓自己的权益、公司的服务标准、投诉途径等。由于服务系统的高度开放性和服务提供的不确定性决定了服务的零缺陷无法实现，顾客在享受服务的过程中，不可避免地要产生抱怨。由于服务抱怨的产生就意味着顾客忠诚瓦解的可能性，如何针对顾客抱怨进行服务补救处理将是服务商们感兴趣的话题，这将有助于提高其服务商对顾客忠诚的理解和把握。毫无疑问，对顾客抱怨的研究可以为企业持续改进服务和重新赢得顾客提供有价值的信息。

服务企业竞争日益激烈，顾客满意与否是永续经营的关键。要达到顾客满意，唯有提高服务的品质才能增加企业自身的竞争力。Goodwin 和 Ross（1992）认为在服务传送时的任何一个服务接触若产生服务失误，则会使得顾客有负面的反应，所以一旦在服务接触过程中发生缺失，则会使顾客不满意而有抱怨行为发生。Firnstahl（1989）认为服务所造成的失误，透过服务补救会使得顾客更满意该企业。Hart，Heskett 和 Sasser（1990）也特别指出服务补救的措施，如果执行不善时，则会增加顾客不满意的机会。因此，在服务失误发生时就需要对失误部分加以补救，让顾客感到满意并增加未来再购买意愿。

早期对顾客抱怨的研究是直接关注顾客抱怨的外在表现，其成果主要集中在对不同行业顾客抱怨率的统计（Hirschman, 1970），总体状况描述（Day and Bouder, 1978），归纳抱怨的性质和方式（Hunt, 1977）等。后来，研究的重点逐渐转移到以下几个方面。

① 顾客抱怨倾向的影响因素：抱怨态度对抱怨行为的影响（Bearden, Crockett and Teel, 1979），个性特征变量对抱怨行为的影响因素（Morganosky and Buckley, 1981），文化因素对抱怨倾向的影响（Triandis, 1989），价值取向对抱怨倾向的影响（范秀成，2003）。

② 顾客抱怨行为的研究（以后可能的行为和实际的行为）（Staubach, 1981）。

③ 抱怨对于管理上的意义（处理抱怨对于营销管理的意义），采用经济理论来分析抱怨管理作为一种防御性销售手段（Fornell and Wernerflet, 1988;

Plymire，1991）。

④ 基于供应商声望和顾客基础的损失，来妥善处理顾客抱怨（Hansen，1997），这些研究都只是静态的研究顾客抱怨，并没有把顾客抱怨与服务补救动态过程结合起来。

由于目前在有关顾客抱怨行为的理论背景中，还没有一种简单、全面的理论能完满解释顾客抱怨行为的机理，所以从服务补救过程到顾客的忠诚水平的变化就没法形成一致的认识。关于顾客抱怨行为和服务补救研究的理论框架主要存在以下几种：

① 关于顾客满意和不满的认证模式方面的理论（Oliver，1980；Day and Grabike，1981；Day，1984）；

② Hirschman（1970）的有关顾客退出（Exit）、抱怨表达（Vice）和忠诚（Loyalty）的理论；

③ Folks（1984）的归因理论。

这些理论主要是解释不满的顾客为什么要抱怨，换句话说主要是解释顾客抱怨的原因。这些理论有助于了理解顾客初始抱怨行为的发生，但是并没有一种理论来研究从顾客初始抱怨到服务补救再到忠诚修复的整个动态过程。

不过，Alexander 和 Ruderman（1987），Bies 和 Shapiro（1987）借助于公平感知理论研究了处于社会冲突形势中个人行为与知觉公平水平如何形成互动。这为研究者理解顾客如何动态反应服务商的服务补救提供了一个很好的框架。Blodgett 等（1993）正式将知觉公平的概念应用于服务补救的动态过程，并得出知觉公平水平的变化直接影响服务补救后顾客满意的修复，知觉公平水平是一个能很好衡量服务补救动态过程的态度目标参数（服务补救满意度的衡量标准），它与服务补救维度形成一一对应关系。然而 Morgan 和 Hunt（1994）认为关系品质对顾客的口碑与重购意向以及未来的预期有明显的影响。因此，研究服务补救动态过程中顾客知觉公平对关系品质以及顾客行为意向的影响，有助于指导服务补救具体实施，有助于服务商评估自己的服务补救绩效，这正是本研究的动机。

从理论和实践的角度出发，本研究选取服务行业（移动通信行业）来研究服务补救与知觉公平、关系品质、顾客行为意向的关系。

1.2 研究内容

本研究选取服务提供商为研究背景，结合知觉公平来研究服务补救、关系品质以及抱怨发生后顾客行为意图之间的动态关系，因此拟定以下几方面研究内容：

① 探讨服务补救的内容与知觉公平的关系；

② 探讨服务补救的内容与关系品质的关系；

③ 探讨服务补救的内容与顾客行为的关系；

④ 探讨服务补救过程中，知觉公平、关系品质、顾客行为的作用机理。

1.3 研究贡献

目前国内的实证研究中都是集中在顾客抱怨的方面，服务失误补救方面的实证研究仍嫌不足。企业都认识到服务补救能够使顾客满意度提高，能够保留顾客并促进与顾客的关系。此外，服务失误与服务补救在西方的研究已经比较成熟，而在国内的相关实证研究还不是很多。以往的研究也主要侧重在餐饮、酒店等有限的领域。本研究选取了移动通信行业作为研究对象，旨在通过研究高科技行业的典型性代表来验证西方相关理论是否适用于中国，并借此拓展相关理论在中国的实用性。

通过服务失误补救，企业可以明白问题在哪里，不断提高服务价值传递系统的稳定性，并进而改善服务传递系统的设计以及相关的员工培训，以便让顾客享受到更高质量的服务，提高顾客的满意度和忠诚度，避免顾客过激反应，维护企业的良好公共形象，从而创造企业的竞争优势。Firnstahl（1989）指出，尽管服务补救成本较高，但可以转变为企业改善本身服务系统的机会，将导致更多顾客满意该企业，就良性循环观点来说，服务递送系统的改善，更可降低系统成本。

本研究通过实证的方法研究服务补救与知觉公平、关系品质、顾客行为意向的关系，一方面可以得到大量一手数据，掌握目前移动通信服务业补救措施的实施情况，另一方面可以从中找出移动通信服务业对顾客心理产生影响的规律，这对于移动通信服务业及其他服务行业服务补救措施的实施和基于服务补救改善服务系统，具有十分重要的实践意义。研究结果对于如何有效地提高顾客的二次满意度以及对于服务补救后顾客的行为意向的预测及控制策略的制定都有深入的指导意义。

第 2 章

文献回顾

要研究现实中的问题，必须找到相关的理论支撑，只有这样才能构建一个合理的研究模型。通过对现实的观察，研究理论的研读及分类，我找到了大量有关服务补救与知觉公平、关系品质及行为意向的文献。然而目前在有关顾客抱怨行为的理论背景中，还没有一种简单、全面的理论能圆满解释顾客抱怨行为的机理，所以从服务补救过程到顾客的忠诚水平的变化就没法形成一致的认识。现存的理论主要是解释不满的顾客抱怨的原因，这些理论有助于理解顾客初始抱怨行为的发生，但是并没有一种理论来研究从顾客初始抱怨到服务补救再到忠诚修复的整个动态过程。

Chapter 2

Literature Review

To study issues in reality, we must find the relevant supporting theories. Only this way can we build a reasonable research model. By observing the reality, as well as by reviewing and sorting out research theories, I found a large number of literatures about service recovery, perceived justice, relationship quality, and behavioral intention. Yet among the available theories about the complaining behaviors of customers, currently there isn't a simple but comprehensive theory that can perfectly explain the mechanism underlying the complaining behaviors of customers, so there is no way to form a consensus from the service recovery process to the change of customer loyalty. The existing theories mainly explain why unsatisfied customers complain. These theories help to understand why customers complain in the first place, but there isn't a theory addressing the entire dynamic process from the initial complaints of customers to service recovery and then to loyalty restoration.

2.1 服务失误

2.1.1 服务失误的定义

所谓服务，ISO9000: 2000（2000）的定义[①]是："为满足顾客的需要，供方和顾客之间接触的活动以及供方内部活动所产生的结果。"由此可知，服务包括以下内容：首先，服务的根本目的是为了满足顾客的需要；其次，服务的前提是提供服务的企业要与接受服务的顾客接触；第三，服务的产品形式可以是完全的劳务，即无形产品形式，也可以是与有形产品的制造和提供结合在一起的服务形式；第四，顾客，即服务的接受者，可以是最终消费者，也可以是购货者、使用者或其他受益者。

服务因为具有无形性、异质性、易逝性和不可分割性等特点，所以消费者很难具体描述服务，仅仅能够通过一些形容词来形容 (Crosby，1979)。服务质量也因为服务的特点而增加了其定义和衡量上的困难。探讨服务品质的学者对于服务质量有许多不同的定义。

Gronroos（1982）也认为服务品质可以分成两种形态，一为技术质量（Technical Quality），它是顾客实际接受了服务时的衡量指标，关系到服务结果；另一个是功能质量（Functional Quality），它是服务传递的方式以及服务态度的衡量指标，并且认为服务质量为顾客对服务质量的期望与接受服务的认知相互比较。

Lewis 和 Booms（1983）认为服务质量为顾客对服务质量之期望与接受服务的认知的比较。Shetty 和 Ross（1985）认为服务品质是提供有效率、亲切的、有帮助的且持续的服务给顾客。Parasuraman，Zetithaml 和 Berry（1985）利用顾客期望与顾客认知来定义服务质量感知（Perceived Service Quality），其定义为实际的服务与期望的服务的差距。

服务在本质上是一种无形过程或行为，生产和消费不可分离，但同时顾客积

① ISO8402—2000《质量管理和质量保证——术语》。

极地参与服务的生产和传递过程，这些特性决定了对服务失误的定义较有形产品的缺陷困难得多。服务提供者与服务接受者身份的不同决定了对服务失误的定义有所不同。

Gronroos（1992）将服务失误定义为不按照顾客的期望进行服务。Keaveney（1995）认为当顾客对服务系统不满意时，服务失误就发生了。大多数不满意的顾客（90%~95%）将离开公司，根本不进行抱怨。Smith（1998）认为当服务提供者不能按照顾客的期望提供服务，并且导致其不满的时候，服务失误就发生了。

对企业来讲，服务失误意味着所提供的服务未能达到企业所规定的要求：而对顾客来讲，服务失误意味着所接收到的服务没有到其预期的程度（Smith，1998）。企业导向的服务失误定义与顾客导向的服务失误定义的关键差别在于，后者考虑到了顾客可以对同样的服务感知到不同的质量水平，从而对是否发生服务失误有自己的评价（Westbrook，1981）。

因此，学者们对服务失误的定义一般都是从顾客感知的角度出发，Bitner，Booms 等学者（1990）将服务失误定义为，在服务提供过程中，在服务接触的任一点上，如果顾客认为其需求未被满足，或是低于其预期水平，那么顾客就有可能认为出现了服务失误。雷蒙德 P. 菲斯克（Fisk，1998）也指出，如果企业服务表现未达到顾客对服务的评价标准，就是服务失误。Liu Chunmei（2005）进一步指出感知服务质量是一种具有多维度（Multidimensional）和多层级（Hierachical）的结构。因此，服务失误更强调顾客对服务经历的感知，而非企业认为他们应当提供的服务，所以人们普遍采用顾客导向的服务失误定义方式。

国外关于服务失败与补救的研究始于 20 世纪 90 年代，最近国内学者也对这方面予以了相当的关注，围绕顾客抱怨行为（申跃，赵平，2005），服务失败情景下消费者不满意、信任与转换行为的关系（赵冰等，2005），顾客感知价值（景奉杰等，2005），失败归因与补救效果的关系（宋亦平和王晓艳，2005），顾客对各种类型的失败和补救战略的不同反应（金立印，2005）等的探讨在增多。

2.1.2 服务失误的类型

在目前已有的有关服务营销研究的文献中，几乎一致认定服务失误的类型主要分为两种：结果性失误和过程性失误（Bitner et al., 1990; Honan, Helley et al., 1995; Mohr and Bitner, 1995），因为服务包含服务结果和服务过程（Gronroos, 1988; Parasuraman et al., 1985）。

结果性服务失误主要是指服务商没有实现基本服务内容，也就是说服务结果是否真正让顾客接受到了；而过程性失误是指服务传递方式上的缺陷和不足，也就是说服务是如何被顾客所接受的（Smith, 1999）。从社会交换的角度来说，结果性失误主要是涉及经济性资源的卷入，而过程性失误集中涉及符号性资源的卷入。

如前所述，服务失误客观存在，不可完全避免，且随时发生于顾客与企业接触的任何时点。但它的出现并非无规律可循，国外学者在零售、航空、餐馆等诸多服务行业对此作了研究，其中最著名的是Bitner（1990）等人用关键事件技术法（Critical Incident Technique，简称CIT法），通过对航空公司、旅馆、餐饮等行业的700多件案例的分析，得到服务失误三大类型，见表2-1。

表2-1 服务失误的类型

服务失误类型	具体表现
第一类：服务传送系统失误	正常服务不可获得
	不合情理的延迟服务
	其他核心服务失误
第二类：顾客个别需求之员工反应	对顾客特殊需求的反应不当
	对有特殊偏好顾客的反应不当
	容忍顾客错误的反应不当
	对可能打扰其他顾客的反应不当

续表

服务失误类型	具体表现
第三类：员工自发性行为	对顾客的关心与注意
	非同寻常的员工行为
	由于文化模式不同产生的行为
	姿势手势
	遭受斥责后的反应

资料来源：Bitner M J, Booms B H, Mohr L A. Critical Service Encounters: The Employee's Viewpoint [J]. Journal of Marketing, 1994, 58(4):95–106.

后来 Bitner 等人（1994）延续以前的研究，提出服务失误的第四大类，即问题顾客引起的服务失误，强调了服务失误也不全是企业或服务员工所造成的，顾客本身也可能是服务失误产生的主要原因。

除此之外，学者 Westbrook（1981）和 Kelly 等（1993）针对零售业的研究，Hoffman 等（1995）针对餐饮业的研究得到的结果，都与 Bitner 服务失误分类方法大体相同。

2.1.3 服务失误与顾客抱怨

无论程序、员工训练如何完善、周密，科技如何先进，在各服务接触点服务失误仍有可能发生，并由此引发顾客不满（Hess 等，2003）。

服务失误使顾客感到不满，顾客抱怨的情况也就由此产生。但是不满的顾客并不一定会抱怨。Tax 和 Brown（1998）就指出仅有 5%~10% 的不满顾客会主动抱怨和投诉。究其原因主要有五个方面（Bitner, 2000）：

① 顾客认为企业不会负责；

② 顾客不愿等待和面对造成失误的人员；

③ 顾客无法确定自身权益与企业应尽的义务；

④ 顾客不愿为抱怨花费时间；

⑤ 顾客担心提出抱怨后会得到更差的服务。

本研究界定所讨论的顾客抱怨是广义的抱怨，指顾客不满意时的心理感受以及做出的反应。顾客抱怨时可能有以下几种反应（Lovelock, 2001）。

① 虽然内心不满，但不采取行动。不满意顾客采取容忍与否的态度，取决于购买经历对顾客的重要程度、购买商品的价值高低、采取行动的难易程度及需要额外付出的代价等条件。

② 不再重复购买。

③ 向亲友传递不满信息。

④ 向运营商、消费者权益保护机构表示不满或提出相应要求。如以相关法律为基础，或以运营商内部标准为基准提出索赔要求。

⑤ 如果顾客不满意程度很强烈，就会采取法律行动，向仲裁机构申请仲裁或向法院起诉。

Day（1977）将顾客不满意但不采取行动也看作顾客抱怨的一种，并提出以下分类图（图 2-1）。

Singh 于 1988 年的研究中将消费者抱怨行为分为出声抱怨、私下抱怨、向第三团体反应三类，如图 2-2 所示。

Day（1980）后来又以顾客抱怨行动的目的将顾客抱怨行为分为三大类，分别是寻求赔偿（顾客采取抱怨行动的目的是为了寻求赔偿）、抱怨（目的是把不满情绪传给他人，而并非为了寻求赔偿）、个人抵制（目的是不再购买该产品或服务）。

此外，顾客满意的判断会因为服务失误的严重性而不同（Wagner, 1998），服务失误的程度越大，那么顾客对交换的知觉公平水平和满意程度就越低。因此，服务失误的严重性会影响到顾客对服务补救的评价与感知，同时，服务补救的内容也针对该服务失误的严重性做出调整。

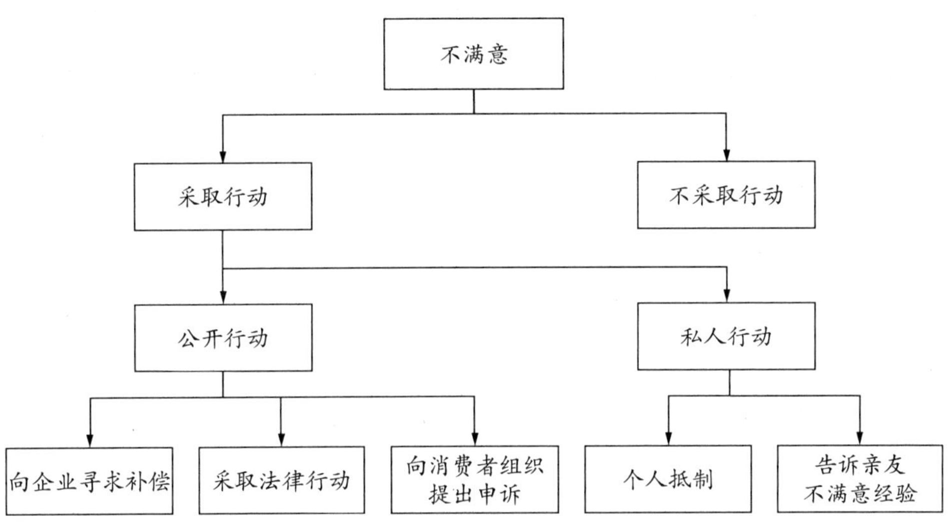

图 2-1 顾客抱怨行为分类 -1

资料来源 :Day R L, Landon E L. Collecting Comprehensive Consumer Complaint Data by Survey Research [J]. Advance in Consumer Research, 1976, 3: 263-269.

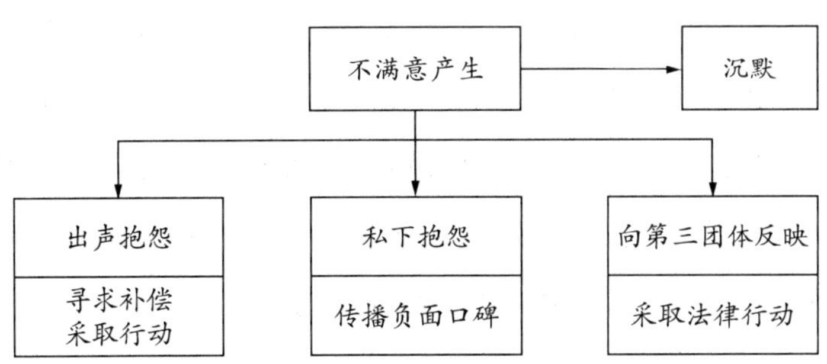

图 2-2 顾客抱怨行为分类 -2

资料来源 : Singh. Consumer Complaint Intertions and Behaviors: Definitional and Taxonomical Issues[J]. Journal of Marketing, 1988, 52(1): 93-107.

2.1.4 服务失误研究小结

服务失误为什么会产生呢？从服务生产和传递的角度来看，服务因为具有无形、异质以及不可储存性等特性，所以顾客在接受服务时常常感受到相当高的不确定性（Uncertainty），尤其当他们面对复杂、不熟悉以及需长期传送的服务时，这种不确定性会更高，而这种不确定性即意味着服务失败及负面结果产生可能会发生在每一个服务接触的地方。

Goodwin 和 Ross（1992）认为服务和消费是同时发生的，服务传送与服务提供者是不可分离的，所以在服务传送时的任何一个服务接触点，如果产生服务失误，都会使得顾客产生负面的反应。从顾客方面来看，现在的顾客需求变化迅速，需求多样、多变造成了服务传递系统的更大不确定性。Power（1991）认为，处于信息时代的顾客拥有许多资讯，其需求的变化速度更常常令服务商们伤透脑筋。

对于服务失误这个问题，研究者们基于不同的理论，从不同的角度对其进行了研究。Westbrook（1981）提出，零售业顾客对企业不满意的原因主要来自三个方面：第一，销售系统（产品和销售系统的提供能力）；第二，购买系统（零售点的布置，实际选择和购买产品）：第三，消费系统（产品购买以后的使用和消费）。服务失误可能产生于产品的来源、实际购买过程到消费者实际使用的一系列过程。

Bitner 等（1990）根据归因理论分析顾客对服务失误的感知。Bolton 等（1999）基于社会交易理论的角度提出：在类似于服务补救的社会交换中，评价服务失误应该从资源（包括经济性和符号性资源）交换的类型和数量方面出发，因为服务失误给顾客造成的损失主要是经济利益和符号性利益的损失。因此，对服务失误的描述应该包含类型维度（失误种类）和数量维度（严重性）。

为了进一步详细回顾已有的相关研究，我将 1990 年以后的主要研究内容进行了整理，并制成表 2–2。

表 2-2 服务失误的相关研究

研究者	时间	主要观点
Bitner	1990	研究发现当顾客感觉服务失误的原因可归因于企业，而且也可能再度发生时，顾客会提高不满意的程度。而员工解释、提供补偿及实体环境等均会影响顾客对服务失误的归因
Bitner,Boom and Tereault	1990	从服务接触的观点来探讨顾客不满意的关键事件，并将其分成三类：①服务传递系统失误；②顾客的需求或要求员工反应；③员工的行为
Bower	1991	服务是“品质、合理价格、良好服务”的综合体
Bitner	1992	认为服务的实体环境会对员工与顾客造成影响，环境的维度包含：①环境状况；②空间；③标识
Goodwin and Ross	1992	服务和消费同时发生，服务传送与服务提供者不可分割，所以在传送的任何一个接触点若产生失误，均会使得顾客产生负面的反应
Bitner, Booms and Mohr	1994	以 CIT 的方法对旅馆、餐厅及航空公司员工的观点做调查，将 744 项关键事件分为：①服务传递系统的错误；②顾客的需要或要求员工反应；③员工的行为；④有问题的顾客行为。研究显示在不满意的部分，员工的角度认为是“有问题的顾客行为”，顾客则认为是“员工的行为”
Kelly and Davis	1994	服务失误应从时间、严重性、频率三个维度来加以深入探讨。失误会发生在顾客与服务人员之任何接触点，而失误的严重性，可以是微不足道或者是非常严重的
Boulder et al.	1996	针对瑞典航空公司及美国航空公司，综合员工及顾客观点，将服务失误事件分为：①在机场发生的服务失误；②在航空器内发生的服务失误
David and Adrian	1998	以航空乘客为研究对象发现，服务失误会造成顾客对公司的承诺急速下降。在顾客的信任方面，初期虽不会急速下降，但若公司持续发生失误或是出现顾客对于补救不满意情形，则在中后期还是会急速下降
Smith Bolton and Wagner	1999	以美国餐饮业和旅店为例，服务失误可以由两个变量来决定：服务失误的类型（过程失误与结果失误）和服务失误的严重性。根据这两个变量可以将服务失误描述为四种模式：不严重结果性失误、严重结果性失误、不严重的过程性失误和严重过程性失误
Bitner	2000	对为何大部分顾客不愿抱怨或投诉的归因进行了研究，认为有 5 个方面的原因阻碍顾客进行抱怨：一是顾客认为企业不会负责；二是顾客不愿等待和面对造成失误的人员；三是顾客无法确定自身权益与企业应尽的义务；四是顾客不愿为抱怨花费时间；五是顾客担心提出抱怨后会得到更差的服务
Weun	2004	服务失误严重程度指的是顾客感知到的服务问题的强度

续表

研究者	时间	主要观点
卢东，李雁晨	2010	服务的有形性对服务失误责任归因和稳定性归因都存在显著的正面影响；顾客参与对服务失误责任归因存在负面影响，但对稳定性归因存在正面影响
罗劲	2010	服务失误的严重性、可控性和稳定性都会显著地促使消费者满意度降低，其中，严重性的影响程度最大
张秀红	2012	服务质量是企业生存的根本，但对于最卓越的企业而言，服务失误也无法根本杜绝
迟焕鹏，张乾	2012	服务失误发生后，如何采取服务补救，将会影响顾客的购后行为意向

2.2 服务补救

2.2.1 服务补救的定义

国外研究普遍引用Gronroos（1988）的观点定义服务补救（Service Recovery）：服务补救亦可称为顾客抱怨处理，它是服务提供者在服务缺陷或失误发生后，所采取的一些补救反应与措施。

Zeithaml和Bitner（1990）认为，服务补救是服务性企业在对顾客提供服务出现失败和错误的情况下，对顾客的不满和抱怨当即做出的补救性反应。其目的是通过这种反应，重新建立顾客满意和忠诚。

Zeithaml, Berry和Parasuraman（1993）三位学者认为，服务补救或称抱怨处理是服务提供者针对顾客感觉到的服务传输低于顾客的“容忍阀”的情况所采取的反应措施。这里，“容忍阀”代表了顾客期望的服务水平与顾客认为足够的服务水平之间的差距。

Bell和Zemke（1987）认为，有效的服务补救措施不应仅仅被看作“损失的控制”，更是公司的一个战略重点。通过服务补救可以与顾客有更多交流的机会，从而有机会强化顾客对企业的忠诚（Berry and Parasuraman，1991）。

Hart，Heskett 与 Sasser（1990）三位学者认为，服务失误是服务业的重要事件，即使最好的服务公司也避免不了服务失误的发生，而服务补救即是企业用来解决顾客抱怨，并通过抱怨处理建立顾客对企业信任的策略。因此，服务补救措施对于顾客在衡量企业及其行为时，会产生正面影响，进而加强企业与顾客之间的关系。

在 1995 年之前的定义，多把服务补救视为服务失误发生且经顾客抱怨以后的事情，与顾客抱怨处理一致。近来的服务补救定义越来越重视主动性和事前反应，倾向于把服务补救看作主动发现和处理服务失误的过程（何会文，2006）。

Tax 和 Brown（1998）将服务补救定义为：服务补救是一种管理过程，它首先要发现服务失误，分析失误原因，然后在定量分析的基础上，对服务失误进行评估并采取恰当的管理措施予以解决。

Smith，Bolton 和 Wagner 等学者于 1999 年明确指出："服务补救比顾客抱怨处理包含了更广泛的活动内容，因为其所处理的状况包括了服务差错已经发生但顾客并未提出抱怨的情境。"

美国的雷蒙德 · P. 菲斯克等人（2001）定义服务补救是企业为重新赢得因服务失误而已经失去的顾客好感而做的努力。

韦福祥（2002）认为，服务补救是服务企业在出现服务失误时所做出的一种即时性和主动性的反应。其目的是通过这种反应，将服务失误在顾客感知服务质量、顾客满意和员工满意方面所造成的负面影响减少到最低限度。

陈忠卫和黄晓波（2005）在综合各种定义的基础上认为服务补救有狭义和广义之分。狭义的服务补救是指服务的提供者对服务过失采取的行动。这个意义上的服务补救强调的是对具体问题、过失实施行动的过程。广义的服务补救是指组织全体成员共同参与的对服务系统中可能出现的过失进行矫正，对顾客进行补偿，以维持长远的顾客关系和不断完善服务系统的一系列活动的总和。

本研究关于移动通信服务业服务失误的定义沿用学者 Gronroos（1998）的观点，并且由于前述顾客抱怨的广义性，特定义文中提到的顾客抱怨处理与服务恢复、服务补救皆为同一概念，不做进一步区分。

2.2.2 服务补救的方式

服务补救是当顾客发生不满时，企业采取行动以抚平顾客的不满情绪，同时再创顾客满意的机会。有效的服务补救能提高顾客满意度，建立顾客忠诚和提高顾客保留率，但是失败的服务补救和不采取任何补救措施一样糟糕，甚至更坏。对服务补救策略的研究从两个层面进行：一是从微观的具体业务层面来探讨服务失误发生后的补救措施的具体实施；二是从宏观的企业运营角度探讨服务补救的系统管理与实施。鉴于服务补救的重要性，越来越多的学者对此领域进行研究，试图找出企业应采取何种服务补救方式才能达到最好的效果。

Bell 和 Zemke（1987）提出服务补救的 5 大要素为：

① 道歉，当事第一人的道歉优于企业道歉，了解失误发生原因的人最好也能出现；

② 紧急恢复，企业应当迅速进行服务补救，即使在不可能改正的情况下，也应当勇于尝试快速解决问题；

③ 同情，真诚地表达对顾客处境的理解；

④ 象征性补偿，补偿形式可以包括免费服务或提供未来的免费服务或折扣；

⑤ 追踪，服务补救以后与顾客电话联系以确定顾客对补救过程是满意的。

Bitner 等人（1990）通过对多个服务行业的 700 多个关键事件的调研发现，并不是服务失误本身使顾客不满，大多数顾客是可以接受服务失误的，真正引起顾客不满的是企业对该服务失误事件的反应（或者缺乏反应）。持同样意见的还有

Feinberg 等人（1998），他们建议成功的服务补救应当包括以下 4 个关键因素：

① 承认企业存在服务失误或发生了问题；

② 解释服务失误的原因；

③ 在合适时向顾客道歉；

④ 给予顾客补偿，如免费券、免费食物或饮料等。

Boshoff（1997）随机选取了 540 个国际旅行者，调查常见的服务失误，并从 27 种解决办法中随机选一种提供给顾客。他发现最成功的方法按顺序是：

① 企业尽可能高职位的人员对服务失误的快速反应；

② 快速反应的同时，给顾客全额退款或一定数额的补偿；

③ 由高级别管理人员提供的高额补偿。

Boshoff（1997）发现，道歉在服务补救上的效果比较有限，除非伴随一定形式的补偿。

Kenney（1995）认为，企业对顾客实施的服务补救主要是两个方面的补救：一方面是心理方面的补救，如道歉、解释以消除消费者的不满；另一方面是物质方面的补救，如对顾客所遭受的损失给予实物的补偿。企业对顾客抱怨处理的方式也可分为解释与补偿两类。解释包括外部解释与内部解释，补偿分为物质补偿（服务补偿与金钱补偿）和非物质补偿（采取道歉的方式）。

Conlon 与 Murray（1996）对解释的方式进行了研究，他们将解释细分成六种，以探讨不同的顾客抱怨处理方式对顾客满意度与再购率是否存在显著的影响。他们所提出的解释方式包括：道歉、证明正当、找借口、避免发生、道歉并加以证明正当、公司需要更多信息才能处理等六种方式。Christo（1997）的研究重点则在有形的服务补偿上，以飞机乘客为研究对象，探讨不同的服务补救方式对顾客满意度的影响。他将服务补救方式分为三种：道歉、道歉加上同等的补偿、道歉外再给予超额补偿。研究结果发现，有形的补偿对顾客满意度有一定程度的影响，但并非顾客满意的必要条件；抱怨回应时间与满意度成反比，等待时间越长，顾客的满意度越低。

Johnston 和 Fern（1999）建议服务补救方法应当按失误的程度和对补救效果的要求而定。他们将服务补救进一步分为对服务失误的处理和对顾客抱怨的不合适反应的处理。前者又被作者称为“单偏差”，后者被称为“二次失误”或“双偏差”，表明失误程度更加严重。在这两种不同的情况下，同样的补救方式却可能取得不同的效果。快速反应和改正是所有服务补救方式的基础。一封道歉信可以给经历过偏差的顾客带来惊喜，而经历了双偏差的顾客，道歉可能也不能使他们满意，他们可能更期望企业能提供一些特殊的照顾。在这两种不同的情况下，信息传达的方式也不一样：在单偏差情况下，企业口头保证类似事件不再发生就可以了，而在双偏差情况下，最好用书面承诺和解释的方式才能达到效果。管理者介入也是补救的有效性的因素之一，但是只有在双偏差情况下才有必要。补偿也非常重要，对于单偏差情况，常规的补偿就足够了，而经历了双偏差的顾客更期望有超出常规的额外补偿。

2.2.3 服务补救研究小结

根据 Gronroos（1988）的定义，服务补救是指服务提供者执行一些动作来回应服务失败。只要有一次服务失败就可能导致顾客的不满意，并寻求替代者，所以服务组织者必须采取有效的补救行动来显示出其和竞争者的不同。它包含了重新解决问题，转变不满意顾客的负面态度，最终保留住这些原本对于服务不满意的顾客。服务提供者必须努力让第一次接受服务的顾客留下好印象，但由于环境及人为因素的困难，错误的发生是难免的，而服务补救即是提供一个机会去弥补这些错误并提供一个让顾客留下正面服务经验的机会。

最近国内学者也对服务补救这方面予以了相当的关注。金立印（2006）通过情景模拟试验考察了服务严重程度及顾客归因对补救预期的影响，结果发现，顾客对服务失败原因的“位置所在”归因影响其在补救结果方面的预期。研究还发现，服务失败与补救情景中的补救预期、补救成就感知及两者间的不一致对顾客满意均有显著影响。宋亦平和朱涛（2006）通过情景模拟试验法，对投诉者与不投诉者对服务补救的评价及服务补救对两类顾客所产生的效果进行比较分析，结果发现，对于同样的服务补救措施，投诉者对于补救水平的评价并不低于不投诉者，且相对于投诉者而言，投诉者的满意度和再购买意愿也并非更难恢复。

表 2–3 列出近年来有关服务补救的相关研究，下面大体上回顾一下。

表 2–3 服务补救相关研究

学者	时间	主要观点
Fimstahl	1989	指出顾客希望前缘人员即被授与解决问题的能力
Hart et al.	1990	指出一半以上对于顾客抱怨的努力，实际上只是增加了顾客对服务的负面反应
Hart, Heskett and Sasser	1990	虽然补救行动是因为服务失败而仓促进行，但这样的行动通常会对顾客评价及行为有正面的影响，并可加强顾客与组织间的联系，对公司而言重新解决问题对于顾客满意有很高的回报
Reichheld and Sasser	1990	顾客对于服务的满意和问题之解决有密切的关系，而问题的重新解决可视为公司的正面、负面声誉及顾客的保持之主要因素
Halstead and Page	1992	研究发现对于抱怨结果满意的顾客有较高的再购意愿
Power	1992	提出公司增进 20% 之顾客保持（Customer Retention）在利润上的影响和减少 10% 的成本是相同的
Boulding et al.	1993	指出失败若发生在顾客的服务组织关系之早期，因为顾客没有之前的成功经验来抵销这个失败，所以将对组织的整体评价有较大的影响
Blodget et al.	1993	指出服务补救的效果直接与顾客公平感知的水平相关
Kelley and Davis	1994	研究指出顾客对于服务补救的期望会受到认知的服务品质及顾客组织的承诺之影响
Christo	1996	以飞机乘客为研究对象，研究发现顾客抱怨回应的时间与满意度成反比，服务补救对顾客满意有一定的影响，但并不是顾客满意的必要条件

续表

学者	时间	主要观点
Tax and Brown	1998	研究中提出服务补救的四个阶段为：①确认服务失误；②解决顾客问题；③服务失误的沟通与分类；④整合资料与改善整体服务
Smith Bolton and Wagner	1999	在 Hart 等（1990）的基础上增添了一个维度：补救的主动性
郑绍成	1999	研究发现服务补救会对于顾客购买意图产生影响，而给予顾客实体补救的顾客满意效果大于只有口头抱歉
Miller et al.	2000	主要提出服务补救的检视程序，程序中说明服务补救的期待会受到失败严重性、认知的服务、顾客忠诚度以及服务保证的影响。而补救的方式有实质性及心理性两种。至于前缘人员的授权及补救的速度会影响补救的结果，而补救的结果则会表现在顾客的忠诚度及满意度上
McCollough, Berry and Yadav	2000	通过将没有经历服务失误的顾客满意度与补救后满意度进行比较的研究指出，对于某些经历过服务失误的客户来说，不管补救的效果如何，整体满意度会比从没经历过服务失误的人要低
Levesque and McDougall	2000	研究发现补救带来的回报逐渐减少并且如果服务失误重复发生补救会变得更加困难
Maxham	2001	指出适度的高服务补救努力显著地提高了失误后的满意度水平
Yim et al.	2003	将公平理论直接纳入期望差异理论框架，证实了基于公平的补救期望在补救评价中的重要作用
Mattila and Patterson	2004	通过对东亚和美国餐馆顾客的研究，指出两类顾客对情境约束的敏感性不同影响其对服务失误的归因并调节他们对补救过程的满意度
金立印	2005	研究顾客对各种类型的服务失败和补救战略的不同反应
申跃和赵平	2005	从顾客抱怨行为研究服务补救措施
赵冰，涂荣法和符国群	2005	研究服务失败情景下消费者不满意、信任与转换行为的关系
金立印	2006	通过情景模拟试验考察了服务严重失败程度及顾客归因对补救预期的影响，结果发现，顾客对服务失败原因的“位置所在”归因影响其在补救结果方面的预期。研究还发现，服务失败与补救情景中的补救预期、补救成就感知及两者间的不一致对顾客满意均有显著影响
宋亦平和朱涛	2006	通过情景模拟试验法，对投诉者与不投诉者对服务补救的评价及服务补救对两类顾客所产生的效果进行比较分析，结果发现，对于同样的服务补救措施，投诉者对于补救水平的评价并不低于不投诉者，且相对于投诉者而言，投诉者的满意度和再购买意愿也并非更难恢复

续表

学者	时间	主要观点
展晓义	2009	服务失败是由服务的特性所决定的，因而是不可避免的，从两个层面探讨服务补救策略，并把侧重点放在现场服务补救层面，服务补救步骤侧重于企业管理层面，通过管理工具的运用，使服务补救的步骤有效实施来推动服务补救策略的运作，进而提高企业服务管理水平，从而提高顾客的满意度和忠诚度，为企业创造良好的经济效益
朱思思	2011	服务的特殊性使得服务质量并非产品质量那样可以得到有效控制，很多因素都可能引发服务失败，此时，企业必须及时采取补救措施，努力消除顾客的负面情绪，避免顾客的流失。补救措施本身并非无差异，在进行服务补救时，认识服务补救的有效性对企业至关重要
郑红	2013	服务补救是服务企业获得顾客忠诚、提高竞争力的重要方式之一。当前，我国服务业发展滞后，在现有服务业发展规模的基础上，服务企业服务水平差异显著，服务补救意识和能力参差不齐。本文总结了现有研究中对服务补救内涵的认识，分析了服务补救的特点以及服务失误出现的可能性，并对服务补救的研究现状进行综述

资料来源：本文作者整理。

2.3 知觉公平

知觉公平理论是在社会交易理论和公平激励理论的基础上发展而来的，本节先简单介绍知觉公平的概念，然后介绍与顾客抱怨背景相关的知觉公平研究，最后介绍知觉公平与服务补救的研究现状。

2.3.1 公平理论的概述

美国心理学家 Adams（1963）在交易理论的基础上参考相对剥夺理论（Relative Deprivation Theory）以及认知失调理论（Cognitive Dissonance Theory）之后提出了公平激励理论，它主要研究人的动机与知觉之间的关系。公平理论的基本内容包括以下三个方面。

① 公平是激励的动力。人能否受到激励，不但视他们得到了什么而定，还要

视他们所得与别人所得相比较之后，心理是否感到公平而定。因此，人的知觉公平水平与人的行为直接相关。

② 公平理论的基本模式（即方程式）：$Q_P/I_P=Q_O/I_O$。Q_P 代表一个人在社会交易中所得的知觉，I_P 代表一个人对他所付出的知觉，Q_O 代表这个人对参考对象所得的知觉，I_O 代表这个人对参考对象所付出的知觉。知觉公平就是一种公平感知水平，指人们在比较自己的付出与所得和他人的付出与得失之后而得出的一种心理评价。这表明公平首先是一种知觉，然后才是一种参考与对照。

③ 不公平的心理行为。当人们感到不公平待遇时，在心里会产生一种张力，然后会通过语言和其他行为来自我释放。通过这些自我解释的行为进行知觉公平的调整，从而达到一种心理平衡。

2.3.2 公平理论在服务补救中的应用

公平理论（Justice Theory）强调顾客感受到的服务补救的过程和结果的公平性。它的主要假设是顾客的满意程度取决于顾客知觉的公平程度。顾客在接受服务时处于一种交换的关系中，他们将自己的投入，如花费的金钱、时间等与从消费经验中所获得的价值、心理上的满足等作比较，并且也与其他参考群体作比较，若顾客自认为比率不协调，心理就会感到不公平，从而产生不满意。知觉公平程度越高，顾客将越满意。

无论顾客以前有无经历过特定企业的服务失误和补救，人们都有一个普遍公认的衡量标准。顾客把这些普遍标准作为参考，与企业的服务补救表现作比较。另外，服务失误的特性（如类型、重要性）也会影响到顾客的普遍参考标准。普遍标准与补救表现的对比产生顾客的知觉公平。知觉公平还会进一步影响顾客满意。

大约在 20 世纪 70 年代，由于受到西方消费至上主义的影响，早期对顾客抱怨的研究直接关注顾客抱怨的外在表现，其成果主要集中在对不同行业顾客抱怨率的统计（Hirschman，1970），总体状况描述（Day and Bouder，1978），归纳抱怨的性质和方式（Hunt，1977）等。后来，研究的重点逐渐转移到顾客抱怨倾向的影响（Bearden et al.，1979）等因素上，但是以上这些方面的研究还没有揭示顾客抱怨后的心理和行为变化过程，以及顾客会怎样解释、理解和评价服务企业对服务失误的反应。

幸运的是，公平理论为研究者提供了一个框架，知觉公平水平是一个可以很好地解释、预测顾客在抱怨发生后其态度和行为意图的参数（Blodgett et al.，1993；Maxham et al.，1997）。以前，公平理论主要是应用在组织行为和人力资源的研究当中，用来解释和预测企业或组织内部个体如何评价和理解冲突形势。如果人在组织内部发生冲突后，个体会借助与自己相似的参考对象进行付出与得益的比较，从而形成一个知觉公平水平（Blau, 1964; Adams, 1963）。Leventhal（1980）指出：公平理论下所有的社会情境当中，在任何的资源（与酬劳）分配的决策过程中，知觉公平（Perceived Fairness 或 Justice）是个人行为的重要决定因素。

Alexander 和 Ruderman（1987），Bies 和 Shapiro（1987）将知觉公平理论进行了进一步发展，将知觉公平分为补偿性公平、程序性公平和互动性公平。然而首次尝试将公平理论应用于研究组织外部顾客行为的学者是美国学者 Deutsch，他认为一种交换是否公平是顾客满意的首要前提，当顾客与其他人相比，如果自己的知觉公平水平低，那么他将会产生抱怨（Deutsch, 1985）。知觉公平理论的宝贵之处在于它提供了一个认识顾客抱怨过程中心理状态变化的参数（Stephens and Tax, 1997）。Blodgett 和 Tax（1993），Clemmer（1993）等几位学者将公平理论正式引入顾客抱怨的研究当中。他们认为：

① 顾客抱怨行为的产生主要是因为企业与自己的社会交易过程中（如服务失误），让他感觉到自己的付出与所得和别人付出与所得不成比例；

② 在服务失误后，企业可以通过服务补救改变顾客公平认知的输入，从而提高顾客的知觉公平水平，进而修正顾客认知输出的结果——满意的态度；

③ 在顾客抱怨的过程中，知觉公平水平与顾客的后续行为和口碑有直接影响。

学者们将公平理论运用到饭店业的服务补救中，并得到一些结论。Hui M.K. 和 Au K.（2001）研究了跨文化背景下饭店顾客的知觉公平。他们调查了三种补救策略，分别是实物补偿、道歉以及给予发言权。研究结果显示，给予顾客充分的发言权在顾客知觉公平上的影响对中国人要比对加拿大人更大。这是因为中国客人对地位、尊重更为看重，相反，对加拿大客人来讲，补偿对知觉公平的影响更为重要。

Sparks 和 Mccoll-Kennedy（2001）探索了饭店在服务补救时给予顾客的知觉公平，包括给予顾客发言权的程度、给予顾客的关注程度、给予顾客特别对待的程度。他们所得到的结论表明，饭店的服务补救方式强烈影响着顾客的知觉公平，同时也特别指出了顾客对饭店服务补救评价的复杂性。例如，如果饭店本身就有高额补偿的政策，那么这种补偿能够起到正面影响，否则反而会起到负面效果。如果顾客得到不同一般的高额补偿，而且这不是饭店一贯的政策，顾客会觉得不舒服，甚至有犯罪感。相反，如果顾客得到不属于政策范围内的低额补偿（如饮料券），但是他们得到了带有明显补偿特征的特别对待，其影响将是积极的，顾客会觉得这种补偿是公平的。

Schoefer 和 Ennew（2003）采用知觉公平框架来测定顾客对旅游供应商服务补救的评价，发现了当顾客用知觉公平三个方面来评价服务补救的证据与结果时同样显示顾客得到的补偿结果（补偿公平）很重要，但整个服务补救过程（程序公平）和员工行为（互动公平）也起到非常重要的作用。

尽管顾客抱怨研究是近年来的热门话题，但是有关顾客抱怨背景下的公平理论研究的文献仍旧比较少，这些文献主要集中在服务补救效果、顾客公平感知、顾客满意和行为意图这几个概念之间（Maxham et al.，2002）。

2.3.3 服务补救与知觉公平的关系

根据前面对服务补救有关文献的回顾得知，服务补救本质内容应该包含四个要素（Hart et al.，1990）：

① 主动性（Initiation）；

② 结果补偿（Compensation）；

③ 响应速度（Response Speed）；

④ 口头道歉（Apology）。

以上四个维度会如何影响顾客的公平的感知呢？Smith 等（1999）分别就服务补救内容与知觉公平之间的关系进行了详细的探讨，并建构了服务补救与知觉公平之间的关系模型。

自从 1988 年美国学者克莱曼首次提出服务公正性概念以来（克莱曼，1988），公正性理论（Justice Theory）在服务管理中的应用主要集中于诠释服务失败与补救情境中顾客的服务公正性感知如何影响满意感和行为意向。许多学者的研究结果表明：服务公正性包括结果（或分配）公正性、程序公正性和互动（或交往）公正性等三个组成方面。从顾客的角度可以对这三个方面的公正性做如下理解：结果公正性也称为分配公正性，是指顾客对服务结果公平程度的一种主观判断，顾客常根据服务的价格、数量、服务的正确性和卓越性来评估服务结果公正性；服务程序公正性是指顾客在接受服务过程中所感知到的服务过程、服务标准、服务方针等方面的公正程度，顾客经常从自己等待服务的时间、等待服务的过程、企业满足顾客的特殊要求、服务效率、服务承诺和服务差错等六个方面来评估服务程序公正性；互动公正性是指顾客在同服务员工接触过程中所感知到的诚信、有礼、耐心、亲切等人际交往方面的公正程度，顾客常从服务人员礼貌待客、理解顾客要求、不欺骗顾客、关心顾客利益、耐心服务等方面来评估服务互动公正性（Smith et al., 1999）。

根据社会交易理论，补偿性知觉公平是与社会交易成本和经济利得直接相关（Adames, 1965; Deusch, 1975，1987），因此在顾客服务补救中，补偿性知觉公平直接和实现交易资源的分配结果相关。如果把一次服务补救作为一种社会交易，那么服务补救中有形结果的补偿维度（Compensation）主要是对补偿性知觉公平有强相关关系；响应速度（Response Speed）只和程序性知觉公平相关，而与补偿性、互动性知觉公平没有太大相关；道歉（Apology）与主动性（Initiation）的补救内容仅对互动性知觉公平有强影响（Smith and Bolton，1999）。

Hoffman 等（1995）认为企业对失败的服务进行补救时，应从结果（提供物质补偿等）、程序（迅速灵活的处理问题等）及互动（亲切的态度、诚恳的道歉等）等三个方面来提升顾客对服务补救的公正性感知，如果顾客觉得补救过程中受到了不公正待遇，会产生失望、愤怒、不满等情感反应，采取更为强烈的抱怨行为甚至法律措施。相反，如果顾客认为企业处理服务失败不论是在结果上，还是在程序和互动上都是十分公正的，则会对企业产生较高的介入度，强化同企业间的心理承诺，较以前更为忠诚。

服务的生产与消费难以分离的属性，使顾客在接受服务时不可避免地要同服务组织及其员工接触和互动，在一般的服务提供情境中，顾客同企业员工一样会感知到服务的公正性。很多服务的提供过程中（如教育培训，医疗等），顾客参与服务的生产和传递，从这个意义上来讲，顾客不单纯是完全存在于企业外部的服务消费者，还是存在于企业“内部”，并承担着部分服务经历创造活动的“员工”。企业需要像培训和激励内部员工那样培训和激励顾客，通过强化顾客的主观能动性来提升其对服务接触的公正性感知，进而实现企业同顾客间成功的互动（Lovelock and Young, 1979）。因此，一直以来主要用于诠释员工对所属企业组织的特定行为及服务补救情境中顾客反应的服务公正性理论同样适用于解释一般服务提供情境中的顾客行为。

韩小芸和汪纯孝（2003）尝试分析了一般服务情境中顾客的公正性感知与其行为意向之间的关系。Rose 和 Neidermeyer（1999）的研究发现顾客的情感反应及心理承诺等顾客心理方面的因素是影响其不良行为的直接原因。Aquino 等（1999）在组织行为方面关于员工公正性感知与员工情感反应及不良行为之间关系的研究成果，以及 Hoffman 等 （1995）将公正性理论应用于服务补救情境中来解释顾客行为的相关研究都为此研究试图利用公正性理论来解释顾客不良行为提供了理论上的依据。借鉴以上这些现有的研究成果，本研究期待顾客的服务公正性感知可以通过某些顾客心理及情感方面的媒介变量来影响顾客的不良行为。

郭贤达等（2006）将感知公平的三个维度作为消费者对服务补救满意度的前置变量，考察了顾客服务试办不久后的满意度和情感承诺对消费者行为意向的影响。该研究以电信行业为背景，结果显示分配公平和交互公平影响顾客服务失败补救后的满意度，并增强他们对服务提供商的情感承诺。

杜建刚和范秀成（2006）分析了包括顾客信任、顾客感知价值等多个前置变量对服务忠诚度的影响，并研究了公平性变量对以上关系模型的调解作用。

金立印（2006）构建了服务公正性感知、顾客情感反应、心理承诺及顾客不良行为等变量构成的结构方程。结果发现，服务公正性感知对顾客心理承诺有显著影响，程序和互动性感知对顾客的情感反应有显著的影响，特别是服务互动公正性感知不仅通过媒介变量来影响顾客行为，还对顾客行为有直接效应。

2.4 关系品质

关系（Relationship）最好的描述是“介于顾客和公司之间的联结”（Berry,1995; Liljander and Strandvik, 1995；Storbacka et al., 1994）。克兹佩尔认为关系牵涉“交

易伙伴之间相互承认的某种特殊地位”（索斯顿·亨尼格—梭罗等，2003）。

关系品质这个概念萌芽于关系营销理论，它以人际关系研究范式为主，整合了交易成本、关系接触与新古典经济学等多方面的研究方法，运用经济学、社会学和心理学等多学科知识，研究顾客与企业之间的关系满足双方需求的程度，并对关系效果进行认知评价（Hennig-Thurau and Klee, 1997）。

关系品质指与顾客建立良好的关系，以降低顾客对交易的不确定性（Crosby et al., 1990; Fletcher et al., 2000; Smith, 1998），使顾客对销售人员、产品或服务产生依赖或好感（ Jones and Sasser, 1995 ），进而建立顾客忠诚感。

在关系营销领域，通常认为客户的忠诚度依赖长期发展起来的企业与客户间的关系品质，认为关系品质是一种无形的力量增加着产品与服务的价值并导致期望的买卖双方的交易（Clevitt, 1986）。由于产品服务的多样性与异质性，使得顾客在交易的选择上，容易发生不安与不确定性，若能与顾客建立良好的关系品质，便能有效降低不确定性，提高未来持续互动的效果（Crosby et al., 1990）。因此，关系营销的主要目的便在于吸引顾客，与顾客发展持续性的长期关系，进而达成获利的关系。

2.4.1 关系品质的定义

对于关系品质理论性的研究最早开始于 Dumont 和 Wilson （1970），企业通过建立良好的互惠合作关系而获利，以关系导向并充分利用现有资源保持顾客，强调顾客忠诚度，注重与相关个人、组织建立、发展关系和承诺并达到长期合作关系以实现各自目标。关系品质也被视为感知关系的质量（Holmlund, 1996），感知关系品质意味着将评估的结果视为感知并结合个人具体情况的一个过程。若能与顾客建立良好的关系品质，便能有效降低不确定性，提高未来持续互动的效果，关系品质可作为衡量关系程度或强度的重要指标（刘人怀，2005）。

在消费市场领域对于关系品质的定义较多涉及社会属性，认为关系品质是顾客对服务人员的信任感以及顾客对买卖双方关系的满意程度，关系品质就是客户在关系中对于销售人员的信任与满意（Crosby et al., 1990）。在服务营销的文献中，关系被视为一系列的重复购买（Repeated Episodes）（Hakansson, 1995）。

关系品质是关系营销理论中一个比较重要的概念，尽管有关关系品质的文献不少，但对关系品质的定义依旧是不清晰的（刘人怀和姚作为，2005）。下面简要列举部分学者对于关系品质的定义（表 2–4）。

表 2–4 对于关系品质定义的总结

作者	定义
Gummesson(1987)	认为关系品质是企业与客户互动关系的质量，是客户感知质量的组成部分，高的关系品质能够引起客户对质量的正向感知并构建双方的长期业务关系
Crosby et al,(1990)	关系品质是买卖双方关系强度的整体评价，此评价符合双方的需求与期望，而这些需求与期望以双方过去成功的或失败的遭遇或事件为基础
Lagace, Robert Dahl-strom, Gassenheimer (1991)	从社会心理学角度来定义关系品质，认为关系品质是消费者对销售人员的信任，即对关系的满意程度
Jarvelin Lehtinen(1996)	认为关系品质是指客户对于关系是如何满足其期望、预期行为、目标的感知并要求客户关注整个关系
Gemuenden(1997)	认为关系品质就是对纯产品（服务）领域的交换、组织间的联系、个体间交流和组织间权力关系的评价
Hennig-Thurau，Klee (1997)	认为关系品质，如同产品质量的概念，可被视为在满足顾客关系需求上的适合程度
Smith (1998)	认为关系品质是一个包含各种正面关系结果的高阶建构（High-Order Construct），反映出关系的总体强度，以及关系人在需求和期望上的满足程度
汪纯孝等 (1998)	关系品质是买卖双方的满意感和信任感
Joyce A. Young(2000)	提出心理学中的近关系理论来对企业间的合作关系进行研究。近关系理论主要从关系强度、关系的持久性、关系频率、关系的多样性、关系的灵活性与公平性等六个维度来对企业间的合作关系品质进行度量
Maria Holmlund (2001)	认为关系品质的定义来自于服务质量的含义：感知关系品质是公司的双方结合各自个人认知对商务交互关系的一种评估，评估强调了评估双方会通过相似的交互标准来进行潜在的调整

续表

作者	定义
Gronroos(2002)	从顾客的观点定义关系品质，他认为关系品质是指顾客与服务提供者在长期的互动关系中所形成的动态的质量感知，是顾客对服务质量长期的、连续的感知过程
刘人怀和姚作为 (2005)	关系品质是关系主体根据一定的标准对关系满足各自需求程度的共同认知评价。其实质就是指能够增加企业提供物的价值，加强关系双方的信任与承诺，维持长久关系的一组无形利益

资料来源：本文作者整理。

2.4.2 关系品质的维度与模型

Kumar 等（1995）认为关系品质反映出信任（Trust）、承诺（Commiment）、冲突（Conflict）、持续的期望（Expectation of Continuity）及投资的意图（Willingness to Invest）的概念。Smith （1998）指出，关系品质至少应包含满意、信任及承诺三个维度。Holmlund（2001）认为技术的、社会的、经济的三个决定性因素影响关系品质。技术因素是价值创造过程的核心；社会交互因素指某一交易关系中包含的个人之间的交流和接触；经济因素是成本和收益。刘人怀和姚作为（2005）指出不论在什么行业背景下，信任、满意与承诺均是关系品质主要的维度。对于关系品质的维度及其模型的研究，学者们提出了各自的观点，至今尚无一致意见，现将几种主要观点简要介绍如下。

① Crosby 等（1990）认为关系品质可以看成一个高阶的维度（High-Order Construct），至少应该包含信任（Trust）和满意（Satisfaction）两个维度。他们提出了关系品质模型，并针对寿险业销售人员与顾客的关系对 151 名投保客户进行了实证研究。影响关系品质的主要因素包含相似性、专业知识及关系销售行为（图 2-3），几个概念分别说明如下。

◆ 满意（Satisfaction）：一种情感性的评价，是顾客与销售人员间互动经验的响应。

◆ 信任（Trust）：代表顾客认为销售人员值得信任，不会采取对消费者不利的行动。

◆ 相似性（Similarity）：Crosby 等人认为相似性（尤其是态度的相似性）是一种暗示，一方认为对方将会帮助自己实现自己的目的。

◆ 专业知识（Expertise）：顾客所感受到销售人员对产品或服务的相关能力。

◆ 关系销售行为（Relational Selling Behaviors）：是指在销售过程中的一种行为倾向，它可以减少或培养买卖双方的关系，并维持以及增长这一关系。关系销售行为包含三个因素：互动强度、相互揭露以及合作意愿。

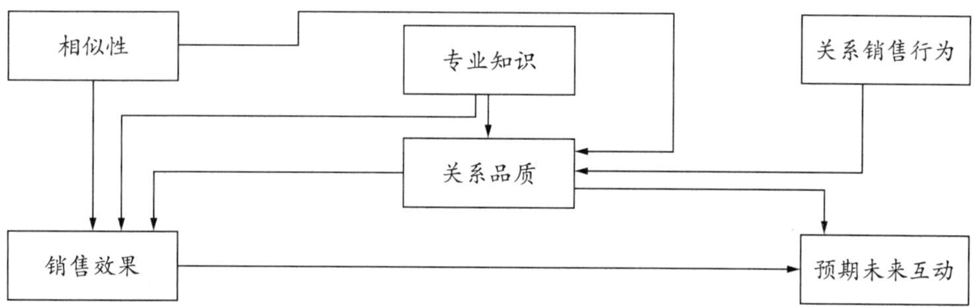

图 2-3 Crosby, Evans 和 Cowles 的关系品质模型

资料来源：Crosby L A, Evans K R, Cowles D. Relationship Quality in Services Selling: An Interpersonal Influence Perspective[J]. Journal of Marketing, 1990, 54(3): 68–81.

② Lagace 等（1991）在其关系品质的模式中，以信任和满意两个维度界定关系品质（图 2–4）。他们认为，如果顾客和销售人员双方对于互动的过程都不满意，那么原本的合作关系可能早已结束；反之，随着时间延长，可能发展出更加信任的关系，故在其模型中假设关系持续时间对于关系质量具有正向的影响。此外，影响

关系质量的主要因素还包含道德行为（Ethical Behavior）、专业知识（Expertise）和关系接触（Relationship Contact）。

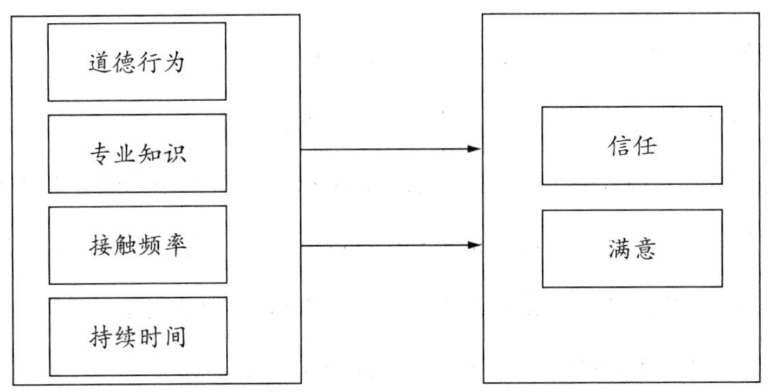

图 2–4 Lagace, Dahlstrom 和 Gassenheimer 的关系品质模型

资料来源：Lagace R R, Dahlstrom R, Gassenheimer J B. The Relevance of Ethical Salesperson Behavior on Relationship Quality: The Pharmaceutical Industry[J]. Journal of Personal Selling & Sales Management, 1991, 11(4):39–48.

③ Storbacka 等（1994）虽未界定关系品质的维度，但提出了相当类似的概念，包含顾客满意（Customer Satisfaction）、关系强度（Relationship Strength）、关系寿命（Relationship Longevity）及关系获利性（Relationship Profitablity）等。他们主要的理论核心建构在以下变量间的关系上：感知价值（Perceived Value）、顾客满意（Customer Satisfaction）、关系强度（Relationship Strength）、关系长度（Relationship Longevity）、顾客关系盈利性（Relationship Profitability）（图 2–5）。

关系强度反映在采购行为及沟通行为(如抱怨)上，内容包括顾客与企业间存在的契约：顾客的承诺是顾客对未来的意图及打算，顾客重复的采购行为是建立在因较强的关系而引发顾客正面的承诺的基础之上。他们认为，关系因企业与顾客的联结 (Bonds) 而加强，较高的服务质量会导致较高的顾客关系盈利性。

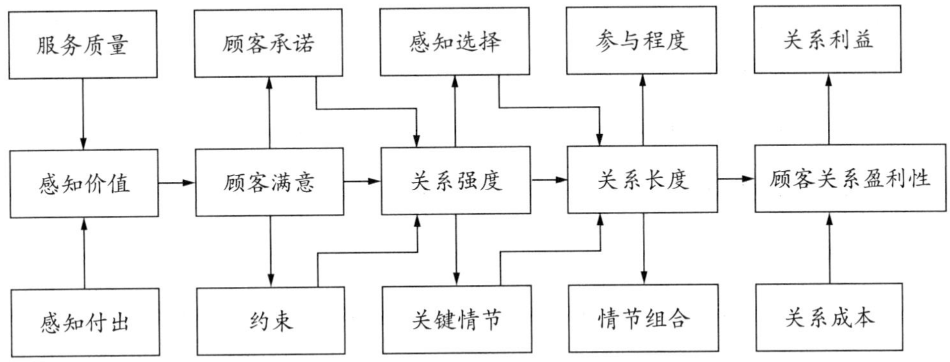

图 2–5 Storbacka, Standvik 和 Gronroos 顾客关系盈利能力模型

资料来源 : Storbacka K, Strandvik T, Gronroos C. Managing Customer Relationships for Profit: The Dynamics of Relationship Quality [J]. International Journal of Service Industry Management, 1994, 5(5):21–38.

④ Kumar 等（1995）认为关系品质反应出信任（Trust）、承诺（Commitment）、冲突（Conflict）、持续的期望（Expectation of Continuity） 以及投资意图（Willingness to Invest）之概念。

⑤ Henning–Thuau 和 Klee（1997）认为关系品质应包括整体感知质量（Overall Quality Perception）、信任 (Trust) 及承诺（Commitment）三个维度（图 2–6）。

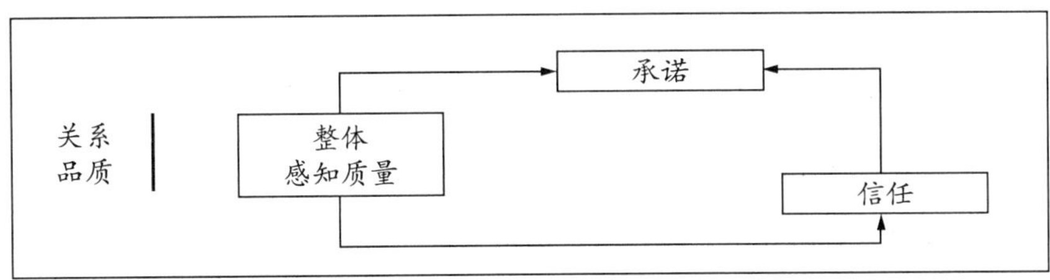

图 2–6 Hennig–Thurau 和 Klee 的关系品质模型

资料来源：Hennig–Thurau T, Klee A. The Impact of Customer Satisfaction and Relationship Quality on Customer Retention: A Critical Reassessment and Model Development[J]. Psychology & Marketing, 1997, 14(18):737–765.

⑥ Smith（1998）综合许多学者的看法认为关系品质至少应该包括满意、信任及承诺三个相关的维度。

从以上研究可以看出，对关系质量的维度，有些学者（Crosby et al.，1990；Hsieh and Hiang，2004；金萍和赵民杰，2005；汪纯孝等，1998）认为满意和信任是关系质量的维度。Morgan 和 Hunt（1994）的研究认为信任与承诺是影响关系质量的关键因素。部分学者（Hennig–Thurau and Klee, 1997; Smith , 1998; 刘人怀和姚作为，2005）则认为，满意、信任、承诺是关系质量最主要的维度。

虽然对于关系品质的维度应该包含哪些内容还没有达成共识，但是从上述学者们所提出的维度可发现到，信任、满意与承诺均是关系质量的主要维度（刘人怀和姚作为，2005）。因此，本研究将引用 Smith （1998）、刘人怀和姚作为（2005）等人的观点，采用满意、信任与承诺作为关系质量的三个维度，以下对此三个维度作一说明。

① 信任（Trust）。信任通常被视为成功关系的必要因素（Berry，1995；Daye et al.，1987；Morgan and Hunt，1994）。在大多数关系营销的研究中，信任一直被当成是一块基石。在信任的定义中，一般会包含相信关系伙伴会以对方的最佳利益来行动。Crosby 等（1990）认为,信任是一种信念，其相信服务人员或销售人员可以依赖，会以顾客长期利益来行动。Moorman 等（1993）认为信任是一种意愿，其意愿有信心信任其交易伙伴。Morgan 和 Hunt（1994）定义信任为对交易伙伴的可靠及正直有信心的认知。对于服务的顾客而言，顾客常面临相当大的不确定性，而当不确定性及风险的程度高，顾客信任的培养就特别重要（Crosby et al., 1990），因为借由信任的建立，可降低或消除此种不确定性。

值得信任的伙伴关系将降低决策的风险并将受到伙伴间交易过程以外的其他因素的直接影响。Anderson 和 Narus （1990）认为信任是合作方相信他的伙伴将完成任务并产生积极的效果，公司不会采取带来消极影响的不期望的行动。Morgan与Hunt（1994）认为信任是对交易伙伴可靠及正直有信心的认知，并指出功能性冲突与不确定性因素的增加会造成信任的缺乏，双方合作的好坏都直接来自组织的承诺与信任，信任也促使将来双方的合作。Wilson（1995）认为大多数伙伴会以对方最佳的利益来行动，因此当不确定性及风险程度高且不具保证时，顾客信任的培养就特别重要。

信任受到不同因素的影响，不仅存在于企业与客户层面上，供应商的规模、双方的接受力、沟通程度，都将影响到客户对企业的信任，进而影响到客户的关系价值。Morgan和Hunt（1994）认为信任发生在个体对交易伙伴的可靠性和忠实度有信心时，认为信任包含三个驱动因素，即能力、一致性和善行。Hakansson和Sharma（1996）认为信任来自于伙伴的专业性、可靠性或是伙伴的意图，并讨论了人与人之间的信任主要受到感知的专业性、真挚、得体、合时与保密的影响。Smith和Barclay (1997)确定了五种信任的来源：关系投资、影响的接受度、沟通的开放程度、控制的减少、机会主义行为的减少。Doney和Cannon（1997）在对供应商信任的相关研究中发现，供应商的规模、供应商定制产品的意愿、对销售人员的信任都将影响顾客对供应商的信任。Walter和Ritter（2003）认为信任包含三个方面：第一，关系成员在他们的行动中表现的仁爱之心；第二，诚实，意思是信任的组织依赖于关系成员的可信度；第三，关系成员获取关系收益的能力。

② 满意（Satisfaction）。Oliver（1996）定义“满意乃是顾客对于和消费相关的事物之喜好程度的评估判断”。Westbrook（1981）则认为“满意是一种情绪状态，其反映出对互动经验的评估”。由此可知满意乃是一种消费者心中主观的情绪感觉，反映出消费者对交易或接触经验喜好的评估。在服务过程中顾客往往会因服务本身的一些因素，例如服务的无形性，当面临不当服务传播的时间很长，绩效可能和期

望不一致时，更可能导致不确定性的提高 (Parasuraman et al.，1985)。

另一方面，顾客常依据服务人员或公司过去的表现来推断其未来的表现，所以顾客对于服务人员或公司的满意与否可视为良好关系的核心。Crosby 等 (1990) 亦指出，当顾客对过去的绩效水平持续感到满意时，其对于销售人员的正直较能够依赖，且对销售人员未来的绩效感到信心。

顾客满意更是衡量整体营销绩效的重要指标之一，顾客满意会增加顾客再次购买的行为，且会购买其他的产品。Anderson 和 Weitz（1992）认为通过与可以信任的、良好声誉的供应商建立关系可以降低购买者的风险。Cronin 和 Taylor（1992）则称顾客满意度一直是影响再次购买的一个主要因素，满意度也被认为是买卖双方关系的重要结果。

③ 承诺（Commitment）。承诺乃是交易伙伴之间对于关系的持续之暗示或公开的誓约（Dwyer and Oh,1987）。Moorman 等（1992）认为承诺乃是想要持续维持有价值关系的一种愿望，而 Hennig-Thurau 和 Klee（1997）则定义承诺是顾客对于关系长期维持的导向，不论是对关系的情绪联结，或者是基于保持关系能产生较高利益的现实考量。由此可知，承诺是维持良好及长期关系的重要表征，也是一种想要持续维持关系的意愿，当顾客表现出承诺的意愿时，通常也表示和企业之间具有良好关系。因此，承诺亦是成功的长期关系之重要元素（Dwye et al., 1987；Morgan and Hunt，1994；Sharma and Patterson，1999）。

Morgan 与 Hunt（1994）发展出“承诺—信任理论”，认为关系承诺与信任为关系营销最主要的中间变数，其中“关系承诺”的定义为彼此认定双方关系值得长久维持的程度，“信任”则为彼此认为其交换伙伴可靠与诚信程度。高的关系中止成本、关系利益与分享价值，会有较高的关系承诺并进而造就高的合作行为与默许认同。承诺是在合作双方认为彼此的关系值得继续的前提下产生的，若没有信任作为基础是无法建立的，因此承诺与信任在关系的建立上扮演着十分重要的角色。Thorsten（1997）、Wong（2002）等研究了信任与承诺的关系，信任可以导致承诺的提高。吴强军（2004）认为关系承诺包含了经济性承诺与情感性承诺，是价值规范、服务质量、相互依赖和关系枢纽等因素通过对顾客的经济性承诺和情感性承诺的中介影响而形成的。Walter 等（2003）认为承诺有三个不同的驱动因素：情感承诺描述了对未来存在的关系的一种正面的态度；当一些形式的投资（时间或其他资源）出现在关系中时，手段承诺将会呈现；最后，承诺的短暂驱动因素表明关系总是存在的。

基于以上文献研究，本文选取信任、满意、承诺作为关系品质的三个维度，并对其进行测量与研究。

2.5 顾客行为意向

行为意愿（Behavior Intention）是指消费者在消费后，对于产品或企业所可能采取的特定活动或行为倾向（Engel et al., 1995），即行为意愿指个人从事某些行为的主观概率或可能性。在 Engel 等（1995）针对信念、感觉、态度、行为意愿与行为间的关系研究中，认为顾客对某一标实物（Object）的整体评估是由其对该标实物的信念与感觉所决定的，顾客对某一标实物的态度会进而决定顾客的行为意愿。Oliver（1996）认为顾客对一项产品或服务的态度是由个人以往的经验而来，而顾客对此产品或服务的态度则会影响其购买意愿。

2.5.1 顾客行为意向基本模式

行为意向（Behavior Intention）的概念来自于态度理论（Attitude Theory），态度主要由认知（Cognitive）、情感（Affective）以及意动（Conative）三种要素（Component）组成。

所谓认知要素即个体对态度标识参数（Attitude Object）的知识与信念（Brief），

而情感要素即表现出个体对态度标实物的感觉，意动要素则是指个体对态度标实物的行动或是行为意向（Engel et a1., 1995）。

在态度理论中，认知要素以及感情要素被视为态度的决定因子，即个体对态度标实物的整体评估决定于个体对标实物的感觉，意动要素则不被视为态度的决定因子，反而是态度决定了意动，即个体的行为意向是由态度来决定的（Engel and Blackwell，1995）。

对企业而言，了解顾客的行为意愿，能够预测顾客的需求，并维持长期的顾客关系。Parasuraman 等（1996）认为所谓的行为意愿，可以区分为正向与负向的行为意愿。顾客对企业有正向行为意愿时，会称赞该企业，对该企业产生偏好，增加对企业产品或服务的购买数量；反之，有负面的行为意愿时，则会选择离开公司，减少购买数量，最后离开企业。

行为意向是态度和行为之间的中介，主要体现为未来的重复购买意向、交叉购买意向和口碑传播意向三个方面。本文测量的是重购意向和口碑传播意向。

① 重购意向（Intention to Remain）。简单地说，重购意向指的是未来再次光顾服务提供者的可能性。顾客保留或重购意向是营销领域中最重要的概念之一，最流行的出版物经常出现强调顾客保留率重要性的文章（Heskett et a1.，1994；Jones and Sasser, 1995; Reichheld and Sasser, 1990）。Reichheld 和 Sasser（1990, P.107）为顾客保留率对商业成功的重要影响作用提供了一个非常有说服力的例子："当顾客流失率下降时，利润会上升。顾客流失率降低 5%，银行系统的利润上升了 85%，保险业的利润增加了 50%，汽车服务业的利润增加了 30%。研究发现顾客流失率改进 5% 将使顾客平均价值提升 125%。"因此，顾客保留率可以被视为提高企业利润和长期绩效的关键因素之一。

② 口碑传播意向（Willingness to Refer）。口碑传播的重要性已经被服务领域

的研究文献很好地证明过了（Day, 1980; Zeithaml et al., 1985, 1993）。口碑向顾客提供了关于企业的重要信息，而这些信息经常能帮助消费者决定是否光顾这家企业。研究表明，口碑传播对顾客购买过程有着极其有力的影响（Richins, 1983）。例如，有调查发现，在向 60 种不同产品的消费者询问什么因素影响他们的购买决策时，回答他人推荐的人数是回答广告人数的 3 倍。从这个意义上说，口碑传播在促使消费者转换品牌的过程中也起着非常重要的作用。口碑传播具有这样的影响是因为从面对面的方式中获得的信息比其他不太生动的方式传达的信息更有影响。需要注意的是，一方面，对企业有利的正面口碑传播会有助于企业获得新顾客，而不需要企业为此花费任何成本。而另一方面，对企业不利的负面口碑却会产生非常强的消极影响，能极大地削弱公司广告和沟通的有效性。口碑传播尤其对服务提供商的成功起着关键的作用。服务的无形性以及生产和消费的同步性，使得对服务进行营销比对有形产品进行营销更加困难，而口碑传播为这一问题的解决提供了一个特殊的方法。虽然消费者在消费之前无法完全了解一项服务，但他会从有经验的信息员 (亲戚、朋友或同事等) 那里寻找口碑信息。同时，来自有经验的信息员的口碑能够帮助消费者解决在服务购买中存在的低可比性和难以寻觅质量信息的问题。由于口碑被认为是没有偏见的(在保证传播者没有为此得到相应的商业利益回报的前提下)，从而当服务中的信息难于评估时，就会更依赖于口碑的作用。因此，口碑在服务购买决策中扮演着极为重要的角色。

2.5.2 服务补救与顾客行为意向之间的关系

企业几乎能够从任何失误中恢复过来且保留顾客未来再次从企业进行购买的意愿（Goodwin and Ross, 1992）。从公平理论观点出发，企业在服务失误之后能够通过有效地满足顾客的感知公平从而成功地提高顾客较低的购买意愿。类似地，有研究者指出企业能通过公平地回应服务失误而维持顾客保留（Oliver and Swan, 1989;

Seiders and Berry, 1998）。这些研究结果表明，当实施了有效的服务补救时，购买意愿会保持稳定，并可能会提高。而另一方面，差劲的服务补救努力会降低顾客从失误企业再次购买的意愿。

企业还能够通过公平地响应服务失误重拾顾客的推荐意向（Goodwin and Ross, 1992; Seiders and Berry, 1998）。但当顾客感知到企业对服务失误的回应不公平时，不仅不会向他人推荐，还很有可能会传播负面的口碑（Seiders and Berry, 1998）。其他一些学者表示服务补救和口碑传播之间存在正向关系（Blodgett et al., 1993, 1997），也就是说服务补救的水平越高，顾客的正面口碑传播意向就越高，而服务补救的水平越低，顾客的负面口碑传播意向就越高。因此，有效的服务补救可以导致正面的口碑，或者至少能够降低与糟糕的服务补救有关的负面口碑的传播。

2.5.3 关系品质与顾客行为意向之间的关系

Crosby 等（1990）实证发现，顾客对未来互动的预期，决定于其与企业之间的关系品质。Boles 等（1997）亦指出，当顾客和企业的关系较佳时，顾客有较高的重购意图（Intention to Remain）、较好的口碑（Willingness to Refer）。Beatty 等（1996）则在和销售员及顾客深度访谈后指出，保有良好关系的顾客对销售代表及公司表现出高度的忠诚及口碑。Morgan 和 Hunt（1994）对顾客与企业间的关系加以探讨，发现较高的关系承诺及信任能减少顾客离去的倾向（Propensity to Leave）及促进合作。Wetzels 等（1998）则针对服务关系（Service Relationship），探讨满意、信任、承诺和顾客留存意向（Intention to Stay）之间的关系，经实证后发现，信任和承诺皆和顾客留存意向有正向关系。Parasuraman 等（1996）指出，当顾客喜爱公司的服务，和公司维持长期且有价值的关系时，较愿意购买额外的服务并散布口碑。且由于顾客认为维持关系有价值，公司可能可以收取比其他公司更高的费用，而和公司保持良好关系的顾客也较不会对他人散布不利公司的信息。因此，维持良好的关系品质，应能增进顾客正面的意向(如：正面口碑、忠诚、付较高价)，减少负面意向(如：离去、散布不利讯息)。

2.5.4 知觉公平与顾客行为意向之间的关系

Deutsch（1985）认为一种交换是否公平是顾客满意的首要前提，当顾客与其他人相比，认为自己的知觉公平水平低，那么他将会产生不满意甚至抱怨。然而不满意的态度或抱怨又可以对顾客行为意向产生影响，所以知觉公平水平决定着顾客抱怨后的行为意向。

Blodgett 等(1993)认为，顾客的程序性知觉公平和负面口碑、重购意图之间有很强的相关关系。在 1997 年，他们把研究进一步拓展，认为知觉公平的三个维度（程序性知觉公平、补偿性知觉公平和互动性知觉公平）都独立地对口碑和重购意图有显著性的影响（Blodgett et al., 1997）。研究还发现互动性公平感知相比其他两个维度来说，对顾客行为意向有更大的影响。Maxham 和 Netemeyer（2002）在 Blogdgett 等人的基础上将模型进一步发展，尽管知觉公平与顾客行为有很强的相关关系，但是知觉公平并不直接对顾客行为意向起作用，而是间接通过补救满意和累积性总体满意这两个中间变量来影响的。

不过 Fourie 和 Mick（1999）认为，尽管顾客满意是对具体交易判断与感知的一个指示器，但是多年来几乎所有消费者行为的研究文献并没有证明：顾客满意是导致顾客行为意向的唯一必然前提，因此没有必要把顾客满意当成顾客行为的必经路径。

消费者的行为意愿主要包括三种类型:重购意愿、口碑和溢价购买（董大海和金玉芳，2003）。在实际操作中，西方学者对消费者行为意愿的具体构成并没有达成统一的意见。

第 3 章

研究模型及研究假设

本研究的目的是研究服务补救与知觉公平、关系品质、抱怨后行为意向的关系。通过文献研究来看，服务补救的因素有很多种，这里我们选择了对本研究适用的三个因素：响应速度、心理补救、有形补偿。与此同时，确定了三个因变量：知觉公平、关系品质以及行为意向的不同构面。由于三个自变量（响应速度、心理补救、有形补偿）各自有两个水平（快、慢，高、低，多、少），因此本研究共有 2×2×2 个处理水平的结合。同时三因素完全随机设计能检验更多的假设，包含了两次交互作用以及三次交互作用。多因素多变量设计可以研究更为复杂的变量关系。本研究共提出了 38 个假设。

Chapter 3

Research Model and Hypotheses

The purpose of this study is to explore the relationships between service recovery and perceived justice, relationship quality and post-complaint behavioral intention. Literature review shows that service recovery has many different factors. Here three factors suitable for this study are selected by us: response speed, psychological remedy, and tangible compensation. At the same time, three dependent variables are identified: perceived justice, relationship quality, and the different facets of behavioral intention. Because each of the three independent variables (response speed, psychological remedy, and tangible compensation) has two levels (fast, slow; high, low; more, less), this study has a combination of $2 \times 2 \times 2$ processing levels. Also, the three factors are completely randomly designed, so that they can test more hypotheses, including two interactions and three interactions. The multivariate design allows the study of more complex relationships between variables. This study comes up with a total of 38 hypotheses.

根据前面的相关文献来设计本研究的基本架构，然后在所提出的架构基础上进行与架构相应的研究假设。

3.1 研究模型

本文的研究目的是研究服务补救与知觉公平、关系品质、抱怨后行为意向的关系。希望本研究的结果，能为电信移动服务商提供合适的建议，并为日后的管理改进提供参考。研究模型如图 3–1 所示。

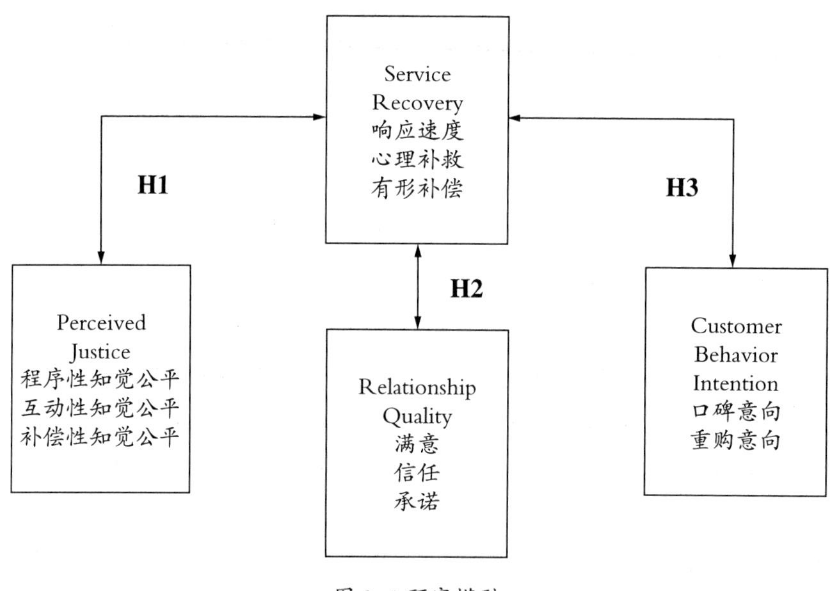

图 3–1 研究模型

本研究是一个典型的三因素完全随机实验设计，实验设计的基本条件如下：

① 研究中有三个自变量（响应速度、心理补救、有形补偿），每个自变量各有两个水平（快、慢，高、低，多、少）。

② 由于实验中的三个因素都有两个水平级，则本研究共有 2×2×2 个处理水

平的结合。

③ 三因素完全随机设计能检验更多的假设，它可检验 A、B、C 三个主效应，还可以检验 AB 、AC 、BC、 ABC 四个交互作用。其中，包含两个字母的交互作用叫两次交互作用，包含三个字母的交互作用叫三次交互作用（三次交互作用本研究不做验证）。

④ 本研究包括三个因变量（知觉公平、关系品质、行为意向），多因素多变量设计可以研究更为复杂的变量关系。

研究者选取了 8 种不同的服务补救设计，将 800 个样本随机分为 4 组，每组回答两种不同的服务补救措施，并测试它们对三个因变量的反应。

3.2 假设推导

通过文献研究来看，服务补救的因素有很多种，这里我们选择了对本研究适用的三个因素；与此同时，确定了知觉公平、关系品质、行为意向的不同构面，构建了如图 3–1 所示的模型，确定了研究假设。

本文的研究目的是研究服务补救与知觉公平、关系品质、抱怨后行为意向的关系。希望本研究的结果，能对服务商提供合适的建议，并作为日后的管理改进提供参考。

服务补救本质内容应该包含四个要素（Hart , Heskett 和 Sasser, 1990）：响应速度（responsive speed）、有形补偿（compensation），心理补偿，主动道歉（Initiation），以上 4 个维度会如何影响顾客的公平的感知呢？ Smith 和 Bolton(1999) 分别就服务补救内容与知觉公平之间的关系进行了详细的探讨，并建构了服务补救与知觉公平之间的关系模型。

Alexander 和 Ruderman（1987）. Bies 和 Shapiro （1987）将知觉公平理论进行

了进一步的发展，将知觉公平分为补偿性公平、程序性公平和互动性公平，这为研究者理解顾客如何动态反应服务商的服务补救提供了一个很好的框架。

Smith(1998) 等则认为关系品质是由满意、信任、承诺三个构面组成的。也有学者（Hennig–Thurau & Klee, 1997）指出，关系品质应包括整体品质的认知、信任和承诺三个构面。虽然对于关系品质的构面没有出现一致性结论，但从文献回顾看，多数学者都提到了满意、信任和承诺这三个构面。本研究也认为，满意、信任、承诺的构面划分较好地概括了关系品质的内容，因此在后面的研究中我们将以这三个构面为基础。

行为意向 (Behavior Intention) 的概念来自于态度理论（Attitude Theory），态度主要由认知（Cognitive）、情感（Affective）以及意动（Conative）三种要素（Component）所组成。

根据以上理论模型以及准实验研究设计，本文做出了以下假设（表 3–1）：

表 3–1 研究假设

编号	假设
H1	服务商服务补救措施与顾客知觉公平正相关
H1.1	响应速度越快，顾客的知觉公平感知越高
H1.2	心理补救越高，顾客的知觉公平感知越高
H1.3	有形补偿越多，顾客的知觉公平感知越高
H1.4	响应速度对顾客知觉公平的不同构面影响存在差异
H1.5	心理补救对顾客知觉公平的不同构面影响存在差异
H1.6	有形补偿对顾客知觉公平的不同构面影响存在差异
H2	服务商服务补救措施与关系品质正相关
H2.1	响应速度越快，顾客的关系品质越高
H2.2	心理补救越高，顾客的关系品质越高
H2.3	有形补偿越多，顾客的关系品质越高
H2.4	响应速度对顾客关系品质的不同层面影响存在差异
H2.5	心理补救对顾客关系品质的不同层面影响存在差异
H2.6	有形补偿对顾客关系品质的不同层面影响存在差异
H3	服务商服务补救措施与行为意向正相关
H3.1	响应速度越快，顾客的行为意向越高

续表

编号	假设
H3.2	心理补救越高，顾客的行为意向越高
H3.3	有形补偿越多，顾客的行为意向越高
H3.4	响应速度对顾客行为意向的不同层面影响存在差异
H3.5	心理补救对顾客行为意向的不同层面影响存在差异
H3.6	有形补偿对顾客行为意向的不同层面影响存在差异
H4	响应速度与心理补救对知觉公平、关系品质、行为意向存在二次交互作用
H4.1	响应速度与心理补救对知觉公平存在二次交互作用。响应速度快的情况下，心理补救越高，顾客知觉公平感知越强
H4.2	响应速度与心理补救对关系品质存在二次交互作用。响应速度快的情况下，心理补救越高，顾客与运营商关系品质越高
H4.3	响应速度与心理补救对行为意向存在二次交互作用。响应速度快的情况下，心理补救越高，顾客行为意向越好
H4.4	响应速度与心理补救对知觉公平的不同构面存在二次交互作用
H4.5	响应速度与心理补救对关系品质的不同构面存在二次交互作用
H4.6	响应速度与心理补救对行为意向的不同构面存在二次交互作用
H5	响应速度与有形补偿对知觉公平、关系品质、行为意向存在二次交互作用
H5.1	响应速度与有形补偿对知觉公平存在二次交互作用。响应速度快的情况下，有形补偿越多，顾客知觉公平感知越强
H5.2	响应速度与有形补偿对关系品质存在二次交互作用。响应速度快的情况下，有形补偿越多，顾客与运营商关系品质越高
H5.3	响应速度与有形补偿对行为意向存在二次交互作用。响应速度快的情况下，有形补偿越多，顾客行为意向越好
H5.4	响应速度与有形补偿对知觉公平的不同构面存在二次交互作用
H5.5	响应速度与有形补偿对关系品质的不同构面存在二次交互作用
H5.6	响应速度与有形补偿对行为意向的不同构面存在二次交互作用
H6	心理补救与有形补偿与知觉公平、关系品质、行为意向存在二次交互作用
H6.1	心理补救与有形补偿对知觉公平存在二次交互作用。心理补救较高的情况下，有形补偿越多，顾客知觉公平感知越强
H6.2	心理补救与有形补偿对关系品质存在二次交互作用。心理补救较高的情况下，有形补偿越多，顾客与运营商关系品质越高
H6.3	心理补救与有形补偿对行为意向存在二次交互作用。心理补救较高的情况下，有形补偿越多，顾客行为意向越好
H6.4	心理补救与有形补偿对知觉公平的不同构面存在二次交互作用
H6.5	心理补救与有形补偿对关系品质的不同构面存在二次交互作用
H6.6	心理补救与有形补偿对行为意向的不同构面存在二次交互作用

第 4 章

研究方法

本研究采用问卷调查的方式，对研究所涉及的所有变量进行数据采集。在问卷的设计过程中，本次研究是在已有的相关研究问卷的基础之上，根据调研企业所提供的服务产品特性专门设计的问卷。调研所获问卷采用 SPSS15.0 进行运算。本研究选取了 8 种不同的服务补救设计，将 800 个样本随机分为 4 组，每组回答两种不同的服务补救措施，并测试了它们对三个因变量的反应，并按照调研的前后顺序对每个环节进行了详尽的说明。

Chapter 4

Research Methods

This study uses questionnaires to collect data for all the variables involved. The questionnaires used in this study are designed according to the unique features of the service products provided by the companies surveyed based on the existing questionnaires used in relevant studies. The returned questionnaires are analyzed using SPSS15.0. This study chooses 8 different service recovery designs and randomly puts 800 samples into 4 groups. Each group is asked to answer questions about two different service recovery measures and tested for their response to the three dependent variables. A detailed explanation is provided for each process according to the sequence of the survey.

本研究采用问卷调查的方式，对研究所涉及的所有变量进行数据采集。在问卷的设计过程中，本次研究是在已有的相关研究问卷的基础之上，根据调研企业所提供的服务产品特性专门设计的问卷。调研所获问卷拟采用 SPSS15.0 进行运算。下面按照调研的前后顺序对每个环节进行详尽的说明。

4.1 变量测量

本章首先定义本研究框架中所涉及的变量，然后依据研究框架和变量来进行问卷设计，并根据所回收到的问卷进行样本数据分析，最后介绍为验证本研究假设所用的方法。

本研究中的变量主要包括：①服务补救；②关系品质；③知觉公平；④行为意向。下面逐一对每个变量的定义和测量方式加以说明。

4.1.1 服务补救

Hart 等(1990)的研究认为服务补救的内容应该包括: 有形补偿(Compasention)、响应速度(Response Speed)和道歉(Apology)。前两者是属于社会交易的经济性维度，而后者是属于符号性维度。Smith 等（ 1999 ）又将服务补救的内容增添了一个维度：补救的主动性，它主要反应服务补救的触发是由交易的哪一方发起（ 企业或顾客 ）的。服务补救的具体维度如下所述。

① 有形补偿（ Compensation ）。有形补偿的内容主要包括赔偿、赠券与赠品、折扣处理和小礼物等方式。Tax 等（ 1998 ）研究发现有形补偿是服务补救 4 个维度中最为重要的维度，他对顾客的行为意图有最大的影响。

② 响应速度（ Response Speed ）。在顾客抱怨时候，抱怨被处理和响应的速度。其主要的衡量指标是顾客等待抱怨被处理的时间。Smith 等（ 1999 ）研究发现，响应速度对顾客的程序性知觉公平的影响最大，而对其他两个知觉公平维度有很小的

相关性。

③ 道歉(Apology)。Berscheid 和 Walaster (1973) 认为，道歉是一种符号性资源(声誉、尊重)的再交换，道歉主要代表着一种人际处理和沟通的符号，所以主要对互动性知觉公平产生影响（Blodgett and Tax, 1997）。

④ 补救的主动性（Recovery Initiation）。服务补救包含了比顾客抱怨处理更为广泛的内容，因为它还包括顾客不抱怨时企业对服务失误的主动性态度（Smith et al., 1999）。在服务失误出现的那一刻，顾客有可能不抱怨。如果此刻，企业主动询问所出现的失误给顾客造成的不便，那么顾客将产生更高的满意度。如果顾客自己首先确认服务失误带来的损失，那么抱怨处理的成本将会更高。服务补救的主动性主要是对互动性知觉公平产生影响（Blodgett et al., 1997）。

因此，本研究借鉴 Smith 等（1999）服务补救与知觉公平的关系研究模型，将服务补救的内容变化以 4 个维度衡量：响应速度、道歉、主动性和有形补偿。响应速度分为快、慢两个值。在问卷设计中考虑到被调研对象对反应速度的不同理解，因此，没有采用具体的时间来限定补救速度的快慢，而是依据不同人对速度快慢的感知来测量。而有形补偿以“不退还多收取的费用”及“双倍返还费用”两种选择来代表补偿低、高两个值。依据前面的文献回顾，可以将道歉与主动性归为一个维度：心理补救。这样心理补救分为高、低两个值。在本研究中心理补救程度高是通过服务人员“真诚地道歉”来表示，而“稍示歉意”则表示低心理补救。问卷试图通过改变服务补救不同维度的值来代表服务补救过程的差异。那么，研究中的服务失误补救维度的测量组合表如表 4.1 所示。

4.1.2 知觉公平

在有关公平文献回顾中，可知学者们（Blodgett and Tax，1993；Clemmer, 1993; Bolton and Wagner, 1999; Maxhaxn and Netemeyer, 2002）也借用了相同的三维度方法

表 4-1 服务补救过程的测量

服务失误场景	补救维度	具体补救值	
设定通信服务运营商服务失误场景	响应速度 (Response Speed)	慢	快
		语言描述:“过了很久”	语言描述:“马上”
	心理补救 (Psychological Recovery)	低	高
		语言描述:“稍示歉意”	语言描述:“真诚道歉并积极了解该失误给您造成的不便”
	有形补偿 (Compensation)	少	多
		语言描述:“不退还多收取的费用”	语言描述:“双倍返还费用”

来定义知觉公平:程序性知觉公平、互动性知觉公平和补偿性知觉公平。顾客在社会交易中对知觉公平的感知主要依赖这三个维度,这三个维度彼此独立作用(Blogett et al., 1999)。本部分的测量量表是在 Bolton 和 Wagner (1999) 以及 Blodgett 和 Tax (1993) 所提出的量表的基础上修改而成。

1. 补偿性知觉公平 (Distributive Justice)

由前面的相关文献回顾,可以知道补偿性公平是指处于社会交易 (协议、争辩、涉及多方的决策等) 中的双方或多方,其中一方对于另一方为解决冲突而做出有形补偿结果的一种公平感知态度 (Blodgett et al., 1999), 它主要是反映有形补偿的效果。本部分的量表是在 Maxham 和 Netemeyer (2002) 以及 Bolton 和 Wagner (1999) 所提出的量表的基础上修改而成,具体的量表内容参见表 4-2。

2. 程序性知觉公平 (Procedural Justice)

程序性知觉公平是指关于顾客对组织决策者所使用的政策、程序以及尺度的知觉公平,这种公平水平将影响争端和协议的结果 (Smith et al., 1999) 。程序性知觉公平这个维度反映的是服务补救过程的及时性、灵敏性和方便性。许多研究都提到过顾客会因为等待太长时间感到不公平从而引起顾客负面情感以及造成不满意 (Venkatesan and Anderson, 1985)。本研究没有采用具体的时间来表示等待的过程,而是采用了“马上”及“过了很久”两个词语来衡量。这样测量者可以通过自己对时间长短的感知来评价运营商的程序性公平。本部分的测量量表是在 Bolton 和 Wagner（1999）以及 Clemmer（1993）所提出的量表的基础上修改而成，具体的量表内容参见表 4–2。

表 4–2 知觉公平测量量表

维度	题项	来源
补偿性知觉公平	① 这一补救结果是公平的； ② 补救结果并不能弥补它给我造成的损失； ③ 该失误给我造成了不便，但该服务商弥补了我的损失； ④ 我认为接受这样的补救结果是不正确的； ⑤ 该服务商给我弥补的结果超过了我所失去的	Maxham, Netemeyer（2002） Bolton, Wagner（1999）
程序性知觉公平	① 该服务商管理制度在处理服务失误时效率高； ② 该服务商很在意没有为我准备我所需要的服务； ③ 该服务商的管理机制对于自己失误反应很迅速； ④ 尽管出现这种失误，但该服务商响应迅速； ⑤ 我相信该服务商有一系列公正的管理政策	Blodgett and Tax（1993） Clemmer（1993）
互动性知觉公平	① 工作人员恰当地体谅我的难处； ② 工作人员并没有努力帮助我解决麻烦； ③ 工作人员与我沟通得很好； ④ 工作人员服务的态度很谦逊	Bolton, Wagner（1999） Blodgettand Tax（1993）

3. 互动性知觉公平（Interactional Justice）

互动性知觉公平是指在冲突被解决的过程中，人们感到自己被对方看待和处理的方式的一种公平感知，比如说对方处理和看待自己的方式是否谦逊和尊重（Bies, Moag, 1986; Bies, Shapiro, 1987），其基本内容：

① 诚实、坦诚、关注程度以及是否给予解释；

② 礼貌、友好、兴致以及敏感性和亲密性；

③ 信心和情感认同；

④ 努力程度。

本研究通过控制服务补救的道歉和主动性维度来反映互动知觉公平的影响。本部分的测量量表是在 Bolton 和 Wagner（1999）以及 Blodgett 和 Tax （1993）所提出的量表的基础上修改而成，具体的量表内容参见表 4-2。

4.1.3 关系品质

根据文献探讨的资料可知，满意、信任以及承诺是多数学者所赞同的主要关系维度（Crosby et al., 1990; Henning-Thurau, Klee, 1997; Smith, 1998），因此关系品质的量表内容应该包含满意、信任以及承诺三个部分。在本研究中满意部分的量表是借用 Crosby 等（1990）所提出的，信任部分的量表是在 Morgan 和 Hunt（1997）所提出的量表的基础上根据本次研究目的所提供的服务特性制成，承诺部分的量表是在 Bettencourt（1997）以及 Hunt（1994 ）所提出的量表基础上修改而成。

1. 满意（Satisfaction）

根据 Westbrook 的定义：满意是一种情绪的状态，其反映射出对互动经验的评估。可知满意乃是一种消费者心中主观的情绪感觉，反映出消费者对交易或接触经验喜好的评估。在本研究中主要是指顾客对公司总体满意程度，这部分的量表是借用 Crosby 等所提出的，见表 4-3。

2. 信任（Trust）

根据 Morgan 和 Hunt（1997）的定义：信任是顾客对服务商的一种信念，相信服务商可以依赖，相信他们会以顾客长期利益来行动。信任是一种意愿，其愿意与有信心的交易伙伴进行合作，相信服务商正直以及可靠。本部分的量表是在 Morgan 和 Hunt 所提出的量表的基础上修改而成，见表 4-3。

3. 承诺（Commitment）

承诺乃是交易伙伴之间对于关系的持续之暗示或明白的誓约，承诺也是想要持续维持有价值关系的一种愿望。根据 Hennig–Thurau 和 Klee（1997）的定义，承诺是顾客对于关系长期维持的导向，不论是对关系的情绪联结，或者是基于保持关系能产生较高利益的现实考虑。由此可知，承诺是维持良好及长期关系的重要表征，也是一种想要持续维持关系的意愿，当消费者表现出承诺的意愿时，通常也表示厂商与消费者间具有良好关系，本部分的量表是在 Bettencourt（1997）以及 Hunt（1994）所提出的量表修改而成，见表 4–3。

表 4–3 关系品质测量量表

维度	题项	来源
满意	① 对于该服务商的服务，我感到很满意； ② 我很高兴选择了他们的产品； ③ 我很喜欢他们； ④ 使用他们的产品总是很愉快； ⑤ 要是其他产品都像这公司的产品就好了； ⑥ 跟其他产品供应商比起来，我很满意我所选择的服务供应商	Crosby,Evans, Cowles（1990） Lethesser, Kohli（1995） Bettencourt（1997）
信任	① 我相信该服务商会遵守对顾客的承诺； ② 我觉得该服务商很诚实、很实在； ③ 我认为该服务商总能给我详尽的咨询； ④ 该服务商不会隐瞒我应该知道的信息； ⑤ 该服务商会真诚关注我的需要； ⑥ 我相信该服务商总会考虑顾客最佳利益； ⑦ 该服务商总会优先考虑顾客的利益； ⑧ 该服务商很值得信任； ⑨ 我对该服务商很有信心	Morgan, Hung（1997） Doney, Cannon（1997） Crosby，Evans，Cowles（1990）
承诺	① 我是该服务商的忠实顾客； ② 我想继续与该服务商保持关系； ③ 我会努力支持该服务商； ④ 即使有其他的选择，我也不会选择其他服务商； ⑤ 我会很积极维持与该服务商的关系； ⑥ 我会一直购买该服务商的产品； ⑦ 该服务商很值得我和他们保持关系	Bettencourt（1997） Hunt（1994）

4.1.4 顾客行为意向

行为意向是指顾客从事特定行为的意图，在本研究中顾客行为意向是特指顾客口碑和重购意图。本部分采用的量表是在 Maxham 和 Netemeyer（2002），Blodgett and Tax（1993），Clemmer（1993）提出量表的基础上修改而成，参见表 4–4。

表 4–4 顾客行为意向测量量表

维度	题项	来源
重购意向	① 我以后会增加购买该服务商产品的次数； ② 如果有别的选择，我不会选择其他服务商的产品	Blodgett, Tax（1993） Clemmer（1993）
口碑意向	① 如果有人提起该服务商，我会推荐； ② 我会向他人说该服务商的不是	Maxham, Netemeyer （2002）

4.2 问卷设计

4.2.1 服务失误情景的选定

由于对服务补救的调查一直沿用情景设定（准试验）的测量方法，本研究也采用该测量方法。在本次研究中，我从移动通信服务失误的事例中选取了“虚拟网”服务项目。选用该服务失误情景的主要原因有以下几点：

① 该服务项目的受众较宽泛，便于被调研者的选取；

② 该服务失误情景与其他移动通信服务失误情景具有很大的相似性，利于被调研者发挥想象；

③ 该服务失误场景具有较强的普遍性，利于被调研者进入角色；

④ 该服务失误场景是真实案例的再现，具有较强的现实意义及说服力。

根据研究目的，在调研中根据服务补救变量的不同维度进行组合，将整体的问卷调查拆分为 4 个独立的部分。根据服务补救变量的不同状态，制定了 8 个组合，并将两两随机组合进行配对，形成了问卷 A、问卷 B、问卷 C、问卷 D。表 4–5 中将问卷的组合设计进行了介绍。

表 4-5 问卷的组合设计

名称	组合性质	服务补救状态描述		
问卷 A	三高	速度快	真诚道歉	双倍返还
	三低	速度慢	稍示歉意	不退还
问卷 B	速度快	速度快	真诚道歉	不退还
	速度慢	速度慢	真诚道歉	不退还
问卷 C	道歉诚意	速度慢	真诚道歉	双倍返还
	道歉不足	速度慢	稍示歉意	双倍返还
问卷 D	双倍返还	速度快	稍示歉意	双倍返还
	不退还	速度快	稍示歉意	不退还

4.2.2 预调研及问卷改进

本次的调查问卷是在 2006 年 10 月份预调研的基础上进行的调整与完善。在预调研中，被调研者需回答 8 个情景组合所设计的全部问题，即在 8 种不同服务补救的情况下分别填写 18 道题，共计 8 × 18=144 道题。另外加上关系品质（22 道题）、人口统计特征（5 道题）、其他（2 道题），预调研问卷总共为 173 道题。

预调研选取了某高校的大学生作为调研样本，样本总量为 315 人，回收有效问卷 172 份。虽然在调研中对过程进行了较严格的控制，但数据的结果与预期的结论还存在一定的差异。为了完善本研究，预调研之后我对被调查者进行了随机调查，发现了问卷中存在的一些问题（预调研问卷见附录 A）。在此基础上，根据导师的意见，我从以下几个方面对问卷进行了重大调整。

① 分拆问卷。考虑原有问卷的问题过多，且重复性大，严重影响被调研者的兴趣与热情。我将原有的问卷进行了拆分，将 8 个服务补救组合分别放置于不同的

问卷中，每份问卷仅包括两种情景，这样就形成了一个 A、B、C、D 问卷组。每一个被调研者只需填写其中的一份问卷，答题难度大大降低，可以更好地保证问卷的有效性。

② 加入新问题。为了获得被调查者更准确的信息，我还在问卷中加入几个新的问题。如：“您是否亲身经历过类似的情景？”过滤性问题的加入可以将不同的样本特征进行辨别，为后续的研究提供更为丰富的研究发现。

③ 删除多余的问题。在最初的问卷中，人口统计包括职业性质等 5 道题。但是过细的职业区分并不能提供有价值的研究结果，因此，在导师的建议下我将此问题从问卷中剔除。

④ 调整主体结构。调整后的问卷分为三部分，共计 87 个问题。第一部分为情景描述（3 个问题）。第二部分选取了两种服务补救组合进行调查。每一种服务补救组合分别测量了补救措施给消费者带来的不同公平感知，以及对关系品质的影响。其中，知觉公平部分包括 18 个问题，关系品质包括 22 个问题。因此，第二部分共 80 道题 [（18+22）×2]。第三部分为人口特征统计（4 个问题）。

⑤ 问题重新排序。为了避免被调查者回答问题时可能的思维定式，我将知觉公平（18 道题）及关系品质（22 道题）按随机顺序重新排列，将不同维度的问题全部融合在一起，以确保调研结果的准确性与可靠性。

⑥ 完善问卷格式。在预调研中，被调研者反映问卷的格式存在问题，答题时容易出现串行和混乱，降低了答题效率。针对相关问题，我对问卷格式进行了改进。首先，将问题和问题之间明显区分，明确分之，避免错误答题；其次，对问卷的页面做了调整，确保每一部分问题的完整性，提高答题效率；再次，将问卷字号、空格进行了相应的压缩，以降低答题者的心理压力。

本研究的调查问卷主要分为三大部分，下面逐次将第一部分和第二部分问卷的内容分述如下。

（1）问卷第一部分

这部分首先设定一个服务失误场景，然后让填答者先填写3个问题。问题1："该情景刚出现的那一刻，您内心的真实感受是？"该问题是测量被调查者对设定情景的评价程度。问题2："您是否亲身经历过类似的情景？"该问题是个过滤问题，目的是为了增加样本的信息，分辨样本数据的差异性。问题3："您目前选用下面哪一家移动通信服务商提供的服务？"该问题可以为本研究的实践意义提供有益的数据支持。

（2）问卷第二部分

这部分让填答者根据设定的服务失误场景中可能遇到的服务补救措施来回答每一问项。这部分主要是为了了解顾客的知觉公平水平如何随服务商的补救过程的变化而变化，以及顾客的行为意向如何随服务补救过程的变化而变化。下面将8个不同的组合分别叙述如下：

① 如果服务人员马上对该失误向您真诚道歉并积极了解该失误给您造成的不便，此外，同意双倍返还多收的费用；

② 如果服务人员过了很久才对此失误向您真诚道歉并积极了解该失误给您造成的不便，但不退还多收部分的费用；

③ 如果服务人员马上对该失误向您稍示歉意，并同意双倍返还多收的费用；

④ 如果服务人员过了很久才对此失误向您真诚道歉并积极了解该失误给您造成的不便，此外，同意双倍返还多收部分的费用；

⑤ 如果服务人员马上对该失误向您真诚道歉并积极了解该失误给您造成的不便，但不退还多收部分的费用；

⑥ 如果服务人员过了很久才对此失误向您稍示歉意，且不退还多收部分的费用；

⑦如果服务人员马上对该失误向您稍示歉意，且不退还多收部分的费用；

⑧如果服务人员过了很久才对此失误向您稍示歉意，此外，同意双倍返还多收部分的费用。

在以上 8 种不同组合下，每份独立的问卷选定其中的两个组合用来测量顾客对应的知觉公平、行为意向、关系品质三个变量。

顾客对应的知觉公平水平的测量，采用 Bolton 和 Wagner（1999）以及 Blodgett 和 Tax（1993）等人的量表，一共由 14 道题组成。其中，测量程序性知觉公平为 5 道题，互动性知觉公平为 4 道题，补偿性知觉公平为 5 道题。本量表使用李克特 7 点尺度衡量（1= 非常不同意，2= 不同意，3= 不太同意，4= 不知道，5= 有点同意，6= 同意，7= 非常同意），填答者根据每一问项的描述表达其同意程度，以了解该顾客针对这一补救内容相应的知觉公平水平。

行为意向强度的测量，采用 Maxham 和 Netemeyer（2002）的量表，由 4 道题组成。其中，测量重购意向 2 道题，测量口碑意向 2 道题，包括："我以后会增加购买该公司产品的次数""我会向他人说该公司的不是"等。量表采用李克特 7 点尺度衡量（1= 非常不同意，2= 不同意，3= 不太同意，4= 不知道，5= 有点同意，6= 同意，7= 非常同意），填答者根据每一问项的描述表达其同意程度，以了解该顾客针对这一补救内容相应的行为意向强度。

关系品质的测量，采用 Bettencourt（1997）以及 Hunt（1994）等人的量表，共计 22 道题，从三个维度进行测量。

①满意：此部分共分为 6 题，包括："对于服务商的服务，我感到很满意"等问题，采用李克特 7 点尺度衡量（1= 非常不同意，2= 不同意，3= 不太同意，4= 不知道，5= 有点同意，6= 同意，7= 非常同意），填答者根据每一问项的描述表达其同意程度，以了解顾客对该公司的总体满意程度。

②信任：此部分共分为 9 题，包括："我相信这家公司总会考虑顾客最佳利益"等问题，采用李克特 7 点尺度衡量（1= 非常不同意，2= 不同意，3= 不太同意，4= 不知道，5= 有点同意，6= 同意，7= 非常同意），填答者根据每一问项的描述表达其同意程度，以了解顾客对该公司的信任程度。

③承诺：此部分共分为 7 题，包括："我会一直购买这家公司的产品"等问题，采用李克特 7 点尺度衡量（1= 非常不同意，2= 不同意，3= 不太同意，4= 不知道，5= 有点同意，6= 同意，7= 非常同意），填答者根据每一问项的描述表达其同意程度，以了解顾客对该公司的承诺程度。

（3）问卷第三部分

问卷的第三部分主要是调查样本的人口统计特性，通过询问被调查者的年龄、性别、学历、工资收入 4 个问题，来了解本次调研样本的人口特征。

本次调研问卷请参看附录 B。

4.3 问卷调研

4.3.1 确定样本量

人们一直在讨论不同类型研究样本量的大小问题，虽然至今为止还没有公认的标准，但是为了服从特殊的统计分析的要求，研究者也找到了一些参照的标准。

Hair 等（1998）认为，样本数量每个估计参数至少要有 5 个观测值。根据研究的需要设定 $2 \times 2 \times 2=8$ 个场景。本研究测量变量的最大参数为 22，根据最小样本量的计算公式 $5 \times 22 = 110$，从而计算出本研究每个场景组合所需要的最小样本量为 110 个。那么，4 个组合（8 个场景）的总体样本量为 $110 \times 4 = 440$ 个。在确定了总体样本量之后，并考虑到有效样本可能的回收率，本次调研的总体样本量定为 800 个（预计有效回收率不低于 50%）。

4.3.2 选取调研样本

本次研究最大的困难之处在于有效样本的获取。由于被调研的对象可能涉及800人以上，因此，通过何种渠道或途径来获取样本是迫切需要考虑的问题。所幸的是，本人在电信行业工作多年，对移动通信服务业务非常熟悉，同时也积累了一定资源，虽然调研工作难度较大，但是本人对此还是非常乐观。

本研究属于准试验研究，在研究中有8个组合，若将8个组合设计成4个问卷，就意味着需要4组调研样本，为了进行组间效果比较，4个样本组必须存在某一个特质（样本无差异）。解决这个问题的可行办法是从一个母体中随机抽取4个样本组，因此，需要一个抽样的母体成为同质样本的第一道难关。

综合研究需要，本研究最后选取了中国某市的一个电信运营企业的一个服务部门作为抽样的母群。这个部门大约有3000名员工，按照研究需要随机抽取800人（4×200）发放问卷。

4.3.3 调研过程控制

本次调查问卷是于2007年4月28号—4月30日在中国某市电信运营企业进行的。本次的数据收集分4次完成，每次被测者200人，共计800人次。该企业共计3000员工，他们被随机地分配在不同的班组进行工作，每一个班组为500人。在调研中，根据该部门领导提供的名单，兼顾被测者工作需要，从中抽选200人参加调研。每一次抽取200名员工同时填写问卷，每一场的时间为1小时，当场回收问卷。调查样本量为800，问卷的有效回收率为100%，有效问卷为791份（有效回收率达到99%）。

为了提高问卷的有效性，保证数据的真实性和客观性，以提高本文研究结论的科学性。本次调查采取了以下措施：

① 简单介绍本次调研的目的，请被调研者放心填写；

② 向被调研者简述设定的情境，并引导其答题；

③ 告知被调研者设定情境下 8 种可能的补救措施，使其明确其中的差异；

④ 告知被调研者所答问卷中的组合类型，确保其准确答题；

⑤ 维持调研秩序，排除一切可能的影响因素。

4.3.4 数据分析方法

在回收问卷之后，我们首先对无效问卷进行了剔除。剔除的标准为：

① 回答不完整；

② 问题答案有明显的倾向性；

③ 基本人口统计特征缺失。

整理之后获得了 791 份有效问卷，然后将问卷原始数据进行录入，制作成 Excel 文本格式。在原始数据的基础上，本研究进行了三部分的数据分析。

1. 数据预处理

在进行统计检验之前，对调研数据进行预处理。在本研究问卷中存在一些反向计分的题项。李克特正向题项给予 7 分、6 分、5 分、4 分、3 分、2 分、1 分，而反向题的题项计分时，便要给予 1 分、2 分、3 分、4 分、5 分、6 分、7 分。因子分析（Fator Analysis）的第一步骤就是要将题项计分的方式转化成一致的标准。

首先，我将所有题项的结果进行了一个回归检验，将检验值为负的 4 个题项进行了反向计分。它们是："我会向他人说该公司的不是（A04、C04）""工作人员并不努力帮我解决麻烦（A15、C15）""补救结果并不能弥补他给我造成的损失（A16、C16）""我认为接受这样的补救结果是不正确的（A17、C17）"4 道题。

然后，我将提供被测者的人口统计特征，并用卡方检验（Chi-Square Test）来验证被测实验组间的样本无差异。验证被测样本特性相似性之后，我就可以将 8 个实验组的数据进行合并，为下一步的统计运算做准备。

此外，由于每份问卷中包含两个实验设计，共计 $4 \times 2 = 8$ 个实验组合。为了数据统计方便，问卷在发出前进行了编号，分别为 A、B、C、D。那么，4 套问卷的前一部分按照问卷编号顺序设定为实验组合一、实验组合二、实验组合三、实验组合四，4 套问卷的后一部分按照问卷编号设定为实验组合五、实验组合六、实验组合七、实验组合八。为了计算简便，先将对应的变量测量值进行了合并，然后再进行问卷总量的计算。

2. 研究量表的检验

本研究的量表都是采用西方学者的问卷，但是西方的问卷是否适用于中国、是否适用于本研究，都需要用数据来验证。只有验证了量表的信度和结构，才能获得有说服力的研究结论。

因此，实验采用因子分析来计算量表的因子数量、因子的负荷、定义因子。接着对量表进行信度分析，检验量表的稳定性。

3. 假设检验

假设检验是本文的核心部分，这部分的运算主要采用多元方差分析（MANOVA）对 8 个试验组的组间进行比较。

方差分析的特点是可以同时检验两个或多个平均数之间的差异，并且可以解释几个因素水平之间的交互作用。方差分析有力地促进了复杂实验设计的发展，它使研究者有可能通过实验设计深入探讨问题的实质。方差分析也帮助了检验假说，它提供了对各种实验设计中显著性检验的基础。

根据方差分析的要求和步骤，先通过多变量的统计分析来验证变量的交互作用；然后用组间效果比较来验证单变量的主效果。根据交互作用与主效果的分析结果来验证本文的假设，并对结果进行分析。

本研究的数据分析方法流程详见图 4-1。

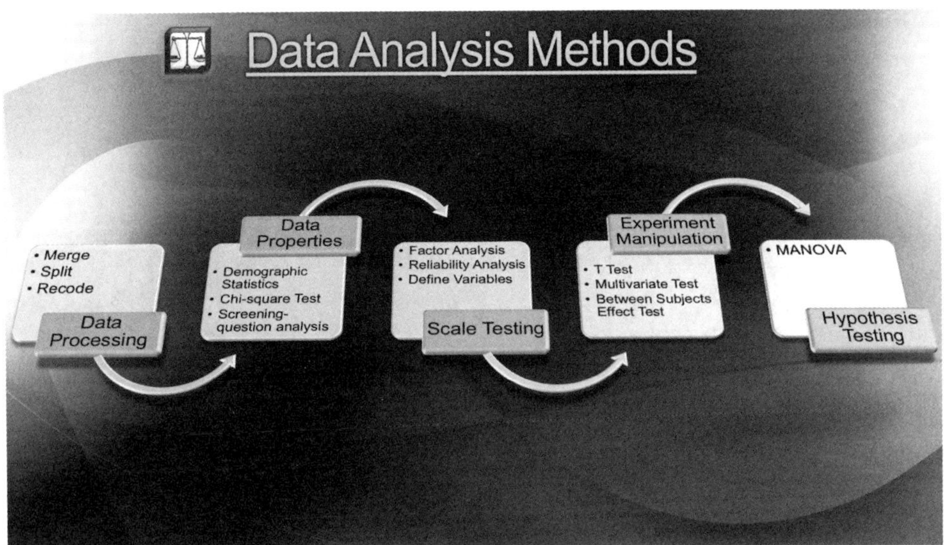

图 4-1 数据分析方法流程

第 5 章

研究结果

通过对问卷调查获取的数据来进行定量分析，根据所研究的内容分别进行描述性统计分析、卡方检验、因子分析、多元方差分析等运算，发现并分析了本研究的问卷与原有的设计存在的一些差异。最后根据分析所得出的数据进行深入探讨，把数据分析的结果与前面的假设进行了比较和验证。

Chapter 5

Research Results

Some differences between the questionnaires used in this study and the original designs are discovered and analyzed by performing quantitative analyses to the data obtained through the questionnaires as well as by performing analyses such as the descriptive statistical analyses, the Chi-Square Goodness of Fit Test, factor analyses, and Multivariate Analysis of Variance (MANOVA) to the subjects studied respectively. Finally, the data obtained through the analyses is discussed, and the results of data analysis are compared with and validated against the aforementioned hypothesis.

本章主要对问卷调查获取的数据来进行定量分析，采用 SPSS15.0，根据所研究的内容分别进行描述性统计分析、卡方检验、因子分析、多元方差分析等运算。根据分析所得出数据进行探讨，然后把数据分析的结果与前面的假设进行比较和验证。

5.1 实验组样本检验

第一节，首先描述本次测试者的人口统计特征， 此外，多因素析因设计中，被试样本必须从总体中随机抽取，因变量在各个单元内的得分相互独立。因此，在进行多元方差分析之前必须对不同实验组样本进行验证。本研究采用卡方检验来验证 4 个对立实验组的被测者具有相似的人口统计特征。

5.1.1 人口统计特征（Demographic Statistics）

本研究设计了 4 个测量人口统计特征的问题：性别、年龄、教育背景、个人年收入（RMB）。表 5–1 是本次被测样本的基本人口统计特征。

表 5–1 体现了本次被测样本的基本特性：①女性为主（女性占 93.9%，男性仅

表 5–1 被测样本人口统计特征

	Gender	Frequency	Percent	Valid Percent	Cumulative Percent
Valid	Male	42	5.3	6.1	6.1
	Female	651	82.3	93.9	100.0
Total		693	87.6	100.0	
Missing System		98	12.4		
Total		791	100.0		
Age		Frequency	Percent	Valid Percent	Cumulative Percent
Valid	18–25	582	73.6	83.7	83.7
	26–35	111	14.0	16.0	99.7
	46–55	2	0.3	0.3	100.0
Total		695	87.9	100.0	
Missing System		96	12.1		
Total		791	100.0		

续表

	Education	Frequency	Percent	Valid Percent	Cumulative Percent
Valid	< high school	52	6.6	7.5	7.5
	High school diploma	316	39.9	45.8	53.3
	Voc tech/some college/AA	321	40.6	46.6	99.9
	≥ 4-year college	1	0.1	0.1	100.0
Total		690	87.2	100.0	
Missing System		101	12.8		
Total		791	100.0		
	Income	Frequency	Percent	Valid Percent	Cumulative Percent
Valid	< 10 000	222	28.1	33.0	33.0
	10 000 – 29 999	444	56.1	66.0	99.0
	40 000 – 59 999	5	0.6	0.7	99.7
	≥ 60 00	2	0.3	0.3	100.0
Total		673	85.1	100.0	
Missing System		118	14.9		
Total		791	100.0		

占 6.1%）；②年轻人为主（18—35 岁占 99.7%，其中 18—25 岁占 83.7%）；③教育水平较低（99.9% 的样本都没有接受大学教育）；④收入较低（99% 的被测者年收入在 3 万元人民币以下）。以上样本的特性体现了本次被测样本可能的偏差，研究结果必然受到这些偏差的影响。

5.1.2 卡方检验

由于实验设计是透过对自变量的操控，然后看因变量的情况。在最简单的情况下，我们只有两个实验情景。这样，如果因变量是“等距尺度”的，我们只需以 t 测试（t–Test）来检定两个实验情景的因变量的平均（Means）是否有差异，便可看出自变量与因变量有关系。如果因变量也是“类别尺度”（例如有没有进步），则可以卡方测试来检定两个实验情景中因变量的比率是否有差异（例如在某一实验情景中进步了的人的比率较高），便可看出自变量是否与因变量有关系。

如果我们的自变量多于一个而且因变量是“等距尺度”的变量，则我们便会以 MANOVA（Multivariate Analysis of Variance）的方法来检定各实验情景中，各因变量的平均（Means）是否有差异，便可看出自变量是否与因变量有关系。本研究设计是多因素多变量的试验设计，因此适用于 MANOVA 分析。

但是多元方差分析需要满足下列条件：各因变量取自同一样本。在自变量（因素）的不同水平上，各因变量（包括变量及协变量）的指标取自同一样本。如果因变量的数值来自不同的样本，多元方差分析的结果就会变得不可靠。因此，在进行多元方差分析之前必须进行卡方检验。

为了符合本研究的设计需要，针对研究对象的特性进行了卡方检验，目的是为了验证不同样本组间的样本特性不存在偏差，为下一步的组间比较研究做好数据准备。

卡方检验的结果（表 5-2）验证了本次调研的 4 个样本组样本无显著差异，可以视为同一调查对象， 因此可以将 8 个组合的数据合并进行假设检验与论证。

5.1.3 预设问题结果分析

表 5-2 实验组样本卡方检验结果

	Chi-Square
Gender	1.756 (p =0 .624)
Age	5.141 (p = 0.526)
Education	12.84 (p =0 .170)
Income	11.606 (p = 0.236)

问卷在讲述了实验情境之后，对被测的总体情况设定了 3 道题进行测量。第一道题是："该情境出现的那一刻，您内心的真实感受是什么？"该题采用 7 点计分法，1 分表示完全不满意，7 分表示完全满意。

791 名被测者中，对情境中所设定的服务失误感到不满意的人最多，达到 263 人次，占 51.17%（缺失数据为 277）。此外感到完全不满意的人数为 22 人，有点不满意的人数为 100 人，对服务失误情境总体不满意的人数为 385 人，占被调查人数的 74.90%。图 5-1 为被测人数对服务失误情境总体感受的分布细节。

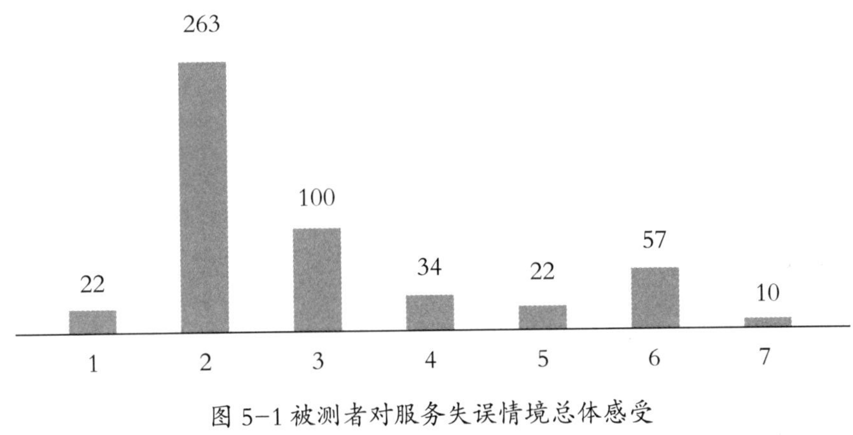

图 5-1 被测者对服务失误情境总体感受

第二个问题是："您是否亲身经历过类似的情境？"答案有两个："有过""没有"。这个问题的目的是想了解在被测者中有多少人亲身经历过类似情境，结果表明，在 791 个被测者中，620 人（78%）没有经历过类似情境，94 人（12%）有过类似经历。图 5-2 描述了这一分布情况。

为了验证对调查情境不同的经历是否对研究结论存在影响，作者将被调查者按照是否具有情境经历分成了两组，并对两组样本进行了 t 检验。t 检验的结果发现，调研对象在 40 道题中只有一道题存在组间差异，其他 39 道题均无组间差异。组间

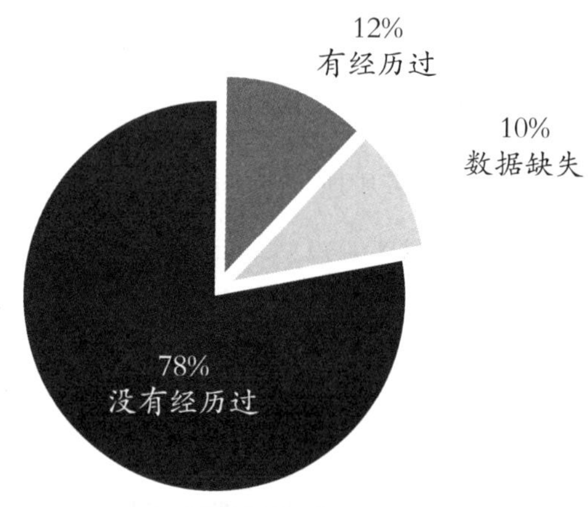

图 5-2 情境经历调查结果

均值比较的结果说明，调研对象是否存在调查问卷中的情境经历对调研结果基本没有影响。

基于以上结果，笔者认为此次调研的对象均为移动通信服务中心的职员，受理客户失误并提供服务补救方案是他们的日常工作，因此，他们对服务失误的各种可能的情境均有深刻的理解，即使他们自身没有问卷中提及的经历，也并不妨碍她们对此场景的合理想象。此外，如果被访者根据亲身经历的回忆印象中的感受作答，不可避免地要出现有些人因遗忘等原因与当时真实的情况有所出入，造成一定的偏差。基于以上判断，笔者坚信被访者的回答具有较高的可信度。

第三个问题是："您目前选用下面哪一个移动通信服务商提供的服务？" 备选答案有四个，分别是：中国移动、中国联通、小灵通、其他。被测者中基本上都选择了中国移动的服务，在 791 个被测者中（缺失值为 57），728 人选择了中国移动，1 人选择了中国联通，3 人使用小灵通，2 人选择了其他。详情可见图（图 5-3）。

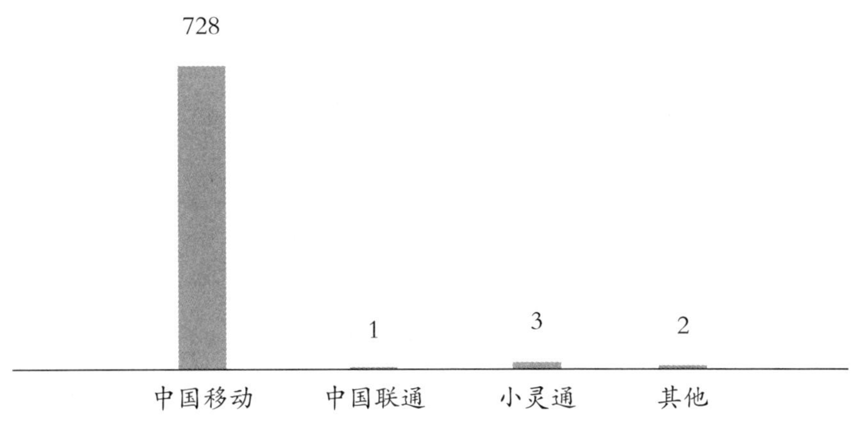

图 5-3 被测者移动服务商的选择

5.2 问卷结构与信度检验

量表的原始数据处理之后，接着要做的是量表的因素分析，研究如何用少数几个因子变量来解释众多原始变量，同时又尽量避免信息丢失。以特征根大于或等于1 为因子抽取原则来决定因子的数量。

在多变量关系中，变量间的线性组合对表现或解释每个层面异数非常有用。主成分分析主要目的即在此。变量的第一个线性组合可以解释最大的变异量。因素分析也是多变量方法的应用之一，在社会科学领域中，应用最广的是把数个很难解释而彼此相关的变量，转化成少数有概念化意义而彼此独立性大的因子（Factor）。因子分析时，主要采用主成分因子分析（Principal Component Analysis, PCA）和方差最大旋转（Varimax Rotation）方法。本研究采用主成分分析方法分别对知觉公平、关系品质、行为意向进行因子分析，以检验三个分量表的结构。

所谓信度（Reliability）是表示一份测验所测变量的可信度或稳定性，也就是测量变量的内部一致性程度，因此一份良好的问卷或量表应具有足够的信度。测量信度的方式有很多种，而其中 Cronbach α 是目前社会科学研究最为常用的信度测量方式，因此，本研究以 Cronbach α 作为衡量问卷信度的方式。

在社会科学领域中，可以接受的最小信度系数为何，是多数研究者最为关注的问题，不过在学者间看法也未尽一致。Guieford（1965）指出了 α 系数大小所代表的可信程度，当 α 小于 0.3 时，表示信度低，不可信；当 α 系数为 0.3~ 0.4 时，表示勉强可信；当 α 为 0.4~0.5 时，表示比较可信；当 α 为 0.5~0.7 时，表示可信，这也是最为常见的范围。Gay（1992）的观点，任何测验或量表的信度关系如果在 0.9 以上，表示检测或量度的信度甚佳。DeVellis（1991）、Nunnally（1978）等人则认为 0.70 以上是可以接受的最小信度值。本文采用 0.70 作为评价依据来判断研究问卷的信度。

5.2.1 知觉公平结构与信度分析

每一个实验组设计了两种不同的服务补救方式，每一个被测者对同一道题分别需要回答两次，因此问卷分析中所有题项值原则上是测试样本的两倍（可能存在缺失值）。测量知觉公平的题项一共为 14 道题，表 5-3 为知觉公平 14 道题的描述统计。

表 5-3 知觉公平题项描述统计

	Mean	Std. Deviation	Analysis *N*
A01	4.21	1.987	1487
A02	4.60	1.767	1487
A03	4.58	1.790	1487
A05	4.28	1.706	1487
A06	4.20	2.065	1487
A08	4.13	1.926	1487
A09	4.42	1.973	1487
A10	4.37	1.760	1487
A11	4.27	1.920	1487
A12	3.72	1.872	1487
A13	4.15	1.755	1487
A15	4.09	1.756	1487

续表

	Mean	Std. Deviation	Analysis *N*
A16	3.65	1.745	1487
A17	4.02	1.881	1487

在进行结构分析之前，先对这 14 道题进行了 KMO and Bartlett's 检验，检验结果（Kaiser-Meyer-Olkin Measure of Sampling Adequacy=0.927; p <0.001）说明这 14 道题适合进行因子分析。表 5-4 是测量知觉公平的 14 道题因子分析结果。

表 5-4 知觉公平量表结构分析结果

	Initial Eigenvalues			Rotation Sums of Squared Loadings		
Component	Total	% of Variance	Cumulative %	Total	% of Variance	Cumulative %
1	6.982	49.873	49.873	4.649	33.209	33.209
2	1.686	12.044	61.917	2.686	20.291	53.500
3	1.003	7.168	69.085	2.182	15.585	69.085
4	0.639	4.567	73.651			
5	0.544	3.889	77.540			
6	0.520	3.712	81.252			
7	0.486	3.474	84.725			
8	0.430	3.069	87.794			
9	0.368	2.627	90.422			
10	0.337	2.409	92.831			
11	0.313	2.236	95.067			
12	0.286	2.046	97.113			
13	0.227	1.620	98.733			
14	0.177	1.267	100.000			

Extraction Method: Principal Component Analysis.

从表 5-4 可以看到，有 3 个因子的特征根大于 1，分别为 4.649、2.686、2.182。3 个因子的累计解释变异量达到 69.085%，分析结果说明 14 道题可以浓缩为 3 个因子。在确定了量表的三维度结构之后，再对该量表进行因子旋转，得到表 5-5 的因子旋转矩阵。

表 5–5 知觉公平因子旋转矩阵[a]

	Component		
	1	2	3
该公司的管理机制对于自己失误反应很迅速	0.815		
尽管出现这种失误，但该公司响应迅速	0.802		
该公司管理制度处理服务失误有效率	0.779		
我相信该公司有一系列公正的管理政策	0.738		
工作人员服务的态度很谦逊	0.728		
该公司很在意没有为我准备我所需要的服务	0.672		
工作人员与我沟通得很好	0.666		
工作人员恰当地体谅我的难处	0.589		
该公司给我弥补的结果超过了我所失去的		0.782	
该失误给我造成了不便，但该公司弥补了我的损失		0.757	
这一补救结果是公平的		0.720	
补救结果并不能弥补它给我造成的损失			0.829
工作人员并不努力帮我解决麻烦			0.817
我认为接受这样的补救结果是不正确的			0.746

Extraction Method: Principal Component Analysis.
Rotation Method: Varimax with Kaiser Normalization.
a：Rotation converged in 5 iterations.

表 5–5 说明，14 道题落在 3 个因子上，无交叉负荷，且所有的负荷值均大于 0.50（最大值为 0.829，最小值为 0.589）。但是，因子分析也发现，14 道题在 3 个因子上的分布与原量表的设计存在差异，因此，根据以上的因子分析结果，对三个维度及整个问卷进行了信度检验，检验结果见表 5–6。

表 5–6 知觉公平信度分析结果

		Corrected Item –Total Correlation	Cronbach's Alpha if Item Deleted
α =0.918（N=1524）	该公司的管理机制对于自己失误反应很迅速	0.807	0.901
	尽管出现这种失误，但该公司响应迅速	0.808	0.901
	该公司管理制度处理服务失误有效率	0.659	0.914
	我相信该公司有一系列公正的管理政策	0.746	0.907
	工作人员服务的态度很谦逊	0.677	0.912

续表

		Corrected Item −Total Correlation	Cronbach's Alpha if Item Deleted
α =0.918 (*N*=1524)	该公司很在意没有为我准备我所需要的服务	0.653	0.914
	工作人员与我沟通得很好	0.770	0.905
	工作人员恰当地体谅我的难处	0.720	0.909
α =0.822 (*N*=1550)	该公司给我弥补的结果超过了我所失去的	0.603	0.825
	该失误给我造成了不便，但该公司弥补了我的损失	0.735	0.694
	这一补救结果是公平的	0.697	0.734
α =0.765 (*N*=1554)	补救结果并不能弥补它给我造成的损失	0.634	0.643
	工作人员并不努力帮我解决麻烦	0.551	0.733
	我认为接受这样的补救结果是不正确的	0.608	0.672
	Total scale reliability		α =0.918

以上的结果表明，补偿性公平、程序性公平、互动性公平三个量表的内部一致性系数 Cronbach's α =0.918(>0.7)，删除任何一道题都不能提高问卷的有效性，因此说明该量表的信度颇佳。

5.2.2 关系品质结构与信度分析

测量关系品质有 22 个题项，下面按照这 22 道题分别进行结构和信度检验。在进行结构分析之前，先对这 22 道题进行了 KMO and Bartlett's 检验，检验结果（Kaiser–Meyer–Olkin Measure of Sampling Adequacy=0.982; p <0.001）说明关系品质量表适合进行因子分析。表 5–7 是测量关系品质的 22 道题的因子分析结果。

表 5–7 关系品质量表结构分析结果 (n =1474)

	Initial Eigenvalues			Rotation Sums of Squared Loadings		
Component	Total	% of Variance	Cumulative %	Total	% of Variance	Cumulative %
1	16.404	74.563	74.563	7.296	33.161	33.161
2	0.877	3.984	78.547	6.750	30.680	63.841
3	0.586	2.663	81.211	3.821	17.369	81.211

续表

	Initial Eigenvalues			Rotation Sums of Squared Loadings		
Component	Total	% of Variance	Cumulative %	Total	% of Variance	Cumulative %
4	0.471	2.142	83.353			
5	0.385	1.752	85.104			
6	0.358	1.627	86.732			
7	0.346	1.572	88.303			
8	0.282	1.283	89.586			
9	0.255	1.161	90.747			
10	0.225	1.023	91.770			
11	0.215	0.978	92.748			
12	0.203	0.923	93.670			
13	0.188	0.855	94.525			
14	0.176	0.802	95.327			
15	0.156	0.710	96.037			
16	0.153	0.696	96.733			
17	0.146	0.665	97.397			
18	0.133	0.603	98.000			
19	0.120	0.544	98.544			
20	0.117	0.533	99.077			
21	0.111	0.504	99.581			
22	0.092	0.419	100.000			

Extraction Method: Principal Component Analysis.

表 5-7 的结果说明关系品质的 22 道题为三维结构（有 3 个因子的特征根大于 1，分别为 7.296、6.750、3.821），3 个因子的累计解释变异量达到 81.211%，分析结果说明 22 道题可以浓缩为 3 个因子。在确定了量表的三维度结构之后，再对该量表进行因子旋转，得到表 5-8 的因子旋转矩阵。

表 5-8 关系品质因子旋转矩阵 [a]

	Component		
	1	2	3
对于该公司的服务，我感到很满意	0.801		
这家公司很值得我和他保持关系	0.795		
我很高兴选择了他们的产品	0.784		
我很喜欢他们	0.739		

续表

	Component		
	1	2	3
我会一直购买这家公司的产品	0.725		
这家公司很值得信赖	0.715		
我会很积极维持与这家公司的关系	0.708		
使用他们的产品总是很愉快	0.672		
这家公司会真诚关注我的需要	0.604		
要是其他产品都像这公司的产品就好了	0.551		
跟其他产品供应商比起来，我很满意我所选择的服务供应商		0.791	
我相信这家公司会遵守对顾客的承诺		0.785	
我对这家公司很有信心		0.745	
我是这家公司的忠实顾客		0.728	
我想继续与这家公司保持关系		0.687	
我相信这家公司总会考虑顾客最佳利益		0.671	
这家公司总会优先考虑顾客的利益		0.668	
我觉得这家公司很诚实、很实在		0.642	
我会努力支持这家公司		0.636	
这家公司不会隐瞒我应该知道的信息			0.797
我认为该公司总能给我详尽的咨询			0.668
即使有其他的选择，我也不会选择其他公司			0.529

Extraction Method: Principal Component Analysis.
Rotation Method: Varimax with Kaiser Normalization.
a：Rotation converged in 5 iterations.

表 5-8 说明，22 道题落在 3 个因子上，无交叉负荷，且所有的负荷值均大于 0.50（最大值为 0.801，最小值为 0.529）。但是，因子分析也发现，22 道题在 3 个因子上的分布与原量表的设计存在差异，因此，根据以上的因子分析结果，对 3 个维度及整个问卷进行了信度检验，检验结果见表 5-9。

表 5-9 关系品质信度分析结果（n =1474）

		Corrected Item −Total Correlation	Cronbach's Alpha if Item Deleted
α =0.972（n=1531）	对于该公司的服务，我感到很满意	0.838	0.971
	这家公司很值得我和他保持关系	0.892	0.968
	我很高兴选择了他们的产品	0.906	0.968
	我很喜欢他们	0.892	0.968

续表

		Corrected Item −Total Correlation	Cronbach's Alpha if Item Deleted
α =0.972（n=1531）	我会一直购买这家公司的产品	0.877	0.969
	这家公司很值得信赖	0.904	0.968
	我会很积极维持与这家公司的关系	0.888	0.968
	使用他们的产品总是很愉快	0.854	0.969
	这家公司会真诚关注我的需要	0.838	0.970
	要是其他产品都像这公司的产品就好了	0.805	0.971
α =0.972（n=1524）	跟其他产品供应商比起来，我很满意我所选择的服务供应商	0.890	0.968
	我相信这家公司会遵守对顾客的承诺	0.897	0.967
	我对这家公司很有信心	0.903	0.967
	我是这家公司的忠实顾客	0.854	0.969
	我想继续与这家公司保持关系	0.880	0.968
	我相信这家公司总会考虑顾客最佳利益	0.851	0.969
	这家公司总会优先考虑顾客的利益	0.867	0.969
	我觉得这家公司很诚实、很实在	0.869	0.969
	我会努力支持这家公司	0.876	0.968
α =0.844（n=1542）	这家公司不会隐瞒我应该知道的信息	0.717	0.776
	我认为该公司总能给我详尽的咨询	0.738	0.755
	即使有其他的选择，我也不会选择其他公司	0.675	0.816
	Total scale reliability		α =0.983

信度分析结果表明，由 22 道题组成的测量关系品质的问卷的内部一致性系数非常高（0.983），删除任何一道题都不能提高问卷的有效性，因此说明该量表的信度非常高。

5.2.3 行为意向结构与信度分析

测量行为意向有 4 个题项，在进行结构效度分析之前，先对这 4 道题进行了 KMO and Bartlett's 检验，检验结果（Kaiser-Meyer-Olkin Measure of Sampling Adequacy=0.701; p <0.001）说明行为意向量表适合进行因子分析。表 5-10 是测量该 4 道题的结构分析结果。

表 5-10 行为意向量表结构分析结果 (n =1553)

	Initial Eigenvalues			Rotation Sums of Squared Loadings		
Component	Total	% of Variance	Cumulative %	Total	% of Variance	Cumulative %
1	2.279	56.980	56.980	2.068	51.688	51.688
2	0.859	21.482	78.461	1.071	26.773	78.461
3	0.576	14.399	92.860			
4	0.286	7.140	100.000			

表 5-10 的结果说明行为意向的 4 道题为二维结构（有 2 个因子的特征根大于 1，分别为 2.068、1.071），两个因子的累计解释变异量达到 78.461%，分析结果说明 4 道题可以浓缩为 2 个因子。在确定了量表的二维度结构之后，再对该量表进行因子旋转，得到表 5-11 的因子旋转矩阵。

表 5-11 行为意向因子旋转矩阵[a]

Item	Component	
	1	2
我以后会增加购买该公司产品的次数	0.854	
如果有人提起该公司，我会推荐	0.831	
如果有别的选择，我也不会选择其他公司的产品	0.793	
我会向他人说该公司的不是		0.977

Extraction Method: Principal Component Analysis.
Rotation Method: Varimax with Kaiser Normalization.
a：Rotation converged in 5 iterations.

因子旋转之后发现，4 道题中有 3 道属于一个因子，另一道题属于其他的一个因子，这与原问卷有所出入。下面继续就 4 道题进行信度分析，分析结果见表 5-12。

表 5-12 行为意向信度分析结果 (n =1553)

Item	Corrected Item-Total Correlation	Cronbach's Alpha if Item Deleted
我以后会增加购买该公司产品的次数	0.658	0.593
如果有人提起该公司，我会推荐	0.680	0.565

续表

Item	Corrected Item–Total Correlation	Cronbach's Alpha if Item Deleted
如果有别的选择，我也不会选择其他公司的产品	0.476	0.694
我会向他人说该公司的不是	0.307	0.789
Total scale reliability	α =0.730	

表 5–12 题项：“我会向他人说该公司的不是。”此条内部一致性系数非常低，仅 0.307。如果删除这道题的话，量表的整体信度将有所提高，因此，下面将这道题剔除再进行一次信度检验，表 5–13 是再验信度的结果。

表 5–13：行为意向再测信度分析结果 (n =1553)

α =.788 (n =1560)	Corrected Item–Total Correlation	Cronbach's Alpha if Item Deleted
我以后会增加购买该公司产品的次数。	0.700	0.642
如果有人提起该公司，我会推荐。	0.684	0.651
如果有别的选择，我也不会选择其他公司的产品。	0.517	0.827
Total scale reliability	α =0.789	

其中，A04 与问卷的相关系数较低（0.307），删除题项 A04 之后，行为意向量表的信度由 0.730 提高到 0.789。结合因子分析与信度检验的结果，本研究决定将此题项删除，仅保留 3 道题，并将该量表定义为行为意向量表。

5.2.4 定义变量

三个因变量的因子分析与信度分析之后，我发现本研究的问卷与原有的设计存在一些差异。每个变量虽然结构与原量表一致。但是，每个维度的问题与原量表都不一样。为了准确地表达出因子的真正内涵，我对每一个量表的维度（因子）重新命名。因子命名的原则主要有：①变化较小的因子，以原量表的名称为主；②变化较大的因子，根据因子负荷较高的题项意义进行重新命名。

在因子分析与信度分析的结果上，结合命名的原则。本研究得到了三个分量表："知觉公平"分量表、"关系品质"分量表、"行为意向"分量表，三个分量表的层面名称、代号与题项如表 5-14。

表 5-14 量表分解图

量表 / 层面名称呼	代号	包含的题项	题数
一、知觉公平量表		（每组问卷中共有两部分值，A + C 对应题项）	
1. 补偿性知觉公平	Dis	A6+A9+A12	3
2. 程序性知觉公平	Pro	A1+A2+ A3+A5+A8+ A10+A11+A13	8
3. 感知性知觉公平[a]	Pre	A15+A16+A17	3
二、关系品质量表		（每组问卷中共有两部分值，B + D 对应题项）	
1. 满意	Sat	B1+ B2+B3 +B4 +B5+B6+B7+B8+B9 +B13	10
2. 承诺	Tur	B14+B15+B16+B17+B18+B19+B20+B21+B22	9
3. 信任	Com	B10+B11+B12	3
三、行为意向量表[b]		（每组问卷中共有两部分值，A + C 对应题项）	
		A14+A18+A7	3

a：这一部分的题项变化较大，根据这三道题的实际含义，重新命名因子名称。
b：在删除一个题项之后，该变量仅保留一维结构，因此沿用原变量的名称。

根据以上计算，得到了 7 个因变量：知觉公平的三个维度变量，即补偿性公平（Dis）、程序性公平（Pro）、感知性公平（Pre）；关系品质三个维度变量，即满意（Sat）、信任（Tur）、承诺（Com）和行为意向变量。

5.3 多变量变异数分析检验（MANOVA）

5.3.1 组间均值比较（t-Tests）

由于本研究的 3 个自变量都包含两个水准：响应速度（快、慢）、心理补救（高、低）、有形补偿（多、少），为了对试验研究操控性进行检验先进行 t 检验，检验结果见表 5-15。

表 5-15 t 检验结果

	响应速度	N	Mean	Std. Deviation	Std. Error Mean	t	Sig. (2-tailed)
知觉公平	慢	785	3.5750	1.23100	0.04394	−20.837	0.000
	快	789	4.7634	1.02144	0.03636		
关系品质	慢	783	3.7611	1.45164	0.05188	−14.044	0.000
	快	787	4.7060	1.20211	0.04285		
行为意向	慢	785	3.6280	1.42720	0.05094	−13.010	0.000
	快	797	3.9891	1.35489	0.04799		
	心理补救	N	Mean	Std. Deviation	Std. Error Mean		
知觉公平	低	777	4.1510	1.31587	0.04721	−0.602	0.547
	高	797	4.1898	1.23885	0.04388		
关系品质	低	775	4.2606	1.44443	0.05189	0.716	0.474
	高	795	4.2095	1.38283	0.04904		
行为意向	低	776	4.1392	1.42727	0.05124	2.137	0.033
	高	797	3.9891	1.35489	0.04799		
	有形补偿	N	Mean	Std. Deviation	Std. Error Mean	t	Sig. (2-tailed)
知觉公平	少	792	3.6760	1.28314	0.04559	−16.810	0.000
	多	782	4.6717	1.05751	0.03782		
关系品质	少	790	3.8333	1.53896	0.05475	−11.838	0.000
	多	780	4.6413	1.13825	0.04076		
行为意向	少	791	3.7012	1.50944	0.05367	−10.753	0.000
	多	782	4.4292	1.15422	0.04127		

从以上的检验结果我们可以看到，响应速度快的组 3 个因变量均值高于响应速度慢的组值（知觉公平 4.7634 vs. 3.575，t=−20.837，p <0.001；关系品质 4.7060 vs. 3.7611，t=−14.044，p <0.001；行为意向 3.9891 vs. 3.6280，t=−13.010，p <0.001）。有形补偿多的组 3 个因变量均值高于有形补偿少的组值（知觉公平 4.6717 vs. 3.6760，t=−16.810，p <0.001；关系品质 4.6413 vs. 3.8333，t=−11.838，p <0.001；行为意向 4.4292 vs. 3.7012，t=−10.753，p <0.001）。

但是，心理补救却显示出相反的结论，因变量知觉公平从均值来看心理补救高的组略高于心理补救低的组（4.1898 vs. 4.1510），但是没有达到统计显著水平，也就是说心理补救高低组间在知觉公平这个变量上不存在显著差异。

心理补救较低的组在关系品质上的均值略高于心理补救较高的组（4.2606 vs. 4.2095）但是，组间不存在差异（t=0.716，p >0.05）。

心理补救对行为意向存在组间差异（4.1392 vs.3.9891，t=2.137，p <0.05），心理补救较低的组在行为意向上反而高于心理补救较高的组。

通过对以上 3 个自变量对因变量影响的均值比较，我们发现，在自变量的不同水准时对因变量基本存在组间差异(心理补救对两个因变量虽然没有通过统计检验，但是组间均值还是存在差异）。以上的结果说明，本研究的实验水准的操控性比较有效，自变量的变化能够带来不同实验组的较大差异。

5.3.3 多变量统计检验（Multivariate Test）

表 5-16 是本研究多变量的描述性统计，分别是 3 个因变量在 3 个自变量不同组间的平均值、标准差及观测值个数。

表 5-16 各细格平均数描述性统计

	响应速度	心理补救	有形补偿	Mean	Std. Deviation	N
知觉公平	慢	低	少	3.0995	1.27257	201
			多	4.1681	1.05996	187
			Total	3.6145	1.28947	388
		高	少	3.0700	1.21259	197
			多	4.0183	0.90338	195
			Total	3.5417	1.16935	392
		Total	少	3.0849	1.24177	398
			多	4.0916	0.98471	382
			Total	3.5779	1.23032	780
	快	低	少	4.1954	1.12651	189
			多	5.1896	0.79932	197
			Total	4.7028	1.09206	386
		高	少	4.3791	0.86215	202
			多	5.2800	0.74685	199
			Total	4.8261	0.92359	401

续表

	响应速度	心理补救	有形补偿	Mean	Std. Deviation	N
知觉公平		Total	少	4.2903	1.00163	391
			多	5.2350	0.77374	396
			Total	4.7657	1.01098	787
	Total	低	少	3.6306	1.32161	390
			多	4.6922	1.06489	384
			Total	4.1573	1.31260	774
		高	少	3.7327	1.23650	399
			多	4.6555	1.04057	394
			Total	4.1912	1.23239	793
		Total	少	3.6822	1.27948	789
			多	4.6736	1.05213	778
			Total	4.1744	1.27234	1567
关系品质	慢	低	少	3.3725	1.55561	201
			多	4.4407	1.30637	187
			Total	3.8873	1.53509	388
		高	少	3.1232	1.44015	197
			多	4.1480	1.04797	195
			Total	3.6330	1.35934	392
		Total	少	3.2491	1.50287	398
			多	4.2913	1.18904	382
			Total	3.7595	1.45407	780
	快	低	少	4.3410	1.42074	189
			多	4.9204	.96437	197
			Total	4.6367	1.24226	386
		高	少	4.5054	1.25398	202
			多	5.0441	0.98704	199
			Total	4.7727	1.15980	401
		Total	少	4.4259	1.33799	391
			多	4.9826	0.97656	396
			Total	4.7060	1.20211	787
	Total	低	少	3.8418	1.56672	390
			多	4.6868	1.16721	384
			Total	4.2610	1.44533	774
		高	少	3.8230	1.51468	399
			多	4.6006	1.11095	394
			Total	4.2093	1.38445	793
		Total	少	3.8323	1.53967	789
			多	4.6431	1.13914	778
			Total	4.2349	1.41463	1567

续表

	响应速度	心理补救	有形补偿	Mean	Std. Deviation	N
行为意向	慢	低	少	3.3085	1.56877	201
			多	4.2941	1.25615	187
			Total	3.7835	1.50779	388
		高	少	3.0321	1.38693	197
			多	3.9214	1.09752	195
			Total	3.4745	1.32668	392
		Total	少	3.1717	1.48614	398
			多	4.1038	1.19099	382
			Total	3.6282	1.42715	780
	快	低	少	4.2293	1.38477	189
			多	4.7631	1.03195	197
			Total	4.5017	1.24496	386
		高	少	4.2541	1.29305	202
			多	4.7236	0.99724	199
			Total	4.4871	1.17800	401
		Total	少	4.2421	1.33650	391
			多	4.7433	1.01356	396
			Total	4.4943	1.21055	787
	Total	低	少	3.7547	1.55061	390
			多	4.5347	1.16891	384
			Total	4.1417	1.42803	774
		高	少	3.6508	1.47168	399
			多	4.3266	1.12114	394
			Total	3.9865	1.35145	793
		Total	少	3.7022	1.51115	789
			多	4.4293	1.14896	778
			Total	4.0632	1.39152	1567

通过表 5-16 报告我们可以总结出以下几个明显的结论：

① 响应速度是影响 3 个因变量的关键性变量，在任何情况下，响应速度快的组因变量得分的均值都高于响应速度慢的组；

② 有形补偿是影响 3 个因变量的关键性变量，在任何情况下，有形补偿多的组因变量得分的均值都高于有形补偿少的组；

③ 心理补救对 3 个因变量的影响却存在差异，3 个因变量的强度与心理补救的

高低并不存在一致性的关系，因变量均值或高或低。

多变量的细格描述性统计虽然体现了 3 个自变量与 3 个因变量的关系存在一些可能的特征，但是并不能体现因变量差异的真正形态。那么，接下来的多变量统计分析就是揭示自变量是如何通过自身及相互影响造成因变量的差异。

在多变量分析中，常用的整体检验有：Hotelling Trace、Wilik's Lambda 、Pillar's Trace、Roy's 最大根准则四种。四种整体效果之统计量各有其不同的特点。在多数多变量分析研究中，出现最多者是 Wilik's Lambda Λ 值，Wilik's Λ 较有韧性，历史也比较悠久。如果组别为多个，变量数也为多个时，显著性就要采用 Λ 加以检验，其中 t、$T2$、F 等检验法，其实都是 Λ 值在特殊情境中使用的方法而已（Tacq, 1997）。鉴于本研究的多组别（8 个组合）、多变量（3 个自变量、3 个因变量）的特征，我们选用 Wilik's Lambda 进行多变量整体检验。表 5-17 为多变量的检验结果。

表 5-17 多变量整体检验结果

	Effect	Value	F	Hypothesis df	Error df	Sig.
Intercept	Pillai's Trace	0.945	8944.365[a]	3.000	1557.000	0.000
	Wilks' Lambda	0.055	8944.365[a]	3.000	1557.000	0.000
	Hotelling's Trace	17.234	8944.365[a]	3.000	1557.000	0.000
	Roy's Largest Root	17.234	8944.365[a]	3.000	1557.000	0.000
响应速度	Pillai's Trace	0.259	181.562[a]	3.000	1557.000	0.000
	Wilks' Lambda	0.741	181.562[a]	3.000	1557.000	0.000
	Hotelling's Trace	0.350	181.562[a]	3.000	1557.000	0.000
	Roy's Largest Root	0.350	181.562[a]	3.000	1557.000	0.000
心理补救	Pillai's Trace	0.011	5.839[a]	3.000	1557.000	0.001
	Wilks' Lambda	0.989	5.839[a]	3.000	1557.000	0.001
	Hotelling's Trace	0.011	5.839[a]	3.000	1557.000	0.001
	Roy's Largest Root	0.011	5.839[a]	3.000	1557.000	0.001

续表

	Effect	Value	*F*	Hypothesis df	Error df	Sig.
有形补偿	Pillai's Trace	0.195	125.441[a]	3.000	1557.000	0.000
	Wilks' Lambda	0.805	125.441[a]	3.000	1557.000	0.000
	Hotelling's Trace	0.242	125.441[a]	3.000	1557.000	0.000
	Roy's Largest Root	0.242	125.441[a]	3.000	1557.000	0.000
响应速度 × 心理补救	Pillai's Trace	0.007	3.556[a]	3.000	1557.000	0.014
	Wilks' Lambda	0.993	3.556[a]	3.000	1557.000	0.014
	Hotelling's Trace	0.007	3.556[a]	3.000	1557.000	0.014
	Roy's Largest Root	0.007	3.556[a]	3.000	1557.000	0.014
响应速度 × 有形补偿	Pillai's Trace	0.019	10.104[a]	3.000	1557.000	0.000
	Wilks' Lambda	0.981	10.104[a]	3.000	1557.000	0.000
	Hotelling's Trace	0.019	10.104[a]	3.000	1557.000	0.000
	Roy's Largest Root	0.019	10.104[a]	3.000	1557.000	0.000
心理补救 × 有形补偿	Pillai's Trace	0.001	0.534[a]	3.000	1557.000	0.659
	Wilks' Lambda	0.999	0.534[a]	3.000	1557.000	0.659
	Hotelling's Trace	0.001	0.534[a]	3.000	1557.000	0.659
	Roy's Largest Root	0.001	0.534[a]	3.000	1557.000	0.659

a：Exact statistic
b：Design: Intercept+speed+concern+compensate+speed * concern+speed * compensate+concern * compensate+speed * concern * compensate

多变量整体统计检验得出以下结论：

（1）响应速度主效果显著，多变量显著性检验的 Wilks' Λ 值= 0.741($p<0.05$) 达到显著水平；

（2）心理补救主效果显著，多变量显著性检验的 Wilks' Λ 值= 0.989($p<0.05$) 达到显著水平；

（3）有形补偿主效果显著，多变量显著性检验的 Wilks' Λ 值= 0.805($p<0.05$) 达到显著水平；

（4）响应速度 × 心理补救交互作用的多变量显著性检验的 Wilks' Λ 值=

0.993(p <0.05)，达到显著水平；

（5）响应速度 × 有形补偿交互作用的多变量显著性检验的 Wilks' Λ 值＝0.981(p <0.01)，达到显著水平；

（6）心理补救 × 有形补偿交互作用的多变量显著性检验的 Wilks' Λ 值＝0.999(p >0.05)，未达到显著水平。

整体检验验证了，3 个自变量的主效果存在，两个（响应速度 × 心理补救，响应速度 × 有形补偿）二次交互作用存在。那么这 3 个自变量与 3 个因变量的主效果如何？两个二次交互作用与 3 个因变量的作用又如何？下面将通过组间效果检验来进一步揭示其中的差异。

5.3.4 组间效果检验（Between-Subjects Effects Test）

进行主要效果比较，此时即直接比较边缘平均数，其结果与个别进行独立样本单因子变异数分析一样。在检验了自变量的交互作用之后，我们再次对 3 个自变量进行单变量显著性检验，检验结果如表 5-18。

表 5-18 组间效果检验结果

Source	Dependent Variable	Type III Sum of Squares	df	Mean Square	F	Sig.
Corrected Model	知觉公平	932.111[a]	7	133.159	129.502	0.000
	关系品质	642.141[b]	7	91.734	57.396	0.000
	行为意向	533.692[c]	7	76.242	47.571	0.000
Intercept	知觉公平	27295.307	1	27295.307	26545.691	0.000
	关系品质	28110.966	1	28110.966	17588.320	0.000
	行为意向	25885.972	1	25885.972	16151.477	0.000
响应速度	知觉公平	537.785	1	537.785	523.015	0.000
	关系品质	339.787	1	339.787	212.596	0.000
	行为意向	285.190	1	285.190	177.944	0.000
心理补救	知觉公平	0.220	1	0.220	0.214	0.644
	关系品质	1.577	1	1.577	0.987	0.321
	行为意向	10.778	1	10.778	6.725	0.010

续表

Source	Dependent Variable	Type III Sum of Squares	df	Mean Square	F	Sig.
有形补偿	知觉公平	374.460	1	374.460	364.176	0.000
	关系品质	252.292	1	252.292	157.852	0.000
	行为意向	202.694	1	202.694	126.470	0.000
响应速度 × 心理补救	知觉公平	5.028	1	5.028	4.890	0.027
	关系品质	16.855	1	16.855	10.546	0.001
	行为意向	9.848	1	9.848	6.145	0.013
响应速度 × 有形补偿	知觉公平	0.363	1	0.363	0.353	0.553
	关系品质	23.259	1	23.259	14.553	0.000
	行为意向	18.586	1	18.586	11.597	0.001
心理补救 × 有形补偿	知觉公平	1.116	1	1.116	1.085	0.298
	关系品质	0.173	1	0.173	0.108	0.742
	行为意向	0.633	1	0.633	0.395	0.530
Error	知觉公平	1603.024	1559	1.028		
	关系品质	2491.710	1559	1.598		
	行为意向	2498.609	1559	1.603		
Total	知觉公平	29841.679	1567			
	关系品质	31236.659	1567			
	行为意向	28902.556	1567			
Corrected Total	知觉公平	2535.135	1566			
	关系品质	3133.852	1566			
	行为意向	3032.301	1566			

a：R Squared =0.368 (Adjusted R Squared =0.365)
b：R Squared =0.205 (Adjusted R Squared =0.201)
c：R Squared =0.176 (Adjusted R Squared =0.172)

组间效果检验得出以下结论：

① 组间效果的检验分别为三个自变量之单变量显著性检验。

② 响应速度单变量显著性检验结果，不同的响应速度在知觉公平、关系品质、行为意向三个变量的 F 值分别为 523.01（p <0.01）、212.59（p <0.01）、177.94（p <0.01），说明响应速度对知觉公平、关系品质、行为意向均有显著差异存在。

③ 心理补救单变量显著性检验结果，不同的心理补救在知觉公平、关系品质、

行为意向三个变量的F值分别为0.214(p >0.05)、0.987(p >0.05)、6. 725(p <0.05)，说明心理补救对知觉公平、关系品质的影响没有显著差异，但是对行为意向的影响存在差异。

④ 有形补偿单变量显著性检验结果，不同的有形补偿在知觉公平、关系品质、行为意向三个变量的 F 值分别为 364.17（ p <0.01 ）、157.852（ p <0.01 ）、126.47（ p <0.01 ），说明有形补偿对知觉公平、关系品质、行为意向均有显著差异存在

⑤ 在所有的 9 个二次交互作用中，5 个二次交互作用符合显著性检验，分别是响应速度 × 心理补救对知觉公平（F=4.890, p =0.027 ）、关系品质（F=10.546, p =0.001 ）、行为意向（F=6.145, p =0.013 ）；响应速度 × 有形补偿对关系品质（F=14.553, p =0.000 ）、行为意向（F=11.597, p =0.001 ）。

5.4 假设检验

基于以上的多元方差分析结果，下面按照因变量的顺序来验证相关的假设。

5.4.1 与知觉公平相关的假设检验

知觉公平是一个核心的因变量，多元方差分析验证了自变量对知觉公平分别存在主效果及交叉效果，因此，以知觉公平为因变量进行单因素多元方差分析来验证相关假设，其分析结果见表 5-19。

表 5-19 知觉公平单因素方差分析结果

Source	Type III Sum of Squares	df	Mean Square	F	Sig.
Corrected Model	941.544[a]	7	134.506	129.674	0.000
Intercept	27378.883	1	27378.883	26395.293	0.000
响应速度	541.333	1	541.333	521.886	0.000
心理补救	0.304	1	0.304	0.293	0.588
有形补偿	380.138	1	380.138	366.482	0.000

续表

Source	Type III Sum of Squares	df	Mean Square	F	Sig.
响应速度 × 心理补救	5.811	1	5.811	5.603	0.018
响应速度 × 有形补偿	0.213	1	0.213	0.205	0.651
心理补救 × 有形补偿	1.086	1	1.086	1.047	0.306
Error	1624.355	1566	1.037		
Total	29944.893	1574			
Corrected Total	2565.899	1573			

a: R Squared =0.367 (Adjusted R Squared =0.364)

从表中可以看到，响应速度、有形补偿、响应速度 × 心理补救对知觉公平存在显著影响（p<0.05），之后再别对这三个假设进一步进行检验。同时，表中的结果也拒绝了假设 H1.2、假设 H5.1 和假设 H6.1。

图 5-4 清楚地说明了响应速度与知觉公平的显著正相关关系（p =0.000），说明响应速度越快，顾客的知觉水平越高。

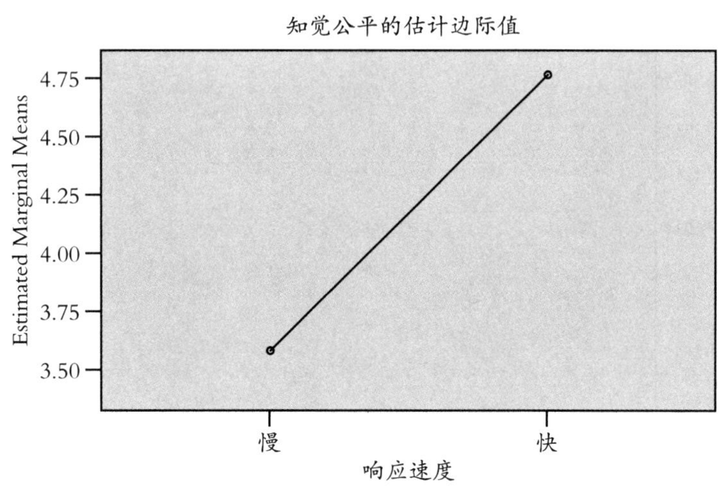

图 5-4 响应速度与知觉公平关系图

这个结论验证假设 H1.1：响应速度越快，顾客的知觉水平越高。

图 5-5 展示了有形补偿与知觉公平的显著正相关关系（p=0.000），说明有形补偿的多少可以提高顾客的知觉公平的感知。

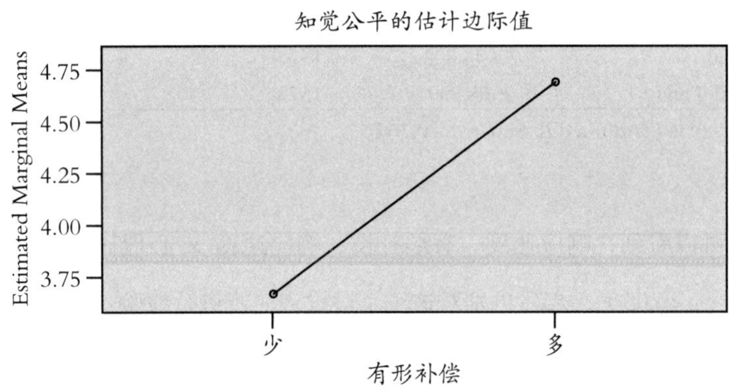

图 5-5 有形补偿与知觉公平关系图

以上结论验证了假设 H1.3: 有形补偿越多，顾客的知觉公平感知越高。

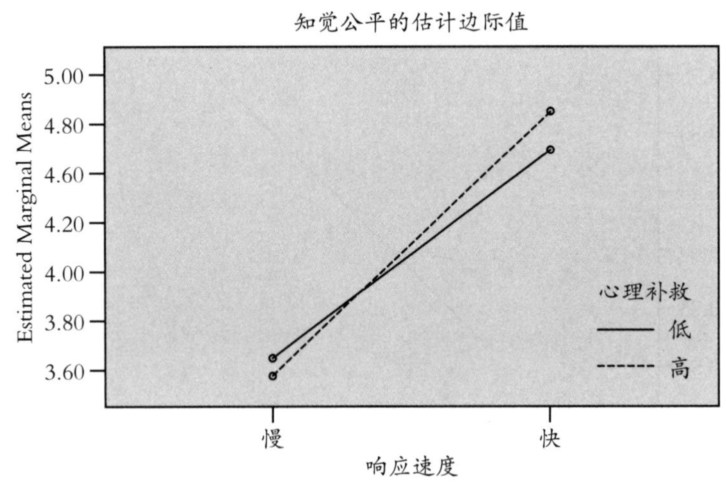

图 5-6 响应速度、心理补救与知觉公平关系图

图 5–6 说明了响应速度 × 心理补救对知觉公平的交互作用：当响应速度慢时，心理补救高并不能提高知觉公平水平；当响应速度快时，心理补救越高知觉公平水平越高。因此，服务商仅为顾客提供心理补救的情况下，响应速度就是影响顾客知觉公平的主要因素。

以上结果验证了假设 H4.1：响应速度与心理补救对知觉公平存在交互作用，在心理补救一定的情况下，响应速度是影响知觉公平的主要变量。

5.4.2 与关系品质相关的假设检验

表 5–20 是以关系品质为因变量进行的单因素多元方差分析结果。

表 5–20 关系品质单因素多元方差分析结果

Source	Type III Sum of Squares	df	Mean Square	*F*	Sig.
Corrected Model	639.917[a]	7	91.417	57.248	0.000
Intercept	28172.647	1	28172.647	17642.635	0.000
响应速度	339.755	1	339.755	212.766	0.000
心理补救	1.470	1	1.470	0.920	0.338
有形补偿	250.989	1	250.989	157.177	0.000
响应速度 × 心理补救	16.523	1	16.523	10.348	0.001
响应速度 × 有形补偿	22.761	1	22.761	14.254	0.000
心理补救 × 有形补偿	0.200	1	0.200	0.125	0.723
Error	2494.280	1562	1.597		
Total	31289.074	1570			
Corrected Total	3134.198	1569			

a：*R* Squared =0.204 (Adjusted *R* Squared = 0.201)

关系品质的多元方差分析结果显示，响应速度、有形补偿、响应速度 × 心理补救、响应速度 × 有形补偿对知觉公平存在显著影响（$p<0.05$），分别对这 4 个假设进一步进行检验，从表 5–20 中结果可以看到，假设 H2.2 与假设 H6.2 没有达到统计显著水平，没有通过假设检验。

图 5-7 说明，响应速度与关系品质显著正相关（ p =0.000 ），响应速度越快，顾客与服务商的关系品质越高。

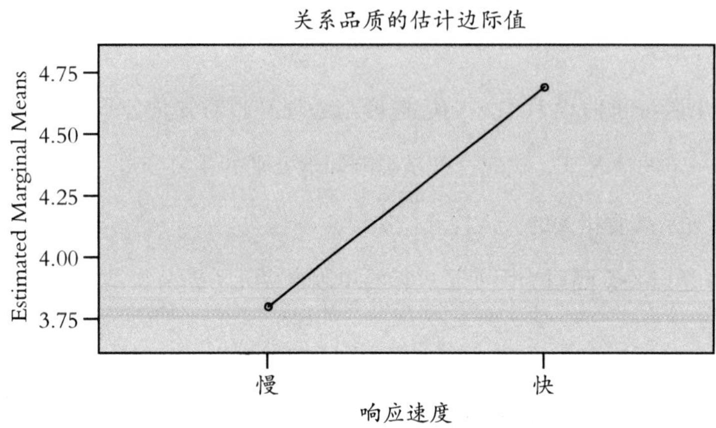

图 5-7 响应速度与关系品质关系图

这个结论验证假设 H2.1：响应速度越快，顾客的关系品质越高。

图 5-8 说明了，有形补偿与关系品质的显著正相关关系（ p =0.000 ），有形补

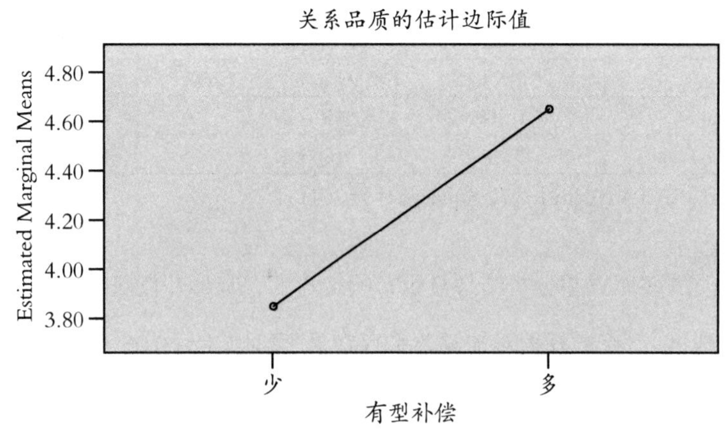

图 5-8 有形补偿与关系品质关系图

偿越多，顾客与服务商的关系品质越高。

这个结论验证了假设 H2.3：有形补偿越多，顾客的关系品质越高。

图 5-9 描绘了响应速度 × 心理补救对关系品质的交互作用。当心理补救高的时候，关系品质随着速度的加快快速上升。因此，当服务补救响应速度快时，顾客的心理状态可以看作是影响关系品质的杠杆。从工作的实践中，我们可以理解为如果运营商能对服务失误快速反应，同时在心理层面关注顾客的感受，那么即使运营商存在服务失误，也能很好地改善和顾客的关系，保持原有的顾客。

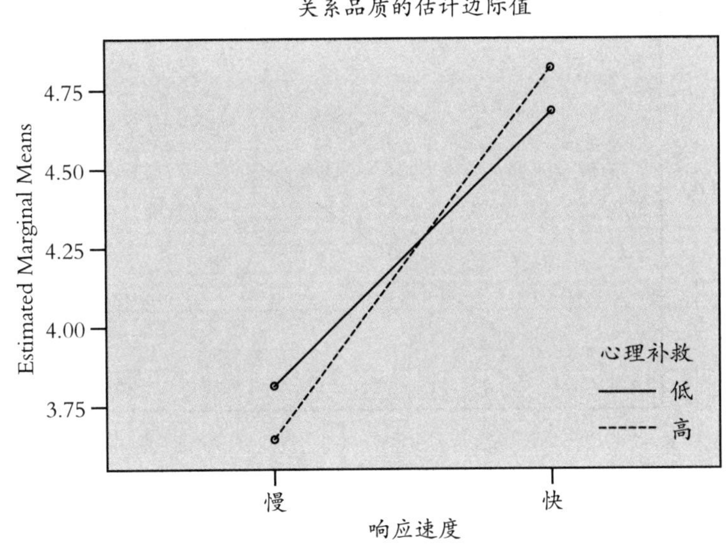

图 5-9 响应速度、心理补救与关系品质关系图

以上验证了假设 H4.2：响应速度快的情况下，心理补救越高，顾客与服务商的关系品质越高。

图 5-10 体现出了在响应速度一定的情况下，有形补偿的不同对关系品质的影

响。图中可以看到，当响应速度不断加快，有形补偿的多少是决定关系品质的主要变量。当有形补偿多的时候，顾客与服务商的关系品质的总体水平高于有形补偿少的状况。在两种不同情况下的关系品质的差距完全是由于有形补偿的多少所导致的，因此在响应速度一致的情况下，有形补偿是决定关系品质的主要变量。同时，我们也发现，当速度较慢时有形补偿的作用更为显著（因为图形左侧的差距要大于右侧的差距）。

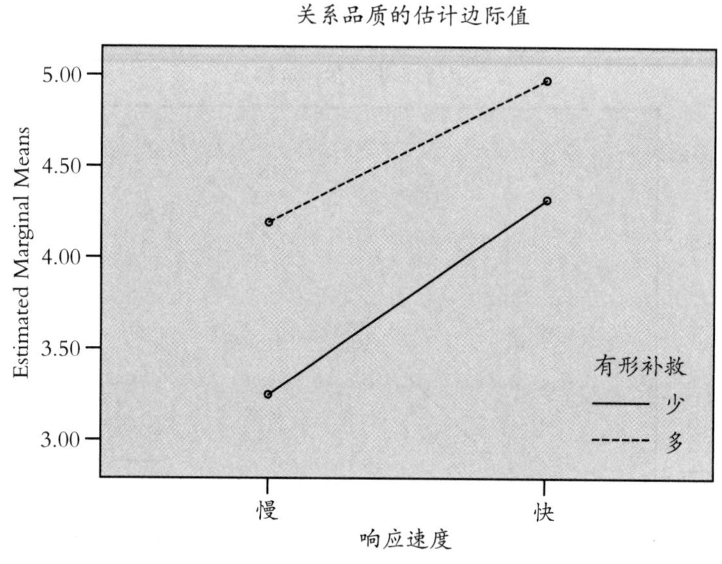

图 5-10 响应速度、有形补偿与关系品质的关系图

以上结论验证了假设 H5.2：响应速度与有形补偿对关系品质存在交互作用。当响应速度一定时，有形补偿越高关系品质越高。

5.4.3 与行为意向相关的假设检验

表 5-21 以行为意向为因变量进行了单因素多元方差分析结果。

表 5-21 行为意向单因素多元方差分析结果

Source	Type III Sum of Squares	df	Mean Square	F	Sig.
Corrected Model	536.552[a]	7	76.650	47.748	0.000
Intercept	25993.379	1	25993.379	16192.275	0.000
响应速度	288.115	1	288.115	179.478	0.000
心理补救	10.210	1	10.210	6.360	0.012
有形补偿	203.748	1	203.748	126.923	0.000
响应速度 × 心理补救	9.797	1	9.797	6.103	0.014
响应速度 × 有形补偿	18.057	1	18.057	11.248	0.001
心理补救 × 有形补偿	0.467	1	0.467	0.291	0.590
Error	2512.287	1565	1.605		
Total	29017.778	1573			
Corrected Total	3048.838	1572			

a：R Squared =0.176 (Adjusted R Squared = 0.172)

行为意向的多元方差分析结果显示，心理补救 × 有形补偿对行为意向没有显著影响（p=0.0590），因而拒绝了假设 H6.3。响应速度、心理补救、有形补偿、响应速度 × 心理补救、响应速度 × 有形补偿对行为意向存在显著影响（p<0.05），那么再分别对这五个假设进一步进行检验。

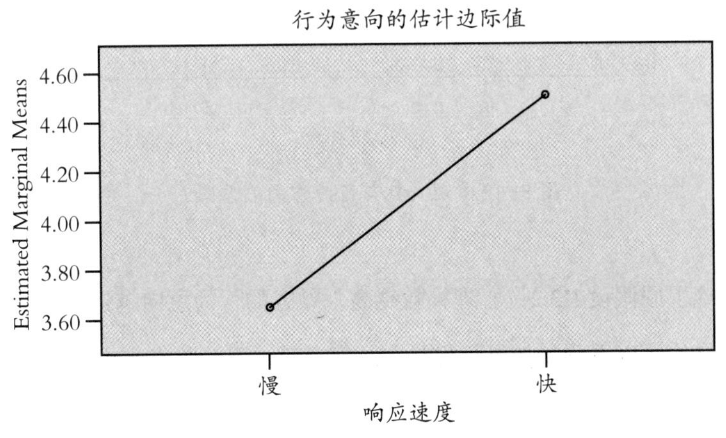

图 5-11 响应速度与行为意向关系图

图 5-11 验证了响应速度与行为意向显著正相关的假设（p=0.000），响应速度的快慢可以影响顾客的行为意向的高低。

以上结论支持了假设 H3.1: 响应速度越快，顾客的行为意向越高。

图 5-12 验证了心理补救与行为意向显著负相关的假设（p=0.012）。心理补救程度越高，反而降低了顾客的行为意向，这与原假设正好相反。

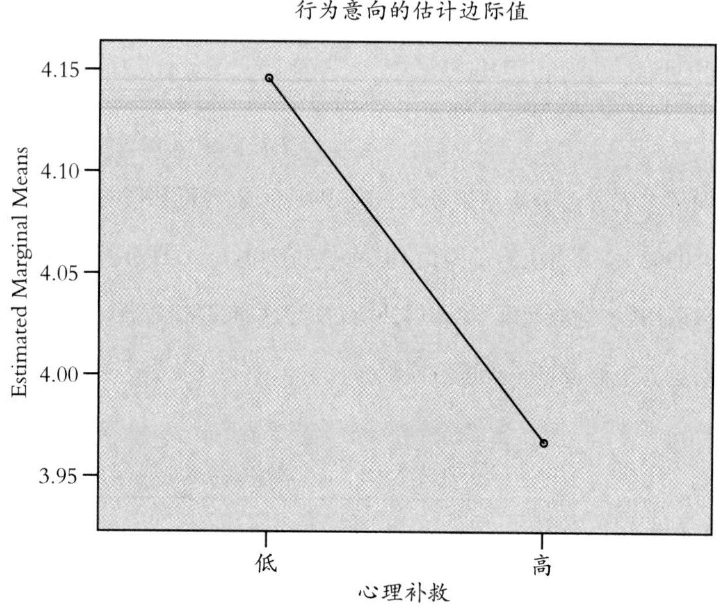

图 5-12 心理补救与行为意向关系图

结论拒绝了原假设 H3.2：心理补救越高，顾客的行为意向越强。

从这个结论可以看到，如果仅仅是向顾客道歉，无论是发自内心的还是客套地表示歉意，都很难改善顾客对服务商的再次购买意向。这个结论从某种意思上说明，仅仅是道歉并不能改变顾客购买意向。

图 5-13 验证了有形补偿与行为意向显著正相关的假设（p=0.000）。有形补偿越多，顾客的行为意向越强。

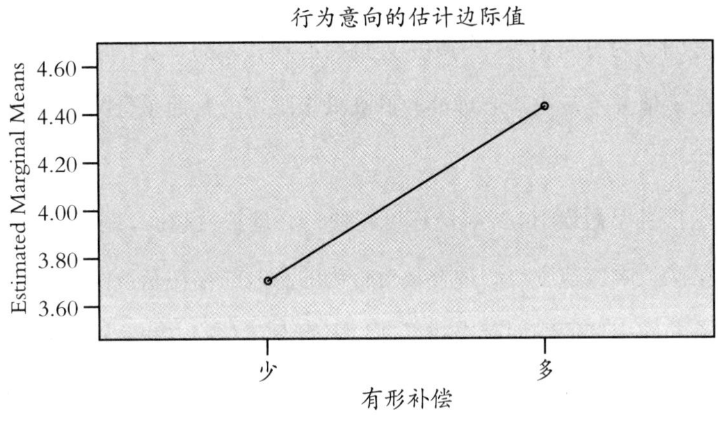

图 5-13 有形补偿与行为意向关系图

这个结论验证了假设 H3.3：有形补偿越高，顾客的行为意向越高。相对与心理安慰而言，有形补偿显然更能打动顾客的心理，同样存在服务失误，实质性的补救措施可以让顾客产生再次购买的意向。

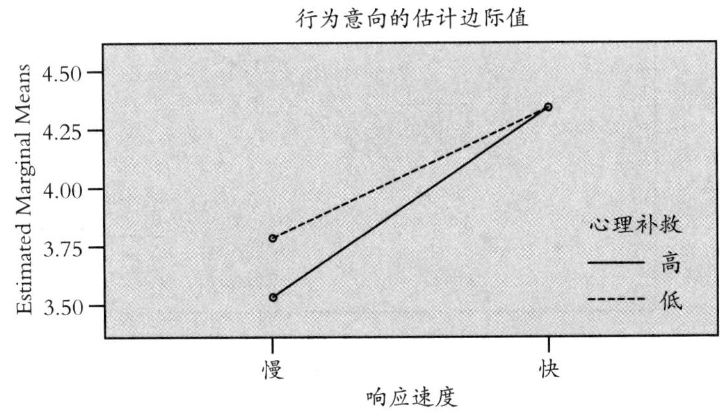

图 5-14 响应速度、心理补救与行为意向关系图

图 5-14 中，当响应速度较慢的时候，心理补救的高低并不能影响到行为意向的提高，心理补救较低的顾客的行为意向水平反而更高，随着响应速度与心理补救的同时提高，顾客的行为意向才越强。当速度达到最快的时候，心理补救的作用为零，此时顾客的行为意向相等。从响应速度与心理补救的交互作用图可以看到，顾客行为意向的差值并不是由于心理补救的高低来决定的，而是受响应速度的快慢影响的。

这个结论推翻了假设 H4.3: 响应速度越快，心理补救越高，顾客与运营商关系品质越高。虽然，响应速度与心理补救对行为的意向的存在交互作用，但是心理补救的作用随着响应速度的增加而递减，这与原假设存在一定的差异。从结果可以看到，响应速度是决定顾客行为意向的主要因素。当响应速度慢时，心理补救与行为意向为负相关的关系。

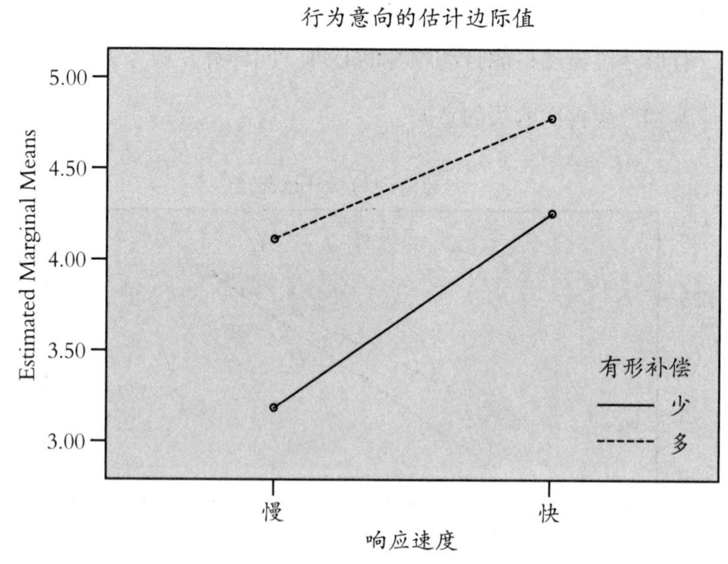

图 5-15 响应速度、有形补偿与行为意向关系图

图 5-15 说明，响应速度与有形补偿共同作用于行为意向，当响应速度相等时，有形补偿的高低可以直接影响顾客行为意向的高低，由此，我们可以看到顾客是否会再次购买原服务商的产品在很大程度上取决于所获得有形补偿的多少。此外，我们也发现有形补偿对行为意向的影响随着响应速度的加快所有降低（两条线段的差距逐渐减小），也就是说响应速度加快可以抵消一部分有形补偿对因为意向的作用。这个结论验证了假设 H5.3: 响应速度、有形补偿对行为意向存在交互作用。当响应速度一定时，有形补偿的多少是影响顾客行为意向的主要因素。

5.4.4 与因变量不同构面相关的假设检验

由于 3 个因变量中有两个自变量是多构面的，因此关注自变量对因变量不同构面的不同作用也同样具有理论与实践意义。由于，本研究中的 3 个自变量都是两个水准级的变量，因此通过单因素多元分析结果中的均值进行比较即可以得出自变量对因变量的差异。表 5-22 为 3 个自变量对因变量不同构面的分析结果。

表 5-22 自变量对因变量不同构面影响的描述性统计

	响应速度	心理补救	有形补偿	Mean	Std. Deviation	*N*
程序性公平	慢	低	少	3.2214	1.50243	201
			多	4.0882	1.36294	187
			Total	3.6392	1.49915	388
		高	少	3.1116	1.36786	196
			多	3.8205	1.07559	195
			Total	3.4652	1.27944	391
		Total	少	3.1672	1.43681	397
			多	3.9516	1.23040	382
			Total	3.5518	1.39503	779
	快	低	少	4.5741	1.19575	189
			多	5.2855	0.86566	197
			Total	4.9372	1.09841	386

续表

	响应速度	心理补救	有形补偿	Mean	Std. Deviation	*N*
程序性公平	快	高	少	4.9202	0.93119	202
			多	5.4868	0.86697	199
			Total	5.2014	0.94247	401
		Total	少	4.7529	1.07988	391
			多	5.3867	0.87107	396
			Total	5.0718	1.02980	787
	Total	低	少	3.8769	1.51979	390
			多	4.7025	1.28245	384
			Total	4.2865	1.46555	774
		高	少	4.0295	1.47569	398
			多	4.6621	1.28281	394
			Total	4.3442	1.41800	792
		Total	少	3.9540	1.49867	788
			多	4.6820	1.28197	778
			Total	4.3157	1.44153	1566
补偿性公平	慢	低	少	2.7877	1.63953	201
			多	4.7148	1.29125	187
			Total	3.7165	1.76638	388
		高	少	2.7449	1.53017	196
			多	4.4462	1.21504	195
			Total	3.5934	1.62188	391
		Total	少	2.7666	1.58462	397
			多	4.5777	1.25848	382
			Total	3.6547	1.69542	779
	快	低	少	3.7743	1.63504	189
			多	5.3046	1.08628	197
			Total	4.5553	1.57889	386
		高	少	3.6782	1.61713	202
			多	5.2915	0.96976	199
			Total	4.4788	1.55944	401
		Total	少	3.7246	1.62444	391

续表

	响应速度	心理补救	有形补偿	Mean	Std. Deviation	*N*
补偿性公平	快	Total	多	5.2980	1.02809	396
			Total	4.5163	1.56848	787
	Total	低	少	3.2658	1.70814	390
			多	5.0174	1.22504	384
			Total	4.1348	1.72621	774
		高	少	3.2186	1.64084	398
			多	4.8731	1.17544	394
			Total	4.0417	1.65013	792
		Total	少	3.2420	1.67359	788
			多	4.9443	1.20157	778
			Total	4.0877	1.68826	1566
感知性公平	慢	低	少	3.0862	1.52835	201
			多	3.8342	1.27628	187
			Total	3.4467	1.45948	388
		高	少	3.2908	1.59982	196
			多	4.1179	1.14688	195
			Total	3.7033	1.45103	391
		Total	少	3.1872	1.56542	397
			多	3.9791	1.21866	382
			Total	3.5755	1.45997	779
	快	低	少	3.6067	1.46186	189
			多	4.8190	1.14109	197
			Total	4.2254	1.44035	386
		高	少	3.6370	1.41194	202
			多	4.7169	1.26008	199
			Total	4.1729	1.44223	401
		Total	少	3.6223	1.43452	391
			多	4.7677	1.20192	396
			Total	4.1986	1.44063	787
	Total	低	少	3.3385	1.51710	390
			多	4.3394	1.30395	384

续表

	响应速度	心理补救	有形补偿	Mean	Std. Deviation	*N*
感知性公平	Total	低	Total	3.8351	1.50049	774
		高	少	3.4665	1.51543	398
			多	4.4205	1.24064	394
			Total	3.9411	1.46463	792
		Total	少	3.4031	1.51665	788
			多	4.3805	1.27211	778
			Total	3.8887	1.48294	1566
满意	慢	低	少	3.2169	1.60938	201
			多	4.3203	1.40633	187
			Total	3.7487	1.61055	388
		高	少	2.9663	1.48841	196
			多	3.9908	1.10976	195
			Total	3.4772	1.40832	391
		Total	少	3.0932	1.55396	397
			多	4.1521	1.27272	382
			Total	3.6125	1.51754	779
	快	低	少	4.1725	1.48814	189
			多	4.9203	1.00493	197
			Total	4.5541	1.31743	386
		高	少	4.3322	1.32530	202
			多	5.0528	1.05356	199
			Total	4.6898	1.24987	401
		Total	少	4.2550	1.40682	391
			多	4.9869	1.03049	396
			Total	4.6233	1.28443	787
	Total	低	少	3.6800	1.62191	390
			多	4.6281	1.25198	384
			Total	4.1504	1.52494	774
		高	少	3.6595	1.56361	398
			多	4.5272	1.20408	394
			Total	4.0912	1.46145	792

续表

	响应速度	心理补救	有形补偿	Mean	Std. Deviation	*N*
满意	Total	Total	少	3.6697	1.59175	788
			多	4.5770	1.22821	778
			Total	4.1204	1.49298	1566
承诺	慢	低	少	3.4820	1.65680	201
			多	4.5888	1.35067	187
			Total	4.0155	1.61309	388
		高	少	3.2602	1.50079	196
			多	4.3390	1.12266	195
			Total	3.7982	1.42998	391
		Total	少	3.3725	1.58361	397
			多	4.4613	1.24419	382
			Total	3.9064	1.52683	779
	快	低	少	4.5250	1.52166	189
			多	5.0288	1.05175	197
			Total	4.7821	1.32567	386
		高	少	4.6947	1.36426	202
			多	5.1513	1.01011	199
			Total	4.9213	1.22170	401
		Total	少	4.6127	1.44313	391
			多	5.0903	1.03156	396
			Total	4.8530	1.27485	787
	Total	低	少	3.9875	1.67413	390
			多	4.8145	1.22496	384
			Total	4.3978	1.52483	774
		高	少	3.9883	1.60134	398
			多	4.7493	1.14087	394
			Total	4.3669	1.44175	792
		Total	少	3.9879	1.63673	788
			多	4.7815	1.18281	778
			Total	4.3821	1.48300	1566
信任	慢	低	少	3.5622	1.55764	201

续表

	响应速度	心理补救	有形补偿	Mean	Std. Deviation	N
信任	慢	低	多	4.3975	1.27260	187
			Total	3.9648	1.48557	388
		高	少	3.3112	1.43861	196
			多	4.0991	1.08165	195
			Total	3.7042	1.33131	391
		Total	少	3.4383	1.50342	397
			多	4.2452	1.18687	382
			Total	3.8340	1.41536	779
	快	低	少	4.3510	1.41536	189
			多	4.5956	1.12310	197
			Total	4.4758	1.27881	386
		高	少	4.5149	1.24857	202
			多	4.6935	1.16744	199
			Total	4.6035	1.21078	401
		Total	少	4.4356	1.33260	391
			多	4.6448	1.14520	396
			Total	4.5409	1.24546	787
	Total	低	少	3.9444	1.53993	390
			多	4.4991	1.20076	384
			Total	4.2196	1.40881	774
		高	少	3.9221	1.47270	398
			多	4.3993	1.16306	394
			Total	4.1595	1.34819	792
		Total	少	3.9332	1.50543	788
			多	4.4486	1.18212	778
			Total	4.1892	1.37837	1566

表 5- 22 说明，响应速度对关系品质的三个构面存在不同的影响，当响应速度快时，顾客承诺水平最高（Mean = 4.85），其次是满意水平（Mean = 4.62），最后是顾客的信任（Mean = 4.54）。当响应速度慢时，顾客承诺水平仍然较高（Mean =

3.91），信任（Mean = 3.83）、满意次之（Mean = 3.61）。总体而言，响应速度对承诺作用最强，然后是信任与满意。响应速度与对知觉公平三个构面的强度依次为程序性公平（Mean = 4.32）、补偿性公平（Mean = 4.09）、感知行公平（Mean = 3.89），响应速度快的组均值均高于响应速度慢的组。

有形补偿对关系品质的影响强度为承诺、信任、满意。有形补偿对知觉公平的三个构面的强度也依次为程序性公平、补偿性公平、感知行公平，且有形补偿多的组均值都高于有形补偿低的组。

心理补救作为一个自变量，它的高低水平不同对 2 个因变量的 6 个构面的影响，也存在一定的差异。

但是，对因变量构面的影响显然不仅仅受到了单个自变量的作用，自变量的交互作用不可忽视，为了进一步揭示自变量对两个因变量的不同构面的影响，本研究将这 6 个构面视为因变量进行多元方差分析，并验证相关假设。

表 5-23 多构面变量整体检验结果

Effect		Value	*F*	Hypothesis df	Error df	Sig.
Intercept	Pillai's Trace	0.951	5039.994[a]	6.000	1553.000	0.000
	Wilks' Lambda	0.049	5039.994[a]	6.000	1553.000	0.000
	Hotelling's Trace	19.472	5039.994[a]	6.000	1553.000	0.000
	Roy's Largest Root	19.472	5039.994[a]	6.000	1553.000	0.000
响应速度	Pillai's Trace	0.324	123.902[a]	6.000	1553.000	0.000
	Wilks' Lambda	0.676	123.902[a]	6.000	1553.000	0.000
	Hotelling's Trace	0.479	123.902[a]	6.000	1553.000	0.000
	Roy's Largest Root	0.479	123.902[a]	6.000	1553.000	0.000
心理补救	Pillai's Trace	0.009	2.452[a]	6.000	1553.000	0.023
	Wilks' Lambda	0.991	2.452[a]	6.000	1553.000	0.023
	Hotelling's Trace	0.009	2.452[a]	6.000	1553.000	0.023
	Roy's Largest Root	0.009	2.452[a]	6.000	1553.000	0.023
有形补偿	Pillai's Trace	0.300	111.122[a]	6.000	1553.000	0.000
	Wilks' Lambda	0.700	111.122[a]	6.000	1553.000	0.000

续表

Effect		Value	F	Hypothesis df	Error df	Sig.
有形补偿	Hotelling's Trace	0.429	111.122[a]	6.000	1553.000	0.000
	Roy's Largest Root	0.429	111.122[a]	6.000	1553.000	0.000
响应速度 × 心理补救	Pillai's Trace	0.020	5.183[a]	6.000	1553.000	0.000
	Wilks' Lambda	0.980	5.183[a]	6.000	1553.000	0.000
	Hotelling's Trace	0.020	5.183[a]	6.000	1553.000	0.000
	Roy's Largest Root	0.020	5.183[a]	6.000	1553.000	0.000
响应速度 × 有形补偿	Pillai's Trace	0.031	8.282[a]	6.000	1553.000	0.000
	Wilks' Lambda	0.969	8.282[a]	6.000	1553.000	0.000
	Hotelling's Trace	0.032	8.282[a]	6.000	1553.000	0.000
	Roy's Largest Root	0.032	8.282[a]	6.000	1553.000	0.000
心理补救 × 有形补偿	Pillai's Trace	0.002	0.420[a]	6.000	1553.000	0.866
	Wilks' Lambda	0.998	0.420[a]	6.000	1553.000	0.866
	Hotelling's Trace	0.002	0.420[a]	6.000	1553.000	0.866
	Roy's Largest Root	0.002	0.420[a]	6.000	1553.000	0.866

a：Exact statistic

多构面变量整体检验结果显示，3 个自变量的主效果显著（响应速度 Wilks'Λ 值 =0.676，p=0.000；心理补救 Wilks'Λ 值 =0.991，p=0.023；有形补偿 Wilks'Λ 值 =0.700，p=0.000)；两个二次交互作用显著（响应速度 × 心理补救 Wilks'Λ 值 =0.980，p=0.000；响应速度 × 有形补偿 Wilks'Λ 值 =0.969，p=0.000）。为了找出具体的变量之间的关系下面将进行组间比较分析。

表 5-24 多构面组间效果检验结果

Source	Dependent Variable	Type III Sum of Squares	df	Mean Square	F	Sig.
Corrected Model	程序性公平	1127.006[a]	7	161.001	118.038	0.000
	补偿性公平	1424.188[b]	7	203.455	104.393	0.000
	感知性公平	545.111[c]	7	77.873	41.887	0.000
	满意	744.487[d]	7	106.355	60.389	0.000
	承诺	641.609[e]	7	91.658	50.996	0.000
	信任	349.310[f]	7	49.901	29.628	0.000

续表

Source	Dependent Variable	Type III Sum of Squares	df	Mean Square	*F*	Sig.
Intercept	程序性公平	29118.573	1	29118.573	21348.408	0.000
	补偿性公平	26214.058	1	26214.058	13450.477	0.000
	感知性公平	23663.959	1	23663.959	12728.702	0.000
	满意	26583.632	1	26583.632	15094.324	0.000
	承诺	30073.958	1	30073.958	16732.285	0.000
	信任	27482.635	1	27482.635	16317.442	0.000
响应速度	程序性公平	887.592	1	887.592	650.742	0.000
	补偿性公平	275.224	1	275.224	141.218	0.000
	感知性公平	146.813	1	146.813	78.970	0.000
	满意	387.999	1	387.999	220.308	0.000
	承诺	340.146	1	340.146	189.248	0.000
	信任	189.635	1	189.635	112.593	0.000
心理补救	程序性公平	0.706	1	0.706	0.517	0.472
	补偿性公平	4.326	1	4.326	2.220	0.136
	感知性公平	4.243	1	4.243	2.282	0.131
	满意	2.028	1	2.028	1.152	0.283
	承诺	0.787	1	0.787	0.438	0.508
	信任	2.022	1	2.022	1.201	0.273
有形补偿	程序性公平	199.151	1	199.151	146.008	0.000
	补偿性公平	1121.348	1	1121.348	575.366	0.000
	感知性公平	365.715	1	365.715	196.716	0.000
	满意	316.244	1	316.244	179.565	0.000
	承诺	242.013	1	242.013	134.649	0.000
	信任	102.409	1	102.409	60.804	0.000
响应速度 × 心理补救	程序性公平	20.917	1	20.917	15.335	0.000
	补偿性公平	1.001	1	1.001	0.514	0.474
	感知性公平	7.670	1	7.670	4.126	0.042
	满意	18.606	1	18.606	10.564	0.001
	承诺	14.269	1	14.269	7.939	0.005
	信任	16.086	1	16.086	9.551	0.002
响应速度 × 有形补偿	程序性公平	2.166	1	2.166	1.588	0.208
	补偿性公平	5.746	1	5.746	2.948	0.086
	感知性公平	12.574	1	12.574	6.763	0.009
	满意	10.634	1	10.634	6.038	0.014
	承诺	36.709	1	36.709	20.424	0.000
	信任	35.211	1	35.211	20.906	0.000

续表

Source	Dependent Variable	Type III Sum of Squares	df	Mean Square	F	Sig.
心理补救 × 有形补偿	程序性公平	2.241	1	2.241	1.643	0.200
	补偿性公平	0.499	1	0.499	0.256	0.613
	感知性公平	0.069	1	0.069	0.037	0.847
	满意	0.276	1	0.276	0.157	0.692
	承诺	0.138	1	0.138	0.077	0.782
	信任	0.314	1	0.314	0.187	0.666
Error	程序性公平	2125.064	1558	1.364		
	补偿性公平	3036.435	1558	1.949		
	感知性公平	2896.481	1558	1.859		
	满意	2743.899	1558	1.761		
	承诺	2800.289	1558	1.797		
	信任	2624.060	1558	1.684		
Total	程序性公平	32419.141	1566			
	补偿性公平	30627.333	1566			
	感知性公平	27122.333	1566			
	满意	30075.900	1566			
	承诺	33514.148	1566			
	信任	30456.111	1566			
Corrected Total	程序性公平	3252.070	1565			
	补偿性公平	4460.623	1565			
	感知性公平	3441.593	1565			
	满意	3488.386	1565			
	承诺	3441.898	1565			
	信任	2973.369	1565			

a：R Squared = 0.347 (Adjusted R Squared = 0.344)
b：R Squared = 0.319 (Adjusted R Squared = 0.316)
c：R Squared = 0.158 (Adjusted R Squared = 0.155)
d：R Squared = 0.213 (Adjusted R Squared = 0.210)
e：R Squared = 0.186 (Adjusted R Squared = 0.183)
f：R Squared = 0.117 (Adjusted R Squared = 0.114)

多构面的组间比较分析结果得出了以下结论。

① 响应速度、有形补偿对 6 个构面的主效果都达到统计显著水平。心理补救没有通过统计检验，因此拒绝了假设 H1.5 和假设 H2.5。

② 18 个二次交互作用中，有 9 个达到统计显著水平，因此拒绝了假设 H1.5、假设 H2.5、假设 H6.4、假设 H6.5。

下面根据组间比较中所显示的符合统计水平的变量进行进一步的假设检验。

（1）响应速度与不同构面关系的假设检验

根据检验结果发现，响应速度与 6 个构面变量都是正相关的关系，即响应速度越快，程序性公平、补偿性公平、感知性公平、满意、承诺、信任都随之增强。由于响应速度是两个水准级的变量，因此我们可以通过组间的均值比较来评价响应速度对不同构面变量影响的强弱。

表 5-25 响应速度对不同构面影响的均值比较

因变量	响应速度（自变量）	Mean	Std. Deviation	*N*
程序性公平	慢	3.5518	1.39503	779
	快	5.0718	1.02980	787
	Total	4.3157	1.44153	1566
补偿性公平	慢	3.6547	1.69542	779
	快	4.5163	1.56848	787
	Total	4.0877	1.68826	1566
感知性公平	慢	3.5755	1.45997	779
	快	4.1986	1.44063	787
	Total	3.8887	1.48294	1566
满意	慢	3.6125	1.51754	779
	快	4.6233	1.28443	787
	Total	4.1204	1.49298	1566
承诺	慢	3.9064	1.52683	779
	快	4.8530	1.27485	787
	Total	4.3821	1.48300	1566
信任	慢	3.8340	1.41536	779
	快	4.5409	1.24546	787
	Total	4.1892	1.37837	1566

表 5-25 可以看到，当响应速度快时，速度对知觉公平三个构面的影响强

度依次为程序性公平、补偿性公平、感知性公平（5.0718>4.5163>4.1986），当响应速度慢时，影响强度依次为补偿性公平、感知性公平、程序性公平（3.6547>3.5755>3.5518）。当响应速度快时，响应速度对关系品质三个构面影响最强的为承诺（Mean = 4.8530），其次是信任（Mean = 4.6233）。当响应速度慢时，影响强度最大的是承诺（Mean = 3.9064），其次是满意（Mean = 3.8340）。

以上结论验证了假设 H1.4，响应速度对顾客的知觉公平的不同构面影响存在差异；假设 H2.4，响应速度对顾客的关系品质的不同构面影响存在差异。

（2）有形补偿与不同构面关系的假设检验

根据检验结果发现，有形补偿与六个构面变量都是正相关的关系，即有形补偿越高，程序性公平、补偿性公平、感知性公平、满意、承诺、信任都随之增强。由于有形补偿是两个水准级的变量，因此我们可以通过组间的均值比较来评价有形补偿对不同构面变量影响的强弱。

表 5-26 有形补偿对不同构面影响的均值比较

因变量	有形补偿（自变量）	Mean	Std. Deviation	N
程序性公平	少	3.9540	1.49867	788
	多	4.6820	1.28197	778
	Total	4.3157	1.44153	1566
补偿性公平	少	3.2420	1.67359	788
	多	4.9443	1.20157	778
	Total	4.0877	1.68826	1566
感知性公平	少	3.4031	1.51665	788
	多	4.3805	1.27211	778
	Total	3.8887	1.48294	1566
满意	少	3.6697	1.59175	788
	多	4.5770	1.22821	778
	Total	4.1204	1.49298	1566
承诺	少	3.9879	1.63673	788
	多	4.7815	1.18281	778
	Total	4.3821	1.48300	1566
信任	少	3.9332	1.50543	788
	多	4.4486	1.18212	778
	Total	4.1892	1.37837	1566

表 5-26 可以看到，当有形补偿多时，对知觉公平三个构面影响的强度依次为补偿性公平、程序性公平、感知性公平（4.9443>4.6820>3.3805）。当有形补偿少时，对知觉公平三个构面影响的强度依次为程序性公平、感知性公平、补偿性公平（3.9540>3.4031>3.2420）。

当有形补偿多时，对关系品质三个构面影响的强弱依次为承诺、满意、信任、（4.7815>4.5770>4.4486）。当有形补偿少时，对关系品质三个构面影响的强弱依次为承诺、信任、满意（3.9879>3.9332>3.6679）。

以上结论验证了假设 H1.6：有形补偿对顾客的知觉公平的不同构面影响存在差异；假设 H2.6: 有形补偿对顾客的关系品质的不同构面影响存在差异。

（3）响应速度、心理补救与不同构面关系的假设检验

要验证响应速度与心理补救对知觉公平不同构面的交互作用，我们根据多元方差分析的交互作用图来表示它们各个的关系并逐一进行分析。图 5-16 是响应速度、心理补救对程序性公平的影响图。

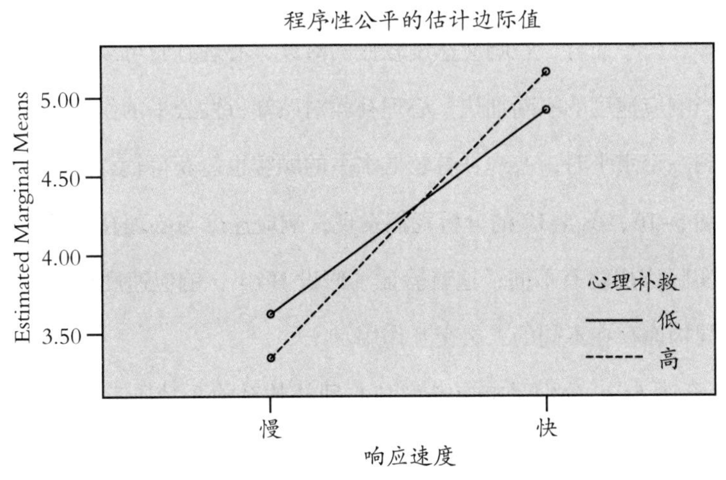

图 5-16 响应速度、心理补救与程序性公平关系图

图 5–17 展现了响应速度是影响程序性公平的主要变量。图中，当响应速度较慢时，即使心理补救的水平较高，顾客的程序性公平的水平并没有达到很高的水平，随着响应速度的加快，顾客的程序性公平感觉随着心理补救水平的提高而快速提升，此时，顾客因为心理补救而提升的程序性公平感知才开始体现出来。

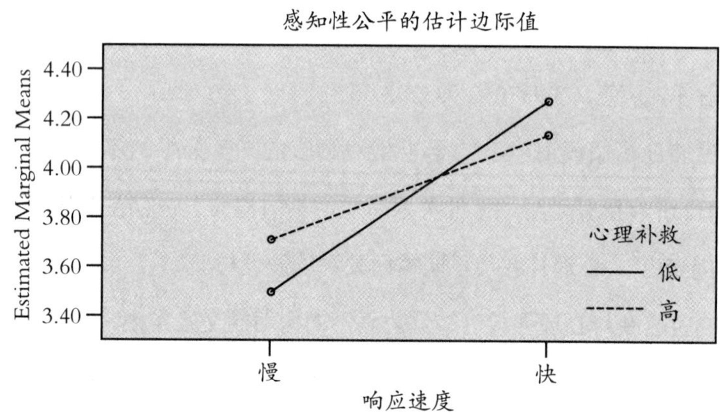

图 5–17 响应速度、心理补救与感知性公平

对于感知性公平而言，在响应速度较慢的时候，心理补救可以提升顾客感知性公平，但是当响应速度的不断加快，心理补救对感知行性公平的作用开始下降，当响应速度达到一定水平时，心理补救较低水平的顾客也能获得较高的感知性公平。

通过对图 5–16、图 5–17 的分析我们发现，响应速度与心理补救对知觉公平的三个构面的实际作用略有不同，这就验证了假设 H4.4 ：响应速度与心理补救对知觉公平的不同构面存在不同的二次交互作用。

图 5–18 至图 5–20 分别是响应速度与心理补救对关系品质三个不同构面的二次交互作用，我们逐一进行分析，探讨其中的异同。

比较图 5–18、图 5–19 和图 5–20 我们不难发现，这三个图的走势基本一致。

图5–18表明，当响应速度加快时，顾客的满意感随着心理补救程度的提高快速增强，这也说明，只有当响应速度达到一定值时，心理补救才会成为提升顾客满意的一个变量，否则，心理补救对顾客满意度不仅起不到应有的作用，反而存在负作用。

图 5–19 与图 5–18 走势基本一致，当响应速度加快时，顾客的承诺随着心理补救程度的提高快速增强，这也说明，只有当响应速度达到一定值时，心理补救才会成为提升顾客承诺的一个变量，否则，心理补救对顾客承诺起不到应有的作用。与图 5–18 相比，顾客的承诺均值要高于顾客满意度，这说明二次交互作用在对两个构面的强弱上还是有些差异的。

图 5–20 也同样说明了心理补救只有当响应速度达到一定值时，顾客的信任才能快速增加。

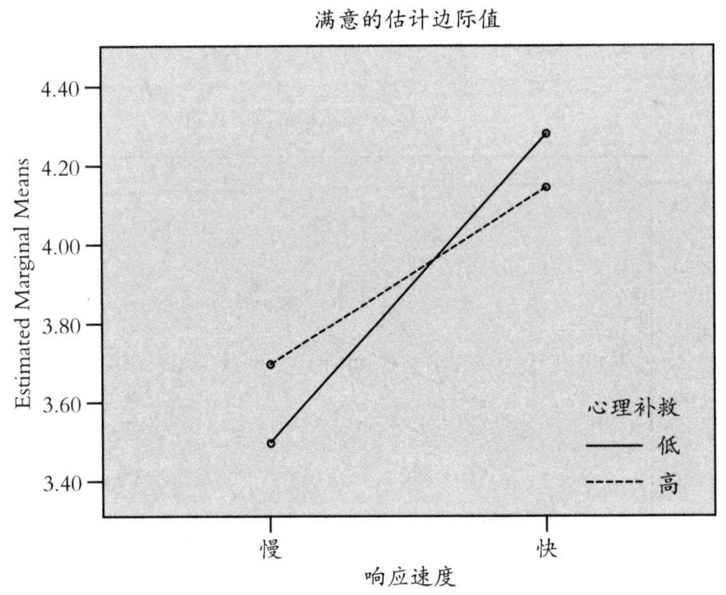

图 5–18 响应速度、心理补救与满意关系图

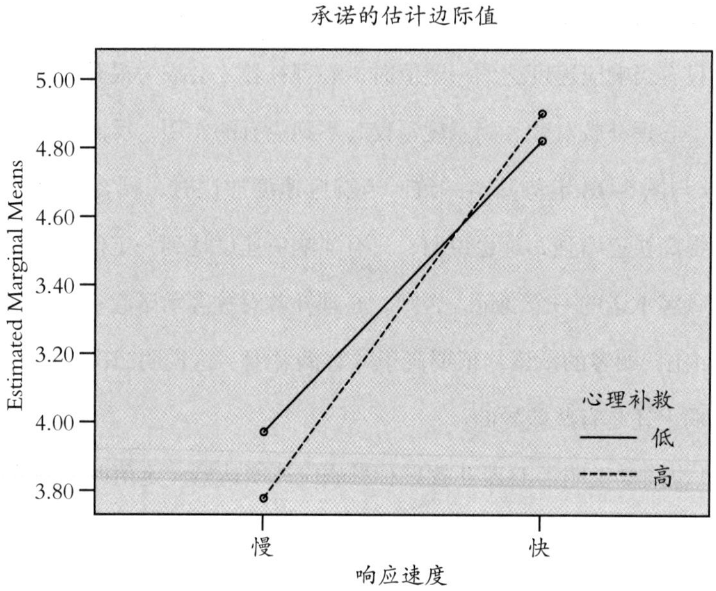

承诺的估计边际值
5.00
4.80
4.60
3.40
3.20
4.00
3.80
Estimated Marginal Means
心理补救
低
高
慢
快
响应速度

图 5-19 响应速度、心理补救与承诺关系图

信任的估计边际值
4.75
4.50
4.25
4.00
3.75
Estimated Marginal Means
心理补救
低
高
慢
快
响应速度

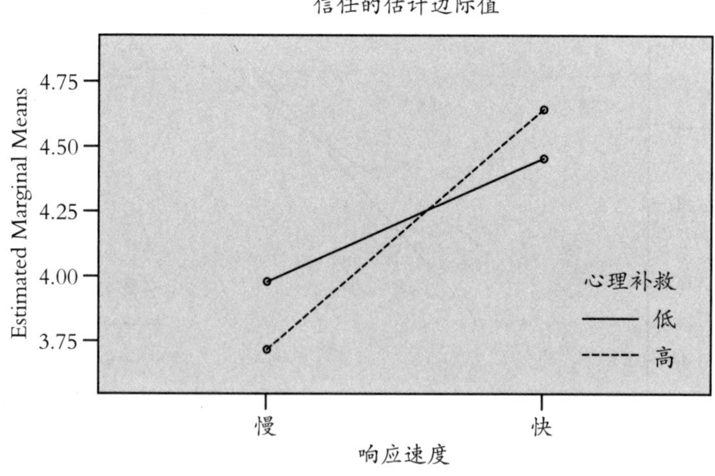

图 5-20 响应速度、心理补救与信任关系图

以上结果说明，响应速度与心理补救对关系品质的三个构面上没有显著的差异，这一结果拒绝了假设 H4.5：响应速度与心理补救的交互作用对关系品质的三个构面存在差异。

（4）响应速度、有形补偿与不同构面关系的假设检验

图 5–21 是描述响应速度与有形补偿对知觉公平三个构面的关系图。

图 5–21 说明了，当响应速度相同时，有形补偿是决定程序性公平、补偿性公平、感知性公平的关键因素。但是，另外两个构面没有通过统计的显著性检验，这个结论验证了假设 H5.4：响应速度与有形补偿对顾客知觉公平的不同构面的影响存在差异。

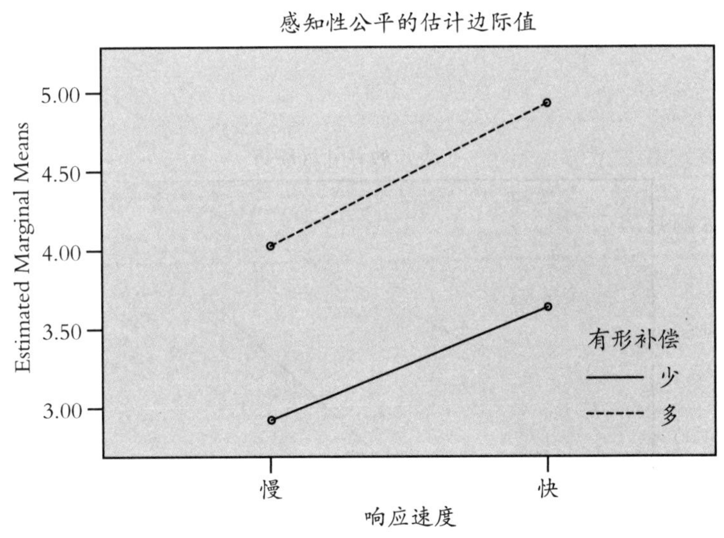

图 5–21 响应速度、有形补偿与感知性公平关系图

图 5–22 至图 5–24 是描述响应速度与有形补偿对顾客关系品质三个构面的关系图。

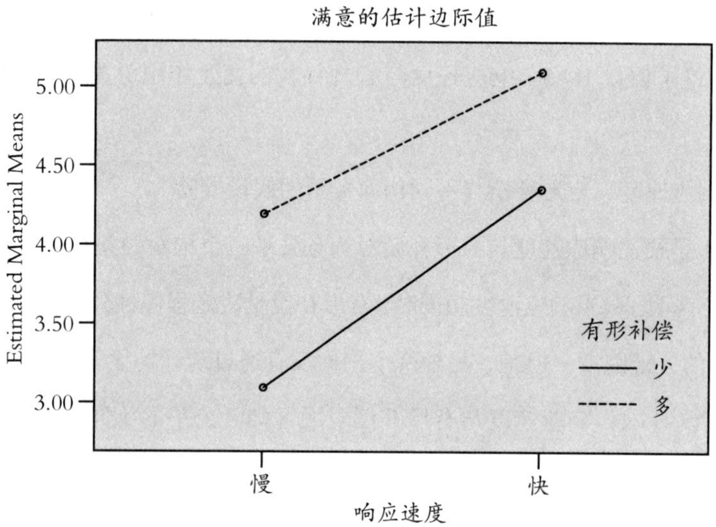

图 5-22 响应速度、有形补偿与满意的关系图

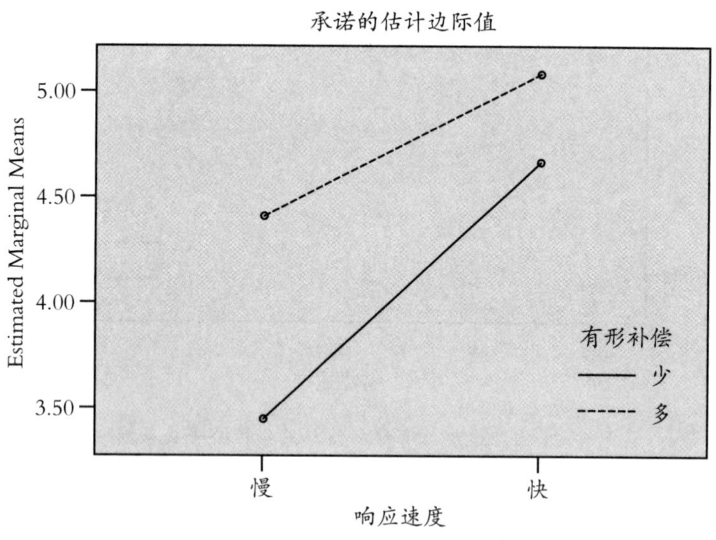

图 5-23 响应速度、有形补偿与承诺的关系图

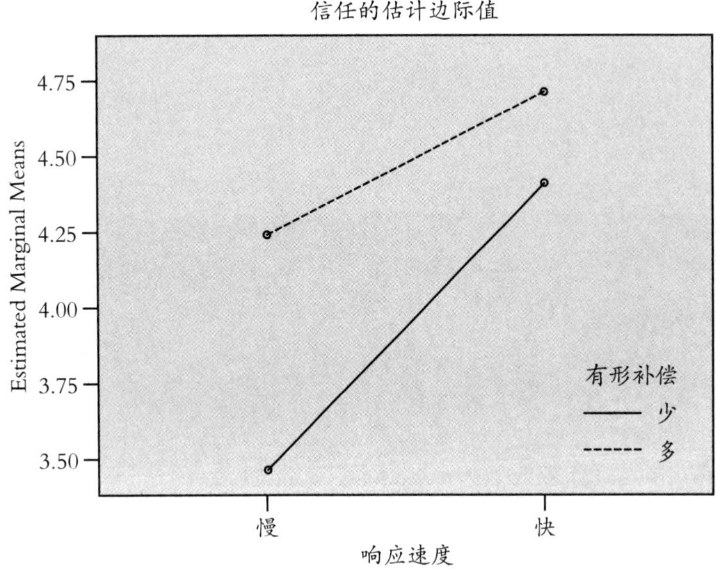

图 5-24 响应速度、有形补偿与信任的关系图

图 5-22、图 5-23 和图 5-24 说明了，当响应速度相同时，有形补偿是影响顾客满意、承诺、信任的主要因素。但是，我们也发现响应速度与有形补偿对这三个不同构面的强弱影响是不一样的，由此也可判断对三个构面的影响还是存在差异，这个结论验证了假设 H5.5：响应速度与有形补偿对顾客关系品质的不同构面的影响存在差异。

第 6 章 讨论与结论

通过上述几章的研究统计分析，本研究得出了一些关键性研究结论。所有与响应速度相关的假设基本都得到了验证，无论是响应速度的主效果还是二次交互作用都得到了证明，同时也证明了响应速度是服务补救的关键，证实了有形补偿的差异能够修补服务失误带来的损伤，无论是有形补偿的主效果还是有形补偿与响应速度的交互作用都具备补偿的作用。与此同时，研究还发现了心理补救与其他两个自变量相互之间的作用机制。

Chapter 6

Discussion and Conclusions

Through the statistical analyses mentioned in the above chapters, this study has obtained some key conclusions. All the hypotheses related to the response speed have basically been validated whether about the main effect of the response speed or about the secondary interactions. It has been proved that the response speed is the key to service recovery. It has been confirmed that the differences in tangible compensation can repair the damages caused by service failures, and that both the main effect of tangible compensation and the interaction between tangible compensation and response speed are compensatory. In the meantime, the study has also found the mechanism for the interaction between psychological remedy and two other independent variables.

通过第五章的统计分析，本研究得出了一些研究结论，本章将对所有的研究结论进行总结，并对其中部分结论进行分析与讨论。

6.1 主要研究结果

本研究主要分为两个部分的检验：第一部分是测量问卷的检验；第二部分是试验研究的假设检验。

6.1.1 量表检验结果

第一部分，我们主要采用因子分析与信度分析来检验问卷的结构与信度。研究发现：三个因变量的结构虽然都与原设计的量表一致（知觉公平的三维结构、关系品质的三维结构、行为意向的两维结构），但是测量题项的因子负荷矩阵与原量表差异较大。所以，虽然维度数量没有发生变化，但是，每个维度的题项都有所改变。为此，本研究根据每个因子的主要内涵重新界定了因子的名称。

此外，行为意向有效维度虽然是两维，但其中测量行为意向中的一个题项："我会向他人说该公司的不是"与其他三道题的共同度最低。仔细考虑之后，笔者认为由于中国人传统的思维模式与语言习惯使得答题者不可避免地对该题产生异议，并可能导致错误的答案，由此可能导致问卷结构的不稳定。基于以上原因，本研究删除了该题项，行为意向在本研究中采用了删除后的一维结构。

笔者认为这个题项应该重新进行翻译，以符合中国人的语言习惯。比如可以翻译为："我会向他人称赞该公司。"修改该题项之后，可能会提升整个量表的信度。

6.1.2 假设检验结果

第二部分检验则采用 MANOVA 进行 8 个试验组的组间比较。研究发现：

① 响应速度 × 心理补救交互作用的多变量显著；

② 响应速度 × 有形补偿交互作用的多变量显著；

③ 响应速度单变量显著性检验结果显著，说明响应速度对知觉公平、关系品质、行为意向均有显著差异存在；

④ 心理补救单变量显著性检验结果显著，其中心理补救对知觉公平、关系品质的影响没有显著差异，但是对行为意向的影响存在差异；

⑤ 有形补偿单变量显著性检验结果显著，说明有形补偿对知觉公平、关系品质、行为意向均有显著差异存在。

在多元方差分析结论上对本研究的假设进行了检验得到以下的结果。

本研究共计 36 个假设，其中 17 个假设得到了验证，19 个假设没能通过假设检验（或未检验）。

表 6-1 假设检验结果

编号	假设	检验结果
H1	服务商服务补救措施与顾客知觉公平正相关	部分验证
H1.1	响应速度越快，顾客的知觉公平感知越高	接受
H1.2	心理补救越高，顾客的知觉公平感知越高	拒绝
H1.3	有形补偿越多，顾客的知觉公平感知越高	接受
H1.4	响应速度对顾客知觉公平的不同构面影响存在差异	接受
H1.5	心理补救对顾客知觉公平的不同构面影响存在差异	拒绝
H1.6	有形补偿对顾客知觉公平的不同构面影响存在差异	接受
H2	服务商服务补救措施与关系品质正相关	部分验证
H2.1	响应速度越快，顾客的关系品质越高	接受
H2.2	心理补救越高，顾客的关系品质越高	拒绝
H2.3	有形补偿越多，顾客的关系品质越高	接受
H2.4	响应速度对顾客关系品质的不同层面影响存在差异	接受
H2.5	心理补救对顾客关系品质的不同层面影响存在差异	拒绝
H2.6	有形补偿对顾客关系品质的不同层面影响存在差异	接受
H3	服务商服务补救措施与行为意向正相关	部分验证
H3.1	响应速度越快，顾客的行为意向越高	接受
H3.2	心理补救越高，顾客的行为意向越高	拒绝
H3.3	有形补偿越多，顾客的行为意向越高	接受
H3.4	响应速度对顾客行为意向的不同层面影响存在差异	未验证[a]
H3.5	心理补救对顾客行为意向的不同层面影响存在差异	未验证[a]
H3.6	有形补偿对顾客行为意向的不同层面影响存在差异	未验证[a]

续表

编号	假设	检验结果
H4	响应速度与心理补救对知觉公平、关系品质、行为意向存在二次交互作用	部分验证
H4.1	响应速度快的情况下，心理补救越高，顾客知觉公平感知越强	接受
H4.2	响应速度快的情况下，心理补救越高，顾客与运营商关系品质越高	接受
H4.3	响应速度快的情况下，心理补救越高，顾客行为意向越好	拒绝
H4.4	响应速度与心理补救的二次交互作用对知觉公平的不同构面存在差异	接受
H4.5	响应速度与心理补救的二次交互作用对关系品质的不同构面存在差异	拒绝
H4.6	响应速度与心理补救的二次交互作用对行为意向的不同构面存在差异	未验证[a]
H5	响应速度与有形补偿对知觉公平、关系品质、行为意向存在二次交互作用	部分验证
H5.1	响应速度快的情况下，有形补偿越多，顾客知觉公平感知越强	拒绝
H5.2	响应速度快的情况下，有形补偿越多，顾客与运营商关系品质越高	接受
H5.3	响应速度快的情况下，有形补偿越多，顾客行为意向越好	接受
H5.4	响应速度与有形补偿的二次交互作用对知觉公平的不同构面存在差异	接受
H5.5	响应速度与有形补偿的二次交互作用对关系品质的不同构面存在差异	接受
H5.6	响应速度与有形补偿的二次交互作用对行为意向的不同构面存在差异	未验证[a]
H6	心理补救与有形补偿与知觉公平、关系品质、行为意向存在二次交互作用	未通过验证
H6.1	心理补救较高的情况下，有形补偿越多，顾客知觉公平感知越强	拒绝
H6.2	心理补救较高的情况下，有形补偿越多，顾客与运营商关系品质越高	拒绝
H6.3	心理补救较高的情况下，有形补偿越多，顾客行为意向越好	拒绝
H6.4	心理补救与有形补偿的二次交互作用对知觉公平的不同构面存在差异	拒绝
H6.5	心理补救与有形补偿的二次交互作用对关系品质的不同构面存在差异	拒绝
H6.6	心理补救与有形补偿的二次交互作用对行为意向的不同构面存在差异	未验证[a]

a：行为意向变量在因子分析与信度检验中未能通过二维结构的验证，因此，在后续的与其不同的构面的假设检验都未进行验证，因此标记为“未验证”，这与“未通过验证（未通过假设检验）”具有不同的含义。

6.2 研究发现与讨论

通过对研究数据的详尽分析，我们得到了一些研究结果，同时也找到了一些有趣的新发现，在此，笔者分别从 3 个自变量在研究中的意义进行分析并对新发现进行讨论。

6.2.1 响应速度是服务补救的关键

本研究中所有与响应速度相关的假设基本都得到了验证。无论是响应速度的主效果还是与其他变量的二次交互作用。

响应速度的快慢可以提高顾客的知觉公平水平、可以改善服务商与顾客关系品质、可以挽留受损顾客的行为意向。同时，只有在保证响应速度的情况下，心理补救才能对其他变量产生作用，有限补偿才能发挥其价值。因此，可以说响应速度是影响服务补救的第一要素，要对服务失误进行有效的补救必须从速度上入手。

随着工作压力的增大、生活节奏的加快，现代人对时间有了新的认识，形成了一些新的时间观念。

① 把握时机。机不可失，时不再来，抓紧时间，可以创造机会。没有机会的人，往往都是任时间流逝的人。很多时候，机会对每一个人都是均等的，行动快的人得到了它，行动慢的人自己错过了它。所以，要抓住机会，就必须与时间竞争。

② 管理时间。现代人从事企业工作，重要的是时间管理，很多企业人十分辛苦，每天早出晚归、疲于奔命，因此很多工作一族都重视有自己的时间安排，抓住关键，掌握重点。

③ 关注时间成本。无效的等待既浪费了自己的时间，也浪费了别人的时间。这些时间，本来安排其他事务，因此不少人计入自己的机会成本。如果没有效益，消费者就会选择放弃。

④ 重视时间效率。时间观念已成为现代管理的重要观念，浪费时间，就是浪

费金钱，就是降低效率。越来越多的人都用正确的时间观念思考问题的行动，节约时间，讲求效率，充当时间的主人，迎接未来的挑战。

现代人重视速度、重视效率，只有提供快速高效的服务，才能维护与顾客良好的关系，才能为顾客增加价值和利益，是真正“想顾客之所想，急顾客之所急”的最佳行为体现。

6.2.2 有形补偿对服务补救贡献突出

研究证明了有形补偿的差异能够修补服务失误带来的损伤，无论是有形补偿的主效果还是有形补偿与响应速度的交互作用，都证明了物质补偿的作用。

人是经济的动物，无限度地改善人的物质条件的欲望被看成是人的内在本质。生产力决定生产关系，经济基础决定上层建筑。我始终相信，只有在物质基础之上，才能分析比较细微的精神差异。当然，物质的丰富不丰富，满足不满足，不是决定精神世界内在的、必然的因素，但有了这个物质基础，也许，我们的精神世界会更快乐。

本研究的结果也很好地证明了，关注物质利益是现代人不可回避的现实。

6.2.3 心理补救对服务补救作用有限

与前两个自变量不同，心理补救在整个研究中的效果非常不显著。心理补救自身没有体现出对服务失误补救的功效，仅有的交互作用也受到了响应速度的限制。

研究中的心理补救是通过道歉的两个维度来测量的：“稍示歉意”与“诚挚道歉”，但是道歉对服务补救的效果没能很好地验证。虽然，该结论说明了心理补救较响应速度、物质补偿而言作用弱，但是我们也不能就此完全否定心理补救对服务补救的可能作用。

当服务失误时，如果对道歉的技巧进行如下改进，或许心理补救的功能就能有所发挥。

第一，道歉应当及时。知道自己错了，马上就要说“对不起”，否则越拖得久，就越会让人家“窝火”，越容易使人误解。道歉及时，还有助于当事人“退一步海阔天宽”，避免因小失大。

第二，道歉并非万能。不该向别人道歉的时候，就千万不要向对方道歉。不然对方肯定不大会领我方的情，搞不好还会因此而得寸进尺，为难我方。即使有必要向他人道歉时，也要切记，更重要的，是要使自己此后的所作所为有所改进，不要言行不一，依然故我。让道歉仅仅流于形式，只能证明自己待人缺乏诚意。

态度决定一切，什么样的态度是受欢迎的？积极的、建设性的、欣赏他人的、包容的、自信的、乐于助人的等，这些构成了一个有感染力的环境，让每个顾客都愿意在这种环境中消费，这样的环境使人的压力减轻，也使事情朝着好的方向发展。工作人员的真诚态度才能让道歉深入顾客心中。

6.3 研究启发与建议

结合前面的分析结果和所归纳的研究结论可以得出以下几点营销启示。

在服务补救过程中，响应速度对知觉公平、关系品质、行为意向有显著性影响，那么服务失误后做出快速高效的反应，可以抑制顾客降低知觉公平水平及关系品质感知，从而提高顾客的行为意向以及未来的预期，所以对顾客的“速度服务”应该成为服务经营管理的基本理念。

有形补偿对修复服务失误有着重要的作用，因此，当服务失误发生之后，应该尽可能地给顾客提供相应的物质补偿，让顾客由于服务失误所造成的损失成本为“0”，甚至损失可以带来超值的服务，以维护与顾客的关系品质，提高顾客的行为意向。

服务人员是直接与顾客进行接触的人，由于他们与顾客的双向互动沟通将直接决定心理补救程度的高低，所以对员工进行相应服务补救知识的培训计划，不要将道歉流于形式，这样才能有助于提高补救效果。

服务补救中的有形补偿与心理补救的作用都受到了响应速度的制约，所以服务型企业应该加强组织柔性，以便于提高组织对服务失误反应的灵敏性，由此才能发挥其他补救措施的整体效能。

有形补偿对知觉公平三个构面影响的强度依次为程序性公平、补偿性公平、感知性公平。应该基于知觉水平来选择合适的有形补偿方式。将关系品质与有形补偿方式进行综合考虑，便于从整体上调整补偿的经济成本。

当响应速度快时，顾客承诺水平最高，其次是满意水平，最后是顾客的信任。有研究证明顾客对移动运营商很难做出承诺，本研究发现当服务失误发生时，要提高顾客的承诺最重要的还是提供快速高效的服务补救措施，从而实现电信服务商与顾客关系强度的改善。

关系品质是代表着顾客对服务企业的一种累计性关系强度，并且根据本研究的结论，它与单次服务补救的效果有着很强的相关性，并且同样的补救措施随着关系品质的高低，其补救效果不同。所以应该采用长远的观点来看待服务补救成本与关系品质建设成本两者之间的关系。

服务补救对顾客满意度的影响很早就受到了学者们的关注。本研究没有单独对此变量进行验证，只是把顾客满意作为关系品质中的一个重要维度来对待。通过自变量对关系品质不同构面的影响也发现了服务补救对顾客满意构面的不同作用结果。比如，当响应速度加快时，顾客的满意感随着心理补救程度的提高快速增强，这也说明，只有当响应速度达到一定值时，心理补救才会成为提升顾客满意的一个变量，否则，心理补救对顾客满意度不仅起不到应有的作用，反而存在负作用。此外，物质补偿与相应速度对顾客的满意度也存在二次交互作用，物质补偿对顾客满意度的影响会随着相应速度的加快而降低。以上结论也说明了，要提高顾客的满意度，主要要从补救速度入手，配合适当的心理及物质补偿就可以实现较好的效果。

从战略上把关系品质建设放在指导服务补救的基础性地位，服务性企业应该发展良好的补救计划，然后把具体的补救措施与顾客公平感知的具体内容对应起来，建立起完善的服务补救制度，只有这样才能全面防止顾客对服务补救的消极感知的出现。

综上所述，服务管理人员在衡量服务补救绩效的时候，不应该只是从自身单纯补救的内容来看待，而应该从补救措施对知觉公平、关系品质、行为意向的强度来发挥服务补救的绩效，并且还应该将服务补救作为一个发展关系品质的战略内容。

6.4 研究的指导意义

近些年服务业顾客满意理论研究焦点逐渐由正向的顾客满意向负向的服务失误研究转移，并进一步向服务失误补救、顾客保留或转移行为等后续行为延伸。而移动服务行业的研究多集中在运营商服务质量评价、服务失误产生原因等方面。鲜少有人从服务补救这一角度入手，研究顾客知觉公平对关系品质及行为意向的影响。而很多服务行业的人员把服务补救看作凭经验积累处理服务失误的手段。虽然通过经验的积累得到一些成果，但并没有得到理论上的证明，也没有人进行这方面的实证研究和概括。鉴于此，对服务补救以及补救后顾客一系列心理及行为活动的研究在电信服务营销领域具有非常现实的理论和实践意义。

6.4.1 理论意义

本研究的理论意义体现在以下几点。

① 在西方已有的研究基础上验证了知觉公平、关系品质、行为意向量表并不完全适用于中国（或本研究）。本文采用因子分析与信度检验确定了知觉公平的三

维结构、关系品质的三维结构，但是由于因子负荷矩阵与原量表的差距较大，因此，本文以原量表为依据重新计算了不同因子的题项并对新因子进行了命名。行为意向则舍弃了原有的二维结构，删除了一个题项，仅保留一维结构进行后续的研究。

② 本研究在对电信行业服务失误、服务补救理论进行综述的同时，结合电信行业的自身特点，归纳出移动通信行业服务失误的类型和服务补救的分类，并阐述其内涵。

③ 根据相关文献梳理以及移动通信行业管理人员访谈的启发，本文建立了电信服务补救对顾客知觉公平、关系品质和行为意向的影响研究理论模型，并提出 8 项假设，通过大样本数据采集，进行实证研究。

④ 将准实验研究运用于电信服务行业，探讨服务补救措施和知觉公平、关系品质、行为意向的关系。该研究方法为服务行业进行相关的理论研究提供了可供借鉴的经验。

⑤ 问卷设计从电信行业顾客的特点出发，针对可能经历过服务补救场景的问题，得到大量一手资料。通过 SPSS 分析，对研究中所有假设一一进行了验证，并得出结论，为日后进一步研究打下基础。

⑥ 在数据处理中，本研究严格按照 MANOVA 的要求，分别对 3 个因变量及因变量的不同构面进行了系统的分析。计算过程严密，计算结果真实可靠，研究结论具有说服力。

6.4.2 实践意义

本研究的实践意义有以下几个方面：

① 揭示了服务补救中不同补救措施对知觉公平、关系品质、行为意向的影响强度，为服务企业提供了服务补救的具体方向与对应的措施；

② 探讨了不同补救措施的组合作用，为服务企业在提供补救措施时有可供借

鉴的整体方案；

③ 研究不同补救措施对变量不同构面的影响，可以使服务企业制定有针对性的服务补救组合，合理规划企业的补救成本；

④ 根据服务企业的现实需求，量身定做最有效率的补救方案，使企业的具体战术完全符合企业战略目标。

6.5 研究局限及未来研究方向

由于实证研究中人力、财力等限制，虽然在研究过程中力求严谨，但仍然有许多不够完善之处，这也是将来研究应当改进和完善的地方。

① 样本偏差。由于本研究是以中国某一个城市的移动用户为例，后续的研究可以扩大国内其他城市和地区，以了解不同地区间的样本可能产生的差异性。也可以以其他行业背景为例进行研究，以了解不同行业之间的样本可能产生的差异性。本次的被测样本主要是年轻的女性，且教育水平、工作收入水平较低，这样的样本特征使得最终的研究结论并不具备广泛的社会说服力。如果有继续研究的可能，在样本选取上应该更多地考虑样本的多样性、广泛性，避免由于样本偏差所带来的研究结论可能的偏颇。

② 被调查者属性偏差。此次被访者是 CALL CENTER 的服务人员，他们的日常工作就是解决顾客投诉并为顾客提高服务解决方案。他们的工作属性可能会让他们对服务失误具有较高容忍性，这一点可能会对本文的研究结论带来一定的影响。

③ 服务失误情境设定偏差。本文问卷调查的被访者基本没有情境设定的经历（87.9%），这就说明了失误场景设定的局限性。虽然，被测者的工作经历可以使他们较好地理解该服务场景，但是，想象经历与现实经历必然会给研究结论带来一定的偏差，进而影响研究结论的普遍意义。

④ 服务补救的三个维度测量不够精准。在问卷中，笔者使用了描述性语言对补救速度（马上、过了很久）与心理补救（稍示歉意、诚挚道歉）来界定补救的不同水准级别。虽然，在设计的过程中考虑了中国顾客对语言的理解与感知，但是非定量的测量有碍于结果的一致性。

⑤ 补救速度测量的操控缺失。补救速度是研究的一个重要变量，尽管笔者使用了描述性语言来测量，但是没有在问卷中设计相应的操控问题。比如“您认为马上解决问题的时间是多少”等。测量操控的缺失可能会模糊不同被访者的心理界限。

⑥ 服务补救类型过于简单。服务补救方式在文中被概括为三大类型(响应速度、心理补救、有形补偿），本文仅仅从这三类（每一类仅两个水准级）出发进行了研究，而未就具体措施进行更深入的探讨，因而使研究结论略显单薄。

⑦ 心理补救的研究可以进一步深化。比如，除了道歉之外，可以引入其他一些具有移情作用的因素来扩展对心理补救测量的广泛性。这样的研究设计可能会使得研究结论与现有的研究结论存在差异，也有可能出现更为显著的效果。

⑧ 改进模型。由于模型上的限制，本研究只考虑了对顾客知觉公平的某些因素。事实上影响顾客知觉公平的因素有很多，如人口统计变量、顾客性格特征、顾客对抱怨价值的事先评估等，都有可能对其产生影响。后续研究可以进一步就这些因素与顾客知觉公平和行为意向的关系进行进一步深入研究。

⑨ 研究方法的改进。在以后的研究中可以采用验证性因子分析方法来验证量表的因子结构及问卷的结构效度，并尝试使用更多的方法对相关问题进行验证。

表格目录

List of Tables

图形目录

List of Figures

参考文献

References

英文部分

1. Adames JS.Towards An Understanding of Inequity[J], The Journal of Abnormal and Social Psychology,1963,67(5):422-436.

2. Albrecht K, Zemke R.Service America![M]. Dow Jones-Irwin, 1985.

3. Anderrson B E, Nilsson S G. Studies in the Reliability and Validity of the Critical Incident Technique[J]. Journal of Applied Psychology, 1964,48(6):398-403.

4. Bejou D, Palmer A. Service Failure and Loyalty: An Exploratory Empirical Study of Airline Customers[J]. Journal of Services Marketing, 1998,12(1):7-22.

5. Bitner M J, Booms B H, Mohr L A. Critical Service Encounters: The Employee's Viewpoint[J]. Journal of Marketing, 1994,58(4):95-106.

6. Bitner M J, Booms B H, Trtreault M S. The Service Encounter: Diagnosing Favorable and Unfavorable Incidens[J]. Journal of Marketing, 1990,54(1):71-84.

7. Blodgett J G, Granbois D H, Walter R G. The Effects of Perceived Justice on Complaints' Negative Word-of-Mouth Behavior and Repatronage Intentions[J]. Journal of Retailing, 1993,69(4):399-427.

8. Blogdett J G, Granbois D H. Toward An Integrated Conceptual Model of Consumer Complaining Behavior[J]. Journal of Consumer Satisfaction, Dissatisfaction and Complaining Behavior, 1992, 5(1):93-103.

9. Bolfing, C P. How Do Consumers Express Dissatisfaction and What Can Service Markers Do about It?[J]. Journal of Services Marketing, 1989,3(2):5-23

10. Brown S P, Beltraminski R F. Consumer Complaining and Word of Mouth Activities:Field Evidence[J]. Advances in Consumer Research, 1989,16:9-16.

11. Callan R J. The Critical Incident Technique in Hospitality Research:An Illustration from the UK Lodge Sector[J]. Tourism Management, 1998,19(1):93-98.

12. Chell E, Pittaway L. A Study of Entrepreneurship in the Restaurant and Café Industry: Exploratory Work Using the Critical Incident Technique as A Methodology:Prize-winning Paper from the IAHMS Conference at Sheffield Hallam Unicersity, England Novrmber 1997[J], International Journal of Hospitality Management, 1998,17(1):23-32.

13. Chen C, Chang S. Researd on Customer Satisfaction Take the Loan Market of the Taiwanese Region as An Example[J]. The Journal of American Academy of Business,

2006,9(1):197-201.

14. Chiu H C. A Study on the Cognitive and Affective Components of Service Quality[J]. Total Quality Management, 2002, 13(2): 265-274.

15. Chowdhary N, Prakash M. Service Quality: Revisiting the Two Factors Theory[J]. Journal of Service Research, 2005, 5(1): 61-75.

16. Ennew C, Schoefer K. Service Failuer and Service Recovery in Tourism: A Review[M]. Christel DeHann Tourism and Travel Research Institute, Nottingham University Business School, 2003.

17. Crosby L A, Evans K R, Cowles D. Relationship Quality in Service Selling: An Interpersonal Influence Perspective[J]. Journal of Marketing, 1990,54(3): 68-81.

18. Day R L. Research Perspectives on Consumer Complaining Behavior[J]. Theoretical Developments in Marketing, 1980: 211-215.

19. Day R L, Landon E L. Toward a Theory of Consumer Complaining Behavior[J]. Consumer and Industrial Buying Behavior. 1977,95: 425-37.

20. Day R L, Bodur M. Consumer Response to Dissatisfaction with Services and Intangibles[J]. Advances in Consumer Research, 1978, (5): 263-72.

21. Edvardsson B. Service Breakdowns: A Study of Critical Incident in an Airline[J]. International Journal of Service Industry Management, 1992,3(4): 17-29.

22. Flanagan J C. The Critical Incident Technique[J]. Psychological Bulletin, 1954,51(4): 327-359.

23. Garbarino E, Johnson M S. The Different Roles of Satisfaction,Trust,and Commitment in Customer Relationships[J]. Journal of Marketing, 1999, 70-87.

24. Gilly M C. Post Complaint Processes: From Organizational Response to Repurchase Behavior, Journal of Consumer Affairs, 1987, 21:293-313.

25. Goodman J. The Nature of Customer Satisfaction[J]. Quality Progress, 1989, 37-40.

26. Goodwin C, Ross I. Consumer Responses to Service Failures : Influence of Procedural and Interactional Fairness Perceptions[J]. Journal of Business Research, 1992,25(2): 149-163.

27. Gronroos C. Service Quality: The Six Criteria of Good Perceived Service[J]. Review of Business, 1988,9(3): 10-13.

28. Hart C W, Heskett J L, Sasser Jr W E. The Profitable Art of Service Recovery[J]. Harvard Business Review, 1989,68(4): 148-156.

29. Hui M K, ,Au K. Justice Perceptions of Complaint-handling: A Cross-cultural Comparison Between PRC and Canadian Customers, Journal of Business Research, 2001.

30. Hoffman K D, Kelley S W, Rotalsky H M. Tracking Service Failures and Employee Recovery Efforts[J]. Journal of Service Marketing, 1995,9(2): 49-61.

31. Chiu H C, Hsieh Y C, Kao C Y. Website Quality and Customer's Behavioral Intention: An Exploratory Study of the Role of Information Asymmetry[J]. Total Quality Management & Business Excellence, 2005, 16(2): 185-197.

32. Tam J L M. Customer Satisfaction, Service Quality and Perceived Value: An Integrative Model[J]. Journal of Marketing Management, 2004, 20(8): 897-917.

33. Jain S K, Gupta G. Measuring Service Quality: Servqual VS. Serperf Scale[J]. The Journal for Decision Makers, 2004, 29(2): 25-37.

34. Kelley S W, Hoffman K D,Davis M A. A Typology of Retail Failures and Recoveries, Journal of Retailing, 1993,69(4): 429-452.

35. Kelly S W, Davis M A. Antecedents to Customer Expectations for Service Recovery[J]. Journal of Academy of Marketing Science,1994,22(1): 52-61.

36. Lapidus R S, Schibrowsky J A. Aggregate Complaint Analysis: A Procedure for Developing Customer Service Satisfaction[J]. Journal of Service Marketing, 1994,8(4): 50-60.

37. Latham G, Saari L M. Do People Do What They Say? Further Studies on the Situational Interview[J]. Journal of Applied Psychology, 1984,69(4): 393-404.

38. Lee M C, Hwan I S. Relationships among Service Quality, Customer Satisfaction and Profitability in the Taiwanese Banking Industry[J]. International Journal of Management, 2005, 22(4): 635-648.

39. Manila A S, Patterson P. The Impact of Culture on Consumers Perceptions of Service Recovery Efforts[J]. Journal of Retailing, 2004,80(3): 196-206.

40. Maute M F, Forrester W R. The Structure and Determinants of Consumer Complaint Intentions and Behavior[J]. Journal of Economic Psychology, 1993,14(2): 219-247.

41. Maxham J G. Service Recovery's Influence on Consumer Satisfaction, Positive Word-of-Mouth, and Purchase Intentions[J]. Journal of Business Research, 2001,54(1): 11-24

42. Morgan R M, Hunt S D. The Commitment-Trust Theory of Relationship Marketing[J]. Journal of Marketing, 1994,58(3): 20-38.

43. Lau P M, Akbar A K. Service Quality: A Study of the Luxury Hotel in Malaysia[J]. Journal of American Academy of Business, 2005, 7(2): 46-55.

44. Danaher P J, Hadderll V. A Comparison of Question Scales Used for Measuring Customer Satisfaction [J]. International of Service Industry Management, 1996, 7(4): 4-26.

45. Pont M, Mcquilken L. An Empirical Investigation of Customer Satisfaction and Loyalty Across Two Divergent Bank Segments[J]. Journal of Financial Service Marketing, 2005, 9(4): 344-359.

46. Suri R,Monros K B. Monroe, The Effects of Time Constrains Onconsumers' Judgments of Prices and Products[J]. Journal of Consumer Research, lnc. 2003,30(1): 92-104.

47. Anna S. Mattila, The impact of service failures on customer loyalty. International Journal of Service Industry Management, 2004, 15(2): 134-149.

48. Sight J. Consumer Complaint Intentions and Behavior: Definitional and Taxonomical Issues[J]. Journal of Marketing, 1988,52(1): 93-107.

49. Sight J. A Typology of Consumer Dissatisfaction Response Styles[J]. Journal of Retailing, 1990,66(1): 57-99.

50. Smith A K, Bolton R N. An Experimental Investigation of Customer Reactions to Service Failure and Recovery Encounters: Paradox or Peril[J]. Journal of Service Research, 1998, 1(1): 65-81.

51. Spreng R A, Harrell G D, Mackoy R D. Service Recovery: Impact on Satisfaction and

Intention[J]. Journal of Service Marketing, 1995,9(1): 15-23.

52. Weun S, Beatty S E, Fones M A. The Impact of Service Failure Service Recovery Evaluations and Post-recovery Relationships[J]. Journal of Services Marketing, 2004, 18(2/3): 133-146.

53. Wirtz J, Mattila A S. Consumer Responses to Compensation, Speed of Recovery and Apology after a Service Failure[J]. International Journal of Service Industry Management, 2004, 15(2): 150-166.

54. Huang Y C, Wu C H, Hsu J C J. Using Importance-Performance Analysis in Evaluating Taiwan Medium and Long Distance National Highway Passenger Transportation Service Quality[J]. Journal of American Academy of Business, 2006, 8(2): 98-104.

中文部分

1. 安静 . 饭店服务补救对顾客满意与行为意向的影响研究 [D]. 浙江大学，2004.

2. 白长虹，刘炽 . 服务企业的顾客忠诚及其决定因素研究 [J]. 南开管理评论，2002，(6): 64−69.

3. 白长虹 . 西方的顾客价值研究及其实践启示 [J]. 南开管理评论，2001，4 (2)51−55

4. 薄湘平，周勤 . 服务补救 : 重建顾客满意的重要手段 [J]. 湖南大学学报，2005，19(1): 58−61.

5. 陈明亮 . 客户重复购买意向决定因素的实证研究 [J]. 科研管理，2003，24(1): 20−23.

6. 陈新跃，杨德礼 . 顾客价值认知与市场信号研究 [J]. 大连理工大学学报，2003(1):42−45.

7. 陈亚锋 . 服务补救——赢得整体顾客满意 [J]. 上海商业，2005(1): 77−79.

8. 陈忠卫，黄晓波 . 服务补救理论述评 [J]. 中外企业家，2005，(4) : 86−91.

9. 杜建刚，范秀成 . 基于公平性调节作用的服务忠诚度前置因素整合模型研究 [J]. 营销科学学报，2006,2(3): 15−29.

10. 范秀成 . 杜建刚 . 服务质量五维度对服务满意及服务忠诚的影响——基于转型期间中国服务行业的一项实证研究 [J]. 管理世界，2006(6): 111−118.

11. 范秀成，赵先德，庄贺均 . 价值取向对服务业顾客抱怨倾向的影响 [J]，南开管理评论，2002，(5): 11−16.

12. 范秀成，刘建华 . 顾客关系、信任与顾客对服务失败的反应 [J]. 南开管理评论，2004，7(6): 9−14.

13. 范秀成，赵先德，庄贺均 . 价值取向对服务业顾客抱怨倾向的影响 [J]. 南开管理评论，2002，1，3−12.

14. 范秀成，赵先德，庄贺军 . 价值取向对服务业顾客抱怨倾向的影响 [J]. 南开管理评论，2002，(5): 11−16.

15. 范秀成 . 顾客满意导向的服务企业顾客抱怨管理体系分析 [J]. 中国流通经济，2002 (2): 40−44.

16. 菲利普·科特勒．营销管理 [M]. 北京：中国人民大学出版社，2001.
17. 桂世功，马克贤．质量管理与质量认证 [M]. 北京：机械工业出版社，2000.
18. 郭贤达，陈荣，谢毅．如何在服务失败后仍然得到顾客的拥护——感知公平、顾客满意、情感承诺对行为意向的影响 [J]. 营销科学学报，2006,2(3): 74–85.
19. 韩经纶，韦福祥．顾客满意与顾客忠诚互动关系研究 [J]，南开管理评论，2001，4(6):8–10.
20. 韩明亮，张娟，李琪．航空公司旅客服务质量实证研究 [J]. 中国民航学院学报，2005，23(1): 29–32.
21. 何会文．服务失败的顾客归因及其启示 [J]. 经济管理，2003(6): 48–55.
22. 何会文．基于战略竞争力的服务补救管理体系 [M]. 天津：南开大学出版社，2006.
23. 黄俊孝，徐伟青．口碑传播的基本研究取向 [J]. 浙江大学学报（人文社会科学版），2004，34(1): 125–132.
24. 姜国平．服务补救流程及其运作策略 [J]. 中国质量，2005(7): 29–32.
25. 解丹琪．用社会交换理论完善企业激励机制 [J]，现代经济探讨，2004(5): 32–34.
26. 金立印．基于服务公正性感知的顾客不良行为模型研究 [J]. 营销科学学报，2006，2(1): 1–17.
27. 金立印．基于关键事件法的服务失败原因及补救效果定性分析 [J]. 管理世界，2005，18(4): 63–70.
28. 金立印．顾客服务补救预期：形成因素及对顾客满意的影响 [J]. 营销科学学报 ,2006，2(2): 1–5.
29. 景奉杰，王毅，彭军锋．基于感知价值的顾客补救后满意的一个整合模型 [J]. 营销科学学报，2005，1(2): 43–52.
30. 景奉杰，曾伏娥．顾客满意水平对顾客行为影响研究的评述 [J]. 商业经济与管理，2004 (10): 21–25.
31. 景奉杰，曾伏娥．顾客满意水平及信念变量对顾客口传行为倾向的影响 [J]. 经济管理，2004 (7): 41–47.
32. 雷蒙德 P 菲斯克，史蒂芬 J 格罗夫，乔比·约翰．互动服务营销 [M]. 张金成，等，译．北京：机械工业出版社，2001.
33. 李金成，何会文．服务补救的认识误区 [J]. 商业经济与管理，2003 (1): 18–21.
34. 李金海，陈慧，张金成．服务业顾客满意概念模式回顾研究 [J]. 河北工业大学学报，2003，32(5): 53–58.
35. 李欣，于渤．服务质量评价特征及服务补救策略 [J]. 管理科学，2004，17(3): 72–75.
36. 李业，曾忻．顾客不满意的反应、影响及抱怨化解策略 [J]. 中国流通经济，2002，16(6): 51–54.
37. 林石平．正确认识和处理航班延误 [J]．中国民用航空，2004，48(12): 44–45.
38. 蔺雷，吴贵生．服务创新 [M]. 北京：清华大学出版社，2003.
39. 卢丹丹．试论航班延误与旅客的赔偿其请求权——从航班延误问题对《中华人民共和国民用航空法》的思考 [J]. 经济师，2005 (1): 59–60.
40. 陆娟，张东蜡，崔明杰．中西方忠诚度测评研究及应用启示 [J]. 商业经济与管理，2003 (10): 17–20.

41. 罗海成 . 基于信任关系的关系营销：心理契约视角 [J]. 经济管理，2003 (16): 73–78.

42. 罗海城 . 基于心理契约的服务忠诚决定因素整合研究 [D]. 南开大学，2005.

43. 马庆国 . 管理统计：数据获取、统计原理、SPSS 工具与应用研究 [M]. 北京 : 科学出版社，2002.

44. 牛宏为，赵黎明 . 服务企业的服务补救管理研究 [J]. 辽宁工学院学报，2005，7(2): 62–65.

45. 彭军锋 . 在服务补救过程中关系品质对顾客知觉公平及行为意向的影响 [D]. 武汉大学，2004.

46. 邵丹 , 杨俊 , 徐中和 . 服务失误与服务补救对客户满意度的影响分析 [J]. 科技进步与对策，2004,21(6): 132–134.

47. 申跃，赵平 . 消费者抱怨行为的比较 [J]. 心理学报，2005，37(3): 397–402.

48. 斯蒂芬 P 罗宾斯 . 组织行为学 [M]. 孙建敏，李原，等，译 . 北京 : 中国人民大学出版社，2012.

49. 宋亦平，王晓艳 . 服务失败归因对服务补救效果的影响 [J]. 南开管理评论，2005，8(4): 12–17.

50. 宋亦平，朱涛 . 顾客投诉于服务补救效果的关联研究 [J]. 营销科学学报，2006，2(3): 75–85.

51. 瓦拉瑞尔 A 泽丝曼尔 , 玛丽 · 乔 · 比特纳 . 服务营销 (原书第 3 版)[M]. 张金成 , 白长虹，译 . 北京 : 机械工业出版社，2004.

52. 汪纯孝，韩小芸，温碧燕 . 顾客满意感与忠诚感关系的实证研究 [J]. 南开管理评论，2003，6(4): 70–74.

53. 汪纯孝，温碧燕，姜彩芬 . 顾客的服务消费经历与行为意向的实证研究 [J]. 中山大学学报 (社会科学版)，2001,4(3): 115–121.

54. 王丽华 . 旅游企业服务利润链理论初探 [J]. 财经问题研究，2001(4): 18–20.

55. 韦福祥 . 对服务补救若干问题的探讨 [J]. 天津商学院学报，2002，22(1): 24–26.

56. 温碧燕，岑成德 . 补救服务公平性对顾客与企业关系的影响 [J]. 中山大学学报 (社会科学版)，2004，44(2): 25–31.

57. 徐伟青，黄孝俊 . 口碑传播的影响力要素及其对营销创新的启示 [J]. 外国经济与管理，2004，26(6): 26–30.

58. 杨俊，刘英姿，陈荣秋 . 服务补救运作策略问题研究 [J]. 外国经济与管理，2002 ，24(7): 45–50.

59. 杨岩，朱丰 . 顾客抱怨的管理对策 [J]. 企业改革与管理，2005 (11): 80–81.

60. 尤建新，杜学美，王艳 . 顾客抱怨管理 [M]. 北京 : 石油工业出版社，2003.

61. 张新安，田澎，朱国锋 . 感知实绩、顾客满意与顾客忠诚——微观层次上的审视 [J]. 南开管理评论，2003，6(5): 46–51.

62. 赵冰 . 服务失败情况下的消费者不满意、信任与转化关系研究 [D]. 北京大学，2005.

63. 赵平，莫亚琳 . 中国耐用消费品行业顾客抱怨行为研究 [J]. 清华大学学报 (哲学社会科学版) ，2002，17(2): 32–38.

64. 展晓义 . 服务补救策略及步骤探讨 [J]. 现代商贸工业，2009，21(18): 119–120.

65. 李雁晨，卢东，周庭锐 . 服务营销组合因素对服务失误归因的影响 [J]. 软科学，2010，24(6):45-50.

66. 罗劲，肖璇 . 服务失误对消费者满意度的影响分析 [J]. 大众商务月刊， 2010 (6): 302-303.

67. 朱思思 . 服务失误归因对服务补救和补救满意度关系的影响 [J]. 南华大学学报（社科版），2011，12(6): 53-56.

68. 迟焕鹏，张乾. 服务失误补救和顾客购后行为意向的理论研究 [J]. 企业导报,2012 (6): 95-95.

69. 张秀红 . 服务失误与服务补救 [J]. 人力资源管理，2012 (11): 189-189.

70. 张晓楠 . 慧锐：63% 中国受访者经历恶劣服务 商家如何抵御差评？ [N/OL].CNET 科技资讯网，2013-11-13[2017-6-1].http://www.cnetnews.com.cn/2013/1113/2995457.shtml.

附录 A

预调查问卷

Appendix A

Pilot Questionnaire

Pilot Test Questionnaire（2–1）

第一部分

您目前选用下面哪一家移动通信服务商提供的服务，请在您所选择答案的编号前打勾“√”。(如有多种选择，请您选最常用的一家)。

①中国移动 ②中国联通 ③小灵通

下列表中的内容是关于您与所选移动通信服务商之间关系的描述性语句，请仔细阅读每一个句子，并在相应的数字上画一个圈。

1	2	3	4	5	6	7
非常不同意	不同意	有点不同意	不能确定	有点同意	同意	非常同意

例题：我很喜欢他们。	1	2	3	④	5	6	7
请细心回答以下每一个问题，不要遗漏。							
1. 对于服务商的服务，我感到很满意。	1	2	3	4	5	6	7
2. 我很高兴选择了他们的产品。	1	2	3	4	5	6	7
3. 我很喜欢他们。	1	2	3	4	5	6	7
4. 使用他们的产品总是很愉快。	1	2	3	4	5	6	7
5. 要是其他产品都像这公司的产品就好了。	1	2	3	4	5	6	7
6. 跟其他供应商比起来，我很满意我所选择的服务供应商。	1	2	3	4	5	6	7
7. 我相信这家公司会遵守对顾客的承诺。	1	2	3	4	5	6	7
8. 我觉得这家公司很诚实、很实在。	1	2	3	4	5	6	7
9. 我认为该公司总能给我详尽的咨询。	1	2	3	4	5	6	7
10. 这家公司不会隐瞒我应该知道的信息.	1	2	3	4	5	6	7
11. 这家公司会真诚关注我的需要。	1	2	3	4	5	6	7
12. 我相信这家公司总会考虑顾客最佳利益。	1	2	3	4	5	6	7
13. 这家公司总会优先考虑顾客的利益。	1	2	3	4	5	6	7

14.	这家公司很值得信赖。	1	2	3	4	5	6	7
15.	我对这家公司很有信心。	1	2	3	4	5	6	7
16.	我是这家公司的忠实顾客。	1	2	3	4	5	6	7
17.	我想继续与这家公司保持关系。	1	2	3	4	5	6	7
18.	我会努力支持这家公司。	1	2	3	4	5	6	7
19.	即使有其他的选择，我也不会选择其他公司。	1	2	3	4	5	6	7
20.	我会很积极维持与这家公司的关系。	1	2	3	4	5	6	7
21.	我会一直购买这家公司的产品。	1	2	3	4	5	6	7
22.	这家公司很值得我和她保持关系。	1	2	3	4	5	6	7

第二部分

下面的情景是您在接受移动通信服务时经常遇到的一个服务失误场景。如果您经历过与此相似的情景，请您按照您的真实体验来填答后面的表格，如果您没有经历与此相似的情景，请您把自己假想成该情景的经历者，并按照自己内心的体会来填答。

情景：

某移动公司推出“虚拟网”服务，即如果成员加入这个“虚拟网”，可享受“虚拟网”内部成员通话每分钟 1 角钱的优惠 (否则通话费为 2 角)。因为你觉得你有非常固定的通话对象群体，无形中就可以减少一笔开销，而平时通话频率最高的就是本群体内部成员之间的通话，于是你将群体内 20 余人的移动号码登记了下来，报送给了移动公司，并与对方签订了“虚拟网”协议书。可是好景不长，自从你加入了这个“虚拟网”，就有很多朋友抱怨，现在的每个月的话费比以前多了不少。你在想，不会吧，可能是因为降价而使得通话次数增多和通话时间加长了，才导致话费的增加。可是，没有过多久，又有很多朋友抱怨，现在的话费就是比以前增加了不少。

你终于来到了移动公司的营业大厅，将你加入“虚拟网”后 3 个月的话费详单打印了出来，仔细地核对详单上的电话号码，发现详单上的与“虚拟网”朋友中的通话，计费标准都是按每分钟 2 角收费的，你又仔细核对当时报送给移动公司的名单，发现这些号码全都准确地抄送给了移动公司。事实上，要是按“虚拟网”收费标准收费，移动公司整整多收了你一倍的费用。

实际情况是，由于移动公司后台工作人员的失误，未将你和你部分朋友的号码完全输入到“虚拟网”中，造成部分人员（大约一半）未正式加入“虚拟网”，于是造成了仍按每分钟 2 角钱收费的情况。于是你当即要求移动公司按照承诺的“话费误差，双倍返还”，或至少退还多收部分的费用。

该情景刚出现的那一刻，您内心的真实感受是，请在您所选择答案相应的数字上画一个圈：

1	2	3	4	5	6	7
非常不同意	不同意	有点不同意	不能确定	有点同意	同意	非常同意

下列表中的内容是关于服务补救的描述性语句，请仔细阅读每一个句子，并在相应的数字上画一个圈。

1	2	3	4	5	6	7
非常不同意	不同意	有点不同意	不能确定	有点同意	同意	非常同意

一、如果该服务人员过了很久才对此失误向您稍示歉意，但是最后还是同意退还多收部分的费用，那么请您根据这种情景给下列内容打分。

例题：该公司管理制度处理服务失误有效率。	1	2	3	④	5	6	7
请细心回答以下每一个问题，不要遗漏。							
1. 该公司管理制度处理服务失误有效率。	1	2	3	4	5	6	7
2. 该公司很在意没有为我准备你所需要的服务。	1	2	3	4	5	6	7
3. 该公司的管理机制对于自己失误反应很迅速。	1	2	3	4	5	6	7
4. 尽管出现这种失误，但该公司响应迅速。	1	2	3	4	5	6	7
5. 我相信该公司有一系列公正的管理政策。	1	2	3	4	5	6	7
6. 工作人员恰当地体谅我的难处。	1	2	3	4	5	6	7
7. 工作人员并不努力帮我解决麻烦。	1	2	3	4	5	6	7
8. 工作人员与我沟通得很好。	1	2	3	4	5	6	7
9. 工作人员服的态度很谦逊。	1	2	3	4	5	6	7
10. 这一补救结果是公平的。	1	2	3	4	5	6	7
11. 补救结果并不能弥补它给我造成的损失。	1	2	3	4	5	6	7
12. 该失误给我造成了不便，但该公司弥补了我的损失。	1	2	3	4	5	6	7
13. 我认为接受这样的补救结果是不正确的。	1	2	3	4	5	6	7
14. 该公司给我弥补的结果超过了我所失去的。	1	2	3	4	5	6	7
15. 我以后会增加购买该公司产品的次数。	1	2	3	4	5	6	7
16. 如果有别的选择，我不会选择其他公司的产品。	1	2	3	4	5	6	7
17. 如果有人提起该公司，我会推荐。	1	2	3	4	5	6	7
18. 我会向他人说该公司的不是。	1	2	3	4	5	6	7

二、如果该服务人员马上对该失误向您真诚道歉并积极了解该失误给您造成的不便，此外，同意双倍返还多收的费用，那么请您根据这种情景给下列内容打分。

例题：该公司管理制度处理服务失误有效率。	1	2	3	④	5	6	7
请细心回答以下每一个问题，不要遗漏。							
1. 该公司管理制度处理服务失误有效率。	1	2	3	4	5	6	7
2. 该公司很在意没有为我准备你所需要的服务。	1	2	3	4	5	6	7
3. 该公司的管理机制对于自己失误反应很迅速。	1	2	3	4	5	6	7
4. 尽管出现这种失误，但该公司响应迅速。	1	2	3	4	5	6	7
5. 我相信该公司有一系列公正的管理政策。	1	2	3	4	5	6	7

续表

6. 工作人员恰当地体谅我的难处。	1	2	3	4	5	6	7
7. 工作人员并不努力帮我解决麻烦。	1	2	3	4	5	6	7
8. 工作人员与我沟通得很好。	1	2	3	4	5	6	7
9. 工作人员服的态度很谦逊。	1	2	3	4	5	6	7
10. 这一补救结果是公平的。	1	2	3	4	5	6	7
11. 补救结果并不能弥补它给我造成的损失。	1	2	3	4	5	6	7
12. 该失误给我造成了不便，但该公司弥补了我的损失。	1	2	3	4	5	6	7
13. 我认为接受这样的补救结果是不正确的。	1	2	3	4	5	6	7
14. 该公司给我弥补的结果超过了我所失去的。	1	2	3	4	5	6	7
15. 我以后会增加购买该公司产品的次数。	1	2	3	4	5	6	7
16. 如果有别的选择，我不会选择其他公司的产品。	1	2	3	4	5	6	7
17. 如果有人提起该公司，我会推荐。	1	2	3	4	5	6	7
18. 我会向他人说该公司的不是。	1	2	3	4	5	6	7

三、如果该服务人员过了很久才对此失误向您稍示歉意，但是同意双倍返还多收的费用，那么请您根据这种情景给下列内容打分。

例题：该公司管理制度处理服务失误有效率。	1	2	3	④	5	6	7
请细心回答以下每一个问题，不要遗漏。							
1. 该公司管理制度处理服务失误有效率。	1	2	3	4	5	6	7
2. 该公司很在意没有为我准备你所需要的服务。	1	2	3	4	5	6	7
3. 该公司的管理机制对于自己失误反应很迅速。	1	2	3	4	5	6	7
4. 尽管出现这种失误，但该公司响应迅速。	1	2	3	4	5	6	7
5. 我相信该公司有一系列公正的管理政策。	1	2	3	4	5	6	7
6. 工作人员恰当地体谅我的难处。	1	2	3	4	5	6	7
7. 工作人员并不努力帮我解决麻烦。	1	2	3	4	5	6	7
8. 工作人员与我沟通得很好。	1	2	3	4	5	6	7
9. 工作人员服的态度很谦逊。	1	2	3	4	5	6	7
10. 这一补救结果是公平的。	1	2	3	4	5	6	7
11. 补救结果并不能弥补它给我造成的损失。	1	2	3	4	5	6	7
12. 该失误给我造成了不便，但该公司弥补了我的损失。	1	2	3	4	5	6	7

续表

13. 我认为接受这样的补救结果是不正确的。	1	2	3	4	5	6	7
14. 该公司给我弥补的结果超过了我所失去的。	1	2	3	4	5	6	7
15. 我以后会增加购买该公司产品的次数。	1	2	3	4	5	6	7
16. 如果有别的选择，我不会选择其他公司的产品。	1	2	3	4	5	6	7
17. 如果有人提起该公司，我会推荐。	1	2	3	4	5	6	7
18. 我会向他人说该公司的不是。	1	2	3	4	5	6	7

四、如果该服务人员过了很久才对此失误向您真诚道歉并积极了解该失误给您造成的不便，同时同意退还多收部分的费用，那么请您根据这种情景给下列内容打分。

例题：该公司管理制度处理服务失误有效率。	1	2	3	④	5	6	7
请细心回答以下每一个问题，不要遗漏。							
1. 该公司管理制度处理服务失误有效率。	1	2	3	4	5	6	7
2. 该公司很在意没有为我准备你所需要的服务。	1	2	3	4	5	6	7
3. 该公司的管理机制对于自己失误反应很迅速。	1	2	3	4	5	6	7
4. 尽管出现这种失误，但该公司响应迅速。	1	2	3	4	5	6	7
5. 我相信该公司有一系列公正的管理政策。	1	2	3	4	5	6	7
6. 工作人员恰当地体谅我的难处。	1	2	3	4	5	6	7
7. 工作人员并不努力帮我解决麻烦。	1	2	3	4	5	6	7
8. 工作人员与我沟通得很好。	1	2	3	4	5	6	7
9. 工作人员服的态度很谦逊。	1	2	3	4	5	6	7
10. 这一补救结果是公平的。	1	2	3	4	5	6	7
11. 补救结果并不能弥补它给我造成的损失。	1	2	3	4	5	6	7
12. 该失误给我造成了不便，但该公司弥补了我的损失。	1	2	3	4	5	6	7
13. 我认为接受这样的补救结果是不正确的。	1	2	3	4	5	6	7
14. 该公司给我弥补的结果超过了我所失去的。	1	2	3	4	5	6	7
15. 我以后会增加购买该公司产品的次数。	1	2	3	4	5	6	7
16. 如果有别的选择，我不会选择其他公司的产品。	1	2	3	4	5	6	7
17. 如果有人提起该公司，我会推荐。	1	2	3	4	5	6	7
18. 我会向他人说该公司的不是。	1	2	3	4	5	6	7

Pilot Test Questionnaire（2–2）

第一部分

您目前选用下面哪一家移动通信服务商提供的服务，请在您所选择答案的编号前打勾“√”。(如有多种选择，请您选最常用的一家)。

①中国移动 ②中国联通 ③小灵通

下列表中的内容是关于您与所选移动通信服务商之间关系的描述性语句，请仔细阅读每一个句子，并在相应的数字上画一个圈。

1	2	3	4	5	6	7
非常不同意	不同意	有点不同意	不能确定	有点同意	同意	非常同意

例题：我很喜欢他们。		1	2	3	④	5	6	7
请细心回答以下每一个问题，不要遗漏。								
1.	对于服务商的服务，我感到很满意。	1	2	3	4	5	6	7
2.	我很高兴选择了他们的产品。	1	2	3	4	5	6	7
3.	我很喜欢他们。	1	2	3	4	5	6	7
4.	使用他们的产品总是很愉快。	1	2	3	4	5	6	7
5.	要是其他产品都像这公司的产品就好了。	1	2	3	4	5	6	7
6.	跟其他供应商比起来，我很满意我所选择的服务供应商。	1	2	3	4	5	6	7
7.	我相信这家公司会遵守对顾客的承诺。	1	2	3	4	5	6	7
8.	我觉得这家公司很诚实、很实在。	1	2	3	4	5	6	7
9.	我认为该公司总能给我详尽的咨询。	1	2	3	4	5	6	7
10.	这家公司不会隐瞒我应该知道的信息.	1	2	3	4	5	6	7
11.	这家公司会真诚关注我的需要。	1	2	3	4	5	6	7
12.	我相信这家公司总会考虑顾客最佳利益。	1	2	3	4	5	6	7
13.	这家公司总会优先考虑顾客的利益。	1	2	3	4	5	6	7

续表

14.	这家公司很值得信赖。	1	2	3	4	5	6	7
15.	我对这家公司很有信心。	1	2	3	4	5	6	7
16.	我是这家公司的忠实顾客。	1	2	3	4	5	6	7
17.	我想继续与这家公司保持关系。	1	2	3	4	5	6	7
18.	我会努力支持这家公司。	1	2	3	4	5	6	7
19.	即使有其他的选择，我也不会选择其他公司。	1	2	3	4	5	6	7
20.	我会很积极维持与这家公司的关系。	1	2	3	4	5	6	7
21.	我会一直购买这家公司的产品。	1	2	3	4	5	6	7
22.	这家公司很值得我和她保持关系。	1	2	3	4	5	6	7

第二部分

下面的情景是您在接受移动通信服务时经常遇到的一个服务失误场景。如果您经历过与此相似的情景，请您按照您的真实体验来填答后面的表格，如果您没有经历与此相似的情景，请您把自己假想成该情景的经历者，并按照自己内心的体会来填答。

情景：

某移动公司推出“虚拟网”服务，即如果成员加入这个“虚拟网”，可享受“虚拟网”内部成员通话每分钟 1 角钱的优惠 (否则通话费为 2 角)。因为你觉得你有非常固定的通话对象群体 , 无形中就可以减少一笔开销，而平时通话频率最高的就是本群体内部成员之间的通话，于是你将群体内 20 余人的移动号码登记了下来，报送给了移动公司，并与对方签订了“虚拟网”协议书。可是好景不长，自从你加入了这个“虚拟网”，就有很多朋友抱怨，现在的每个月的话费比以前多了不少。你在想，不会吧，可能是因为降价而使得通话次数增多和通话时间加长了，才导致话费的增加。可是，没有过多久，又有很多朋友抱怨，现在的话费就是比以前增加了不少。

你终于来到了移动公司的营业大厅，将你加入“虚拟网”后 3 个月的话费详单打印了出来，仔细地核对详单上的电话号码，发现详单上的与“虚拟网”朋友中的通话，计费标准都是按每分钟 2 角收费的，你又仔细核对当时报送给移动公司的名单，发现这些号码全都准确地抄送给了移动公司。事实上，要是按“虚拟网”收费标准收费，移动公司整整多收了你一倍的费用。

实际情况是，由于移动公司后台工作人员的失误，未将你和你部分朋友的号码完全输入到“虚拟网”中，造成部分人员（大约一半）未正式加入“虚拟网”，于是造成了仍按每分钟 2 角钱收费的情况。于是你当即要求移动公司按照承诺的“话费误差，双倍返还”，或至少退还多收部分的费用。

该情景刚出现的那一刻，您内心的真实感受是，请在您所选择答案相应的数字上画一个圈：

1	2	3	4	5	6	7
非常不同意	不同意	有点不同意	不能确定	有点同意	同意	非常同意

下列表中的内容是关于服务补救的描述性语句，请仔细阅读每一个句子，并在相应的数字上画一个圈。

1	2	3	4	5	6	7
非常不同意	不同意	有点不同意	不能确定	有点同意	同意	非常同意

一、如果该服务人员马上就这一失误向您稍示道歉，同时同意退还多收部分的费用，那么请您根据这种情景给下列内容打分。

例题：该公司管理制度处理服务失误有效率。	1	2	3	④	5	6	7
请细心回答以下每一个问题，不要遗漏。							
1. 该公司管理制度处理服务失误有效率。	1	2	3	4	5	6	7
2. 该公司很在意没有为我准备你所需要的服务。	1	2	3	4	5	6	7
3. 该公司的管理机制对于自己失误反应很迅速。	1	2	3	4	5	6	7
4. 尽管出现这种失误，但该公司响应迅速。	1	2	3	4	5	6	7
5. 我相信该公司有一系列公正的管理政策。	1	2	3	4	5	6	7
6. 工作人员恰当地体谅我的难处。	1	2	3	4	5	6	7
7. 工作人员并不努力帮我解决麻烦。	1	2	3	4	5	6	7
8. 工作人员与我沟通得很好。	1	2	3	4	5	6	7
9. 工作人员服的态度很谦逊。	1	2	3	4	5	6	7
10. 这一补救结果是公平的。	1	2	3	4	5	6	7
11. 补救结果并不能弥补它给我造成的损失。	1	2	3	4	5	6	7
12. 该失误给我造成了不便，但该公司弥补了我的损失。	1	2	3	4	5	6	7
13. 我认为接受这样的补救结果是不正确的。	1	2	3	4	5	6	7
14. 该公司给我弥补的结果超过了我所失去的。	1	2	3	4	5	6	7
15. 我以后会增加购买该公司产品的次数。	1	2	3	4	5	6	7
16. 如果有别的选择，我不会选择其他公司的产品。	1	2	3	4	5	6	7
17. 如果有人提起该公司，我会推荐。	1	2	3	4	5	6	7
18. 我会向他人说该公司的不是。	1	2	3	4	5	6	7

二、如果该服务人员马上就这一失误向您真诚道歉并积极了解该失误给您造成的不便，同时同意退还多收部分的费用，那么请您根据这种情景给下列内容打分。

例题：该公司管理制度处理服务失误有效率。	1	2	3	④	5	6	7
请细心回答以下每一个问题，不要遗漏。							
1. 该公司管理制度处理服务失误有效率。	1	2	3	4	5	6	7
2. 该公司很在意没有为我准备你所需要的服务。	1	2	3	4	5	6	7
3. 该公司的管理机制对于自己失误反应很迅速。	1	2	3	4	5	6	7
4. 尽管出现这种失误，但该公司响应迅速。	1	2	3	4	5	6	7

续表

5.	我相信该公司有一系列公正的管理政策。	1	2	3	4	5	6	7
6.	工作人员恰当地体谅我的难处。	1	2	3	4	5	6	7
7.	工作人员并不努力帮我解决麻烦。	1	2	3	4	5	6	7
8.	工作人员与我沟通得很好。	1	2	3	4	5	6	7
9.	工作人员服的态度很谦逊。	1	2	3	4	5	6	7
10.	这一补救结果是公平的。	1	2	3	4	5	6	7
11.	补救结果并不能弥补它给我造成的损失。	1	2	3	4	5	6	7
12.	该失误给我造成了不便，但该公司弥补了我的损失。	1	2	3	4	5	6	7
13.	我认为接受这样的补救结果是不正确的。	1	2	3	4	5	6	7
14.	该公司给我弥补的结果超过了我所失去的。	1	2	3	4	5	6	7
15.	我以后会增加购买该公司产品的次数。	1	2	3	4	5	6	7
16.	如果有别的选择，我不会选择其他公司的产品。	1	2	3	4	5	6	7
17.	如果有人提起该公司，我会推荐。	1	2	3	4	5	6	7
18.	我会向他人说该公司的不是。	1	2	3	4	5	6	7

三、如果该服务人员马上就这一失误向您稍示道歉，同时同意双倍返还多收的费用，那么请您根据这种情景给下列内容打分。

例题：该公司管理制度处理服务失误有效率。		1	2	3	④	5	6	7
请细心回答以下每一个问题，不要遗漏。								
1.	该公司管理制度处理服务失误有效率。	1	2	3	4	5	6	7
2.	该公司很在意没有为我准备你所需要的服务。	1	2	3	4	5	6	7
3.	该公司的管理机制对于自己失误反应很迅速。	1	2	3	4	5	6	7
4.	尽管出现这种失误，但该公司响应迅速。	1	2	3	4	5	6	7
5.	我相信该公司有一系列公正的管理政策。	1	2	3	4	5	6	7
6.	工作人员恰当地体谅我的难处。	1	2	3	4	5	6	7
7.	工作人员并不努力帮我解决麻烦。	1	2	3	4	5	6	7
8.	工作人员与我沟通得很好。	1	2	3	4	5	6	7
9.	工作人员服的态度很谦逊。	1	2	3	4	5	6	7
10.	这一补救结果是公平的。	1	2	3	4	5	6	7
11.	补救结果并不能弥补它给我造成的损失。	1	2	3	4	5	6	7

续表

12. 该失误给我造成了不便，但该公司弥补了我的损失。	1	2	3	4	5	6	7
13. 我认为接受这样的补救结果是不正确的。	1	2	3	4	5	6	7
14. 该公司给我弥补的结果超过了我所失去的。	1	2	3	4	5	6	7
15. 我以后会增加购买该公司产品的次数。	1	2	3	4	5	6	7
16. 如果有别的选择，我不会选择其他公司的产品。	1	2	3	4	5	6	7
17. 如果有人提起该公司，我会推荐。	1	2	3	4	5	6	7
18. 我会向他人说该公司的不是。	1	2	3	4	5	6	7

四、如果该服务人员过了很久才就这一失误向您真诚道歉并积极了解该失误给您造成的不便，同时同意双倍返还多收的费用，那么请您根据这种情景给下列内容打分。

例题：该公司管理制度处理服务失误有效率。	1	2	3	④	5	6	7
请细心回答以下每一个问题，不要遗漏。							
1. 该公司管理制度处理服务失误有效率。	1	2	3	4	5	6	7
2. 该公司很在意没有为我准备你所需要的服务。	1	2	3	4	5	6	7
3. 该公司的管理机制对于自己失误反应很迅速。	1	2	3	4	5	6	7
4. 尽管出现这种失误，但该公司响应迅速。	1	2	3	4	5	6	7
5. 我相信该公司有一系列公正的管理政策。	1	2	3	4	5	6	7
6. 工作人员恰当地体谅我的难处。	1	2	3	4	5	6	7
7. 工作人员并不努力帮我解决麻烦。	1	2	3	4	5	6	7
8. 工作人员与我沟通得很好。	1	2	3	4	5	6	7
9. 工作人员服的态度很谦逊。	1	2	3	4	5	6	7
10. 这一补救结果是公平的。	1	2	3	4	5	6	7
11. 补救结果并不能弥补它给我造成的损失。	1	2	3	4	5	6	7
12. 该失误给我造成了不便，但该公司弥补了我的损失。	1	2	3	4	5	6	7
13. 我认为接受这样的补救结果是不正确的。	1	2	3	4	5	6	7
14. 该公司给我弥补的结果超过了我所失去的。	1	2	3	4	5	6	7
15. 我以后会增加购买该公司产品的次数。	1	2	3	4	5	6	7
16. 如果有别的选择，我不会选择其他公司的产品。	1	2	3	4	5	6	7
17. 如果有人提起该公司，我会推荐。	1	2	3	4	5	6	7
18. 我会向他人说该公司的不是。	1	2	3	4	5	6	7

附录 B

最终调查问卷

Appendix B

Final Test Questionnaire

香港理工大学市场营销项目

调查问卷 A

您好！首先，衷心感谢您参与此项目研究。这份调查问卷由香港理工大学管理及市场学系设计，旨在研究中国移动通信服务消费者在运营商失误情况下对其补救措施的感受及行为倾向，同时也为中国移动通信行业管理层就管理提出建议。所有资料只做科学研究，调查资料将会保密，研究结果只展现组织状态，不涉及任何个人信息。

研究结果的可信赖度取决于阁下对问题认真和客观的回答，请您填写此问卷时，细心阅读各项问题，真实地表达您的感受。您所提供的资料对我们的研究会有很大的帮助，同时也会对中国移动通信服务商工作改进提供依据。

最后，再次对您的参与及帮助表示衷心的感谢！

李 瑾

香港理工大学管理及市场学系

下面的情景是您在接受移动通信服务时经常遇到的一个服务失误场景。如果您经历过与此相似的情景，请您按照您的真实体验来填答后面的表格，如果您没有经历与此相似的情景，请您把自己假想成该情景的经历者，并按照自己内心的体会来填答。

情景：

某移动公司推出“虚拟网”服务，即如果成员加入这个“虚拟网”，可享受“虚拟网”内部成员通话每分钟 1 角钱的优惠 (否则通话费为 2 角)。因为你觉得你有非常固定的通话对象群体 , 无形中就可以减少一笔开销，而平时通话频率最高的就是本群体内部成员之间的通话，于是你将群体内 20 余人的移动号码登记了下来，报送给了移动公司，并与对方签订了“虚拟网”协议书。可是好景不长，自从你加入了这个“虚拟网”，就有很多朋友抱怨，现在的每个月的话费比以前多了不少。你在想，不会吧，可能是因为降价而使得通话次数增多和通话时间加长了，才导致话费的增加。可是，没有过多久，又有很多朋友抱怨，现在的话费就是比以前增加了不少。

你终于来到了移动公司的营业大厅，将你加入“虚拟网”后 3 个月的话费详单打印了出来，仔细地核对详单上的电话号码，发现详单上的与“虚拟网”朋友中的通话，计费标准都是按每分钟 2 角收费的，你又仔细核对当时报送给移动公司的名单，发现这些号码全都准确地抄送给了移动公司。事实上，要是按“虚拟网”收费标准收费，移动公司整整多收了你一倍的费用。

实际情况是 , 由于移动公司后台工作人员的失误，未将你和你部分朋友的号码完全输入到“虚拟网”中，造成部分人员（大约一半）未正式加入“虚拟网”，于是造成了仍按每分钟 2 角钱收费的情况。于是你当即要求移动公司按照承诺的“话费误差，双倍返还”，或至少退还多收部分的费用。

1. 该情景刚出现的那一刻，您内心的真实感受是（请在您所选择答案的编号前打勾“√”）：

7	6	5	4	4	3	1
完全满意	满意	有点满意	不确定	有点不满意	不满意	完全不满意

2. 您是否亲身经历过类似的情景（请在您所选择答案的编号前打勾“√”）：

① 有过　　② 没有

3. 您目前选用下面哪一家移动通信服务商提供的服务，请在您所选择答案的编号前打勾“√”。(如有多种选择，请您选最常用的一家)。

① 中国移动　② 中国联通　③ 小灵通　④ 其他

第一种补救措施：如果服务人员马上对该失误向您真诚道歉并积极了解该失误给您造成的不便，此外，同意双倍返还多收的费用。请仔细阅读每一个句子，并在相应的数字上画一个圈。

第二种补救措施：如果该服务人员过了很久才对此失误向您真诚道歉并积极了解该失误给您造成的不便，但不退还多收部分的费用，那么请您根据这种情景给下列内容打分。

7	6	5	4	4	3	1
完全同意	同意	有点同意	不确定	有点不同意	不同意	完全不同意

例题：我自信有能力完成各项工作任务。	7	6	5	4	3	2	①
请细心回答以下每一个问题，不要遗漏。							
1. 该公司管理制度处理服务失误有效率。	7	6	5	4	3	2	1
2. 我相信该公司有一系列公正的管理政策。	7	6	5	4	3	2	1
3. 工作人员服的态度很谦逊。	7	6	5	4	3	2	1
4. 我会向他人说该公司的不是。	7	6	5	4	3	2	1
5. 该公司很在意没有为我准备我所需要的服务。	7	6	5	4	3	2	1
6. 这一补救结果是公平的。	7	6	5	4	3	2	1
7. 如果有人提起该公司，我会推荐。	7	6	5	4	3	2	1
8. 该公司的管理机制对于自己失误反应很迅速。	7	6	5	4	3	2	1
9. 该失误给我造成了不便，但该公司弥补了我的损失。	7	6	5	4	3	2	1
10. 工作人员与我沟通得很好。	7	6	5	4	3	2	1
11. 尽管出现这种失误，但该公司响应迅速。	7	6	5	4	3	2	1
12. 该公司给我弥补的结果超过了我所失去的。	7	6	5	4	3	2	1
13. 工作人员恰当地体谅我的难处。	7	6	5	4	3	2	1
14. 我以后会增加购买该公司产品的次数。	7	6	5	4	3	2	1
15. 工作人员并不努力帮我解决麻烦。	7	6	5	4	3	2	1
16. 补救结果并不能弥补它给我造成的损失。	7	6	5	4	3	2	1
17. 我认为接受这样的补救结果是不正确的。	7	6	5	4	3	2	1
18. 如果有别的选择，我也不会选择其他公司的产品。	7	6	5	4	3	2	1

下列表中的内容是针对服务商给您提供了第一种服务补救措施之后，您对该移动通信服务商的评价，请仔细阅读每一个句子，并在相应的数字上画一个圈。

7	6	5	4	4	3	1
完全同意	同意	有点同意	不确定	有点不同意	不同意	完全不同意

例题：我自信有能力完成各项工作任务。	7 6 5 4 3 2 ①
请细心回答以下每一个问题，不要遗漏。	

续表

1.	对于该公司的服务，我感到很满意。	7 6 5 4 3 2 1
2.	这家公司很值得我和她保持关系。	7 6 5 4 3 2 1
3.	我很高兴选择了他们的产品。	7 6 5 4 3 2 1
4.	我会一直购买这家公司的产品。	7 6 5 4 3 2 1
5.	这家公司很值得信赖。	7 6 5 4 3 2 1
6.	我很喜欢他们。	7 6 5 4 3 2 1
7.	我会很积极维持与这家公司的关系。	7 6 5 4 3 2 1
8.	这家公司会真诚关注我的需要。	7 6 5 4 3 2 1
9.	使用他们的产品总是很愉快。	7 6 5 4 3 2 1
10.	这家公司不会隐瞒我应该知道的信息。	7 6 5 4 3 2 1
11.	即使有其他的选择，我也不会选择其他公司。	7 6 5 4 3 2 1
12.	我认为该公司总能给我详尽的咨询。	7 6 5 4 3 2 1
13.	要是其他产品都像这公司的产品就好了。	7 6 5 4 3 2 1
14.	我会努力支持这家公司。	7 6 5 4 3 2 1
15.	我觉得这家公司很诚实、很实在。	7 6 5 4 3 2 1
16.	我想继续与这家公司保持关系。	7 6 5 4 3 2 1
17.	我相信这家公司会遵守对顾客的承诺。	7 6 5 4 3 2 1
18.	我是这家公司的忠实顾客。	7 6 5 4 3 2 1
19.	跟其他产品供应商比起来，我很满意我所选择的服务供应商。	7 6 5 4 3 2 1
20.	我对这家公司很有信心。	7 6 5 4 3 2 1
21.	这家公司总会优先考虑顾客的利益。	7 6 5 4 3 2 1
22.	我相信这家公司总会考虑顾客最佳利益。	7 6 5 4 3 2 1

第二种补救措施：如果该服务人员过了很久才对此失误向您真诚道歉并积极了解该失误给您造成的不便，但不退还多收部分的费用，那么请您根据这种情景给下列内容打分。

7	6	5	4	4	3	1
完全同意	同意	有点同意	不确定	有点不同意	不同意	完全不同意

例题：我自信有能力完成各项工作任务。	7	6	5	4	3	2	①
请细心回答以下每一个问题，不要遗漏。							
1. 该公司管理制度处理服务失误有效率。	7	6	5	4	3	2	1
2. 我相信该公司有一系列公正的管理政策。	7	6	5	4	3	2	1
3. 工作人员服的态度很谦逊。	7	6	5	4	3	2	1
4. 我会向他人说该公司的不是。	7	6	5	4	3	2	1
5. 该公司很在意没有为我准备我所需要的服务。	7	6	5	4	3	2	1
6. 这一补救结果是公平的。	7	6	5	4	3	2	1
7. 如果有人提起该公司，我会推荐。	7	6	5	4	3	2	1
8. 该公司的管理机制对于自己失误反应很迅速。	7	6	5	4	3	2	1
9. 该失误给我造成了不便，但该公司弥补了我的损失。	7	6	5	4	3	2	1
10. 工作人员与我沟通得很好。	7	6	5	4	3	2	1
11. 尽管出现这种失误，但该公司响应迅速。	7	6	5	4	3	2	1
12. 该公司给我弥补的结果超过了我所失去的。	7	6	5	4	3	2	1
13. 工作人员恰当地体谅我的难处。	7	6	5	4	3	2	1
14. 我以后会增加购买该公司产品的次数。	7	6	5	4	3	2	1
15. 工作人员并不努力帮我解决麻烦。	7	6	5	4	3	2	1
16. 补救结果并不能弥补它给我造成的损失。	7	6	5	4	3	2	1
17. 我认为接受这样的补救结果是不正确的。	7	6	5	4	3	2	1
18. 如果有别的选择，我也不会选择其他公司的产品。	7	6	5	4	3	2	1

下列表中的内容是服务商给您提供了第二种服务补救措施之后，您对该移动通信服务商的评价，请仔细阅读每一个句子，并在相应的数字上画一个圈。

7	6	5	4	4	3	1
完全同意	同意	有点同意	不确定	有点不同意	不同意	完全不同意

例题：我自信有能力完成各项工作任务。	7	6	5	4	3	2	①
请细心回答以下每一个问题，不要遗漏。							
1. 对于该公司的服务，我感到很满意。	7	6	5	4	3	2	1
2. 这家公司很值得我和她保持关系。	7	6	5	4	3	2	1
3. 我很高兴选择了他们的产品。	7	6	5	4	3	2	1

续表

4. 我会一直购买这家公司的产品。	7	6	5	4	3	2	1
5. 这家公司很值得信赖。	7	6	5	4	3	2	1
6. 我很喜欢他们。	7	6	5	4	3	2	1
7. 我会很积极维持与这家公司的关系。	7	6	5	4	3	2	1
8. 这家公司会真诚关注我的需要。	7	6	5	4	3	2	1
9. 使用他们的产品总是很愉快。	7	6	5	4	3	2	1
10. 这家公司不会隐瞒我应该知道的信息。	7	6	5	4	3	2	1
11. 即使有其他的选择，我也不会选择其他公司。	7	6	5	4	3	2	1
12. 我认为该公司总能给我详尽的咨询。	7	6	5	4	3	2	1
13. 要是其他产品都像这公司的产品就好了。	7	6	5	4	3	2	1
14. 我会努力支持这家公司。	7	6	5	4	3	2	1
15. 我觉得这家公司很诚实、很实在。	7	6	5	4	3	2	1
16. 我想继续与这家公司保持关系。	7	6	5	4	3	2	1
17. 我相信这家公司会遵守对顾客的承诺。	7	6	5	4	3	2	1
18. 我是这家公司的忠实顾客。	7	6	5	4	3	2	1
19. 跟其他产品供应商比起来，我很满意我所选择的服务供应商。	7	6	5	4	3	2	1
20. 我对这家公司很有信心。	7	6	5	4	3	2	1
21. 这家公司总会优先考虑顾客的利益。	7	6	5	4	3	2	1
22. 我相信这家公司总会考虑顾客最佳利益。	7	6	5	4	3	2	1

1. 请问您的性别：①男性　②女性

2. 请问您的年龄：① 18–25 岁　② 26–35 岁　③ 36–45 岁　④ 46–55 岁　⑤ 60 岁以上

3. 请问您的学历：①初中　②高中　③高职（中专）　④大学（包括大专）　⑤研究生及以上

4. 请问您的收入水平（年收入）：① 1 万元以下　② 1 万 –3 万元　③ 4 万 –6 万　④ 7 万 –9 万元　⑤ 10 万元以上

香港理工大学市场营销项目

调查问卷 B

您好！首先，衷心感谢您参与此项目研究。这份调查问卷由香港理工大学管理及市场学系设计，旨在研究中国移动通信服务消费者在运营商失误情况下对其补救措施的感受及行为倾向，同时也为中国移动通信行业管理层就管理提出建议。所有资料只作科学研究，调查资料将会保密，研究结果只展现组织状态，不涉及任何个人信息。

研究结果的可信赖度取决于阁下对问题认真和客观的回答，请您填写此问卷时，细心阅读各项问题，真实地表达您的感受。您所提供的资料对我们的研究会有很大的帮助，同时也会对中国移动通信服务商工作改进提供依据。

最后，再次对您的参与及帮助表示衷心的感谢！

李 瑾

香港理工大学管理及市场学系

下面的情景是您在接受移动通信服务时经常遇到的一个服务失误场景。如果您经历过与此相似的情景，请您按照您的真实体验来填答后面的表格，如果您没有经历与此相似的情景，请您把自己假想成该情景的经历者，并按照自己内心的体会来填答。

情景：

某移动公司推出“虚拟网”服务，即如果成员加入这个“虚拟网”，可享受“虚拟网”内部成员通话每分钟 1 角钱的优惠（否则通话费为 2 角）。因为你觉得你有非常固定的通话对象群体，无形中就可以减少一笔开销，而平时通话频率最高的就是本群体内部成员之间的通话，于是你将群体内 20 余人的移动号码登记了下来，报送给了移动公司，并与对方签订了“虚拟网”协议书。可是好景不长，自从你加入了这个“虚拟网”，就有很多朋友抱怨，现在的每个月的话费比以前多了不少。你在想，不会吧，可能是因为降价而使得通话次数增多和通话时间加长了，才导致话费的增加。可是，没有过多久，又有很多朋友抱怨，现在的话费就是比以前增加了不少。

你终于来到了移动公司的营业大厅，将你加入“虚拟网”后 3 个月的话费详单打印了出来，仔细地核对详单上的电话号码，发现详单上的与“虚拟网”朋友中的通话，计费标准都是按每分钟 2 角收费的，你又仔细核对当时报送给移动公司的名单，发现这些号码全都准确地抄送给了移动公司。事实上，要是按“虚拟网”收费标准收费，移动公司整整多收了你一倍的费用。

实际情况是，由于移动公司后台工作人员的失误，未将你和你部分朋友的号码完全输入到“虚拟网”中，造成部分人员（大约一半）未正式加入“虚拟网”，于是造成了仍按每分钟 2 角钱收费的情况。于是你当即要求移动公司按照承诺的“话费误差，双倍返还”，或至少退还多收部分的费用。

1. 该情景刚出现的那一刻，您内心的真实感受是（请在您所选择答案的编号前打勾“√”）：

7	6	5	4	4	3	1
完全满意	满意	有点满意	不确定	有点不满意	不满意	完全不满意

2. 您是否亲身经历过类似的情景（请在您所选择答案的编号前打勾“√”）：

① 有过　　② 没有

3. 您目前选用下面哪一家移动通信服务商提供的服务，请在您所选择答案的编号前打勾“√”。(如有多种选择，请您选最常用的一家)。

① 中国移动　② 中国联通　③ 小灵通　④ 其他

第一种补救措施：如果服务人员马上对该失误向您稍示歉意，并同意双倍返还多收的费用。请仔细阅读每一个句子，并在相应的数字上画一个圈。

7	6	5	4	4	3	1
完全同意	同意	有点同意	不确定	有点不同意	不同意	完全不同意

例题：我自信有能力完成各项工作任务。	7	6	5	4	3	2	①
请细心回答以下每一个问题，不要遗漏。							
1. 该公司管理制度处理服务失误有效率。	7	6	5	4	3	2	1
2. 我相信该公司有一系列公正的管理政策。	7	6	5	4	3	2	1

续表

3.	工作人员服的态度很谦逊。	7	6	5	4	3	2	1
4.	我会向他人说该公司的不是。	7	6	5	4	3	2	1
5.	该公司很在意没有为我准备我所需要的服务。	7	6	5	4	3	2	1
6.	这一补救结果是公平的。	7	6	5	4	3	2	1
7.	如果有人提起该公司，我会推荐。	7	6	5	4	3	2	1
8.	该公司的管理机制对于自己失误反应很迅速。	7	6	5	4	3	2	1
9.	该失误给我造成了不便，但该公司弥补了我的损失。	7	6	5	4	3	2	1
10.	工作人员与我沟通得很好。	7	6	5	4	3	2	1
11.	尽管出现这种失误，但该公司响应迅速。	7	6	5	4	3	2	1
12.	该公司给我弥补的结果超过了我所失去的。	7	6	5	4	3	2	1
13.	工作人员恰当地体谅我的难处。	7	6	5	4	3	2	1
14.	我以后会增加购买该公司产品的次数。	7	6	5	4	3	2	1
15.	工作人员并不努力帮我解决麻烦。	7	6	5	4	3	2	1
16.	补救结果并不能弥补它给我造成的损失。	7	6	5	4	3	2	1
17.	我认为接受这样的补救结果是不正确的。	7	6	5	4	3	2	1
18.	如果有别的选择，我也不会选择其他公司的产品。	7	6	5	4	3	2	1

下列表中的内容是针对服务商给您提供了第一种服务补救措施之后，您对该移动通信服务商的评价，请仔细阅读每一个句子，并在相应的数字上画一个圈。

7	6	5	4	4	3	1
完全同意	同意	有点同意	不确定	有点不同意	不同意	完全不同意

例题：我自信有能力完成各项工作任务。		7	6	5	4	3	2	①
请细心回答以下每一个问题，不要遗漏。								
1.	对于该公司的服务，我感到很满意。	7	6	5	4	3	2	1
2.	这家公司很值得我和她保持关系。	7	6	5	4	3	2	1
3.	我很高兴选择了他们的产品。	7	6	5	4	3	2	1
4.	我会一直购买这家公司的产品。	7	6	5	4	3	2	1
5.	这家公司很值得信赖。	7	6	5	4	3	2	1

续表

6. 我很喜欢他们。	7	6	5	4	3	2	1
7. 我会很积极维持与这家公司的关系。	7	6	5	4	3	2	1
8. 这家公司会真诚关注我的需要。	7	6	5	4	3	2	1
9. 使用他们的产品总是很愉快。	7	6	5	4	3	2	1
10. 这家公司不会隐瞒我应该知道的信息。	7	6	5	4	3	2	1
11. 即使有其他的选择，我也不会选择其他公司。	7	6	5	4	3	2	1
12. 我认为该公司总能给我详尽的咨询。	7	6	5	4	3	2	1
13. 要是其他产品都像这公司的产品就好了。	7	6	5	4	3	2	1
14. 我会努力支持这家公司。	7	6	5	4	3	2	1
15. 我觉得这家公司很诚实、很实在。	7	6	5	4	3	2	1
16. 我想继续与这家公司保持关系。	7	6	5	4	3	2	1
17. 我相信这家公司会遵守对顾客的承诺。	7	6	5	4	3	2	1
18. 我是这家公司的忠实顾客。	7	6	5	4	3	2	1
19. 跟其他产品供应商比起来，我很满意我所选择的服务供应商。	7	6	5	4	3	2	1
20. 我对这家公司很有信心。	7	6	5	4	3	2	1
21. 这家公司总会优先考虑顾客的利益。	7	6	5	4	3	2	1
22. 我相信这家公司总会考虑顾客最佳利益。	7	6	5	4	3	2	1

第二种补救措施：如果该服务人员过了很久才对此失误向您真诚道歉并积极了解该失误给您造成的不便，此外，同意双倍返还多收部分的费用，那么请您根据这种情景给下列内容打分。

7	6	5	4	4	3	1
完全同意	同意	有点同意	不确定	有点不同意	不同意	完全不同意

例题：我自信有能力完成各项工作任务。	7	6	5	4	3	2	①
请细心回答以下每一个问题，不要遗漏。							
1. 该公司管理制度处理服务失误有效率。	7	6	5	4	3	2	1

续表

2.	我相信该公司有一系列公正的管理政策。	7	6	5	4	3	2	1
3.	工作人员服的态度很谦逊。	7	6	5	4	3	2	1
4.	我会向他人说该公司的不是。	7	6	5	4	3	2	1
5.	该公司很在意没有为我准备我所需要的服务。	7	6	5	4	3	2	1
6.	这一补救结果是公平的。	7	6	5	4	3	2	1
7.	如果有人提起该公司，我会推荐。	7	6	5	4	3	2	1
8.	该公司的管理机制对于自己失误反应很迅速。	7	6	5	4	3	2	1
9.	该失误给我造成了不便，但该公司弥补了我的损失。	7	6	5	4	3	2	1
10.	工作人员与我沟通得很好。	7	6	5	4	3	2	1
11.	尽管出现这种失误，但该公司响应迅速。	7	6	5	4	3	2	1
12.	该公司给我弥补的结果超过了我所失去的。	7	6	5	4	3	2	1
13.	工作人员恰当地体谅我的难处。	7	6	5	4	3	2	1
14.	我以后会增加购买该公司产品的次数。	7	6	5	4	3	2	1
15.	工作人员并不努力帮我解决麻烦。	7	6	5	4	3	2	1
16.	补救结果并不能弥补它给我造成的损失。	7	6	5	4	3	2	1
17.	我认为接受这样的补救结果是不正确的。	7	6	5	4	3	2	1
18.	如果有别的选择，我也不会选择其他公司的产品。	7	6	5	4	3	2	1

下列表中的内容是服务商给您提供了第二种服务补救措施之后，您对该移动通信服务商的评价，请仔细阅读每一个句子，并在相应的数字上画一个圈。

7	6	5	4	4	3	1
完全同意	同意	有点同意	不确定	有点不同意	不同意	完全不同意

例题：我自信有能力完成各项工作任务。		7	6	5	4	3	2	①
请细心回答以下每一个问题，不要遗漏。								
1.	对于该公司的服务，我感到很满意。	7	6	5	4	3	2	1
2.	这家公司很值得我和她保持关系。	7	6	5	4	3	2	1
3.	我很高兴选择了他们的产品。	7	6	5	4	3	2	1
4.	我会一直购买这家公司的产品。	7	6	5	4	3	2	1

续表

5.	5. 这家公司很值得信赖。	7	6	5	4	3	2	1
6.	我很喜欢他们。	7	6	5	4	3	2	1
7.	我会很积极维持与这家公司的关系。	7	6	5	4	3	2	1
8.	这家公司会真诚关注我的需要。	7	6	5	4	3	2	1
9.	使用他们的产品总是很愉快。	7	6	5	4	3	2	1
10.	这家公司不会隐瞒我应该知道的信息。	7	6	5	4	3	2	1
11.	即使有其他的选择，我也不会选择其他公司。	7	6	5	4	3	2	1
12.	我认为该公司总能给我详尽的咨询。	7	6	5	4	3	2	1
13.	要是其他产品都像这公司的产品就好了。	7	6	5	4	3	2	1
14.	我会努力支持这家公司。	7	6	5	4	3	2	1
15.	我觉得这家公司很诚实、很实在。	7	6	5	4	3	2	1
16.	我想继续与这家公司保持关系。	7	6	5	4	3	2	1
17.	我相信这家公司会遵守对顾客的承诺。	7	6	5	4	3	2	1
18.	我是这家公司的忠实顾客。	7	6	5	4	3	2	1
19.	跟其他产品供应商比起来，我很满意我所选择的服务供应商。	7	6	5	4	3	2	1
20.	我对这家公司很有信心。	7	6	5	4	3	2	1
21.	这家公司总会优先考虑顾客的利益。	7	6	5	4	3	2	1
22.	我相信这家公司总会考虑顾客最佳利益。	7	6	5	4	3	2	1

1. 请问您的性别：①男性　②女性

2. 请问您的年龄：① 18–25 岁　② 26–35 岁　③ 36–45 岁　④ 46–55 岁　⑤ 60 岁以上

3. 请问您的学历：①初中　②高中　③高职（中专）　④大学（包括大专）　⑤研究生及以上

4. 请问您的收入水平（年收入）：① 1 万元以下　② 1 万 –3 万元　③ 4 万 –6 万　④ 7 万 –9 万元　⑤ 10 万元以上

香港理工大学市场营销项目

调查问卷 C

您好！首先，衷心感谢您参与此项目研究。这份调查问卷由香港理工大学管理及市场学系设计，旨在研究中国移动通信服务消费者在运营商失误情况下对其补救措施的感受及行为倾向，同时也为中国移动通信行业管理层就管理提出建议。所有资料只作科学研究，调查资料将会保密，研究结果只展现组织状态，不涉及任何个人信息。

研究结果的可信赖度取决于阁下对问题认真和客观的回答，请您填写此问卷时，细心阅读各项问题，真实地表达您的感受。您所提供的资料对我们的研究会有很大的帮助，同时也会对中国移动通信服务商工作改进提供依据。

最后，再次对您的参与及帮助表示衷心的感谢！

李 瑾

香港理工大学管理及市场学系

下面的情景是您在接受移动通信服务时经常遇到的一个服务失误场景。如果您经历过与此相似的情景，请您按照您的真实体验来填答后面的表格，如果您没有经历与此相似的情景，请您把自己假想成该情景的经历者，并按照自己内心的体会来填答。

情景：

某移动公司推出“虚拟网”服务，即如果成员加入这个“虚拟网”，可享受“虚拟网”内部成员通话每分钟 1 角钱的优惠（否则通话费为 2 角）。因为你觉得你有非常固定的通话对象群体，无形中就可以减少一笔开销，而平时通话频率最高的就是本群体内部成员之间的通话，于是你将群体内 20 余人的移动号码登记了下来，报送给了移动公司，并与对方签订了“虚拟网”协议书。可是好景不长，自从你加入了这个“虚拟网”，就有很多朋友抱怨，现在的每个月的话费比以前多了不少。你在想，不会吧，可能是因为降价而使得通话次数增多和通话时间加长了，才导致话费的增加。可是，没有过多久，又有很多朋友抱怨，现在的话费就是比以前增加了不少。

你终于来到了移动公司的营业大厅，将你加入“虚拟网”后 3 个月的话费详单打印了出来，仔细地核对详单上的电话号码，发现详单上的与“虚拟网”朋友中的通话，计费标准都是按每分钟 2 角收费的，你又仔细核对当时报送给移动公司的名单，发现这些号码全都准确地抄送给了移动公司。事实上，要是按“虚拟网”收费标准收费，移动公司整整多收了你一倍的费用。

实际情况是，由于移动公司后台工作人员的失误，未将你和你部分朋友的号码完全输入到“虚拟网”中，造成部分人员（大约一半）未正式加入“虚拟网”，于是造成了仍按每分钟 2 角钱收费的情况。于是你当即要求移动公司按照承诺的“话费误差，双倍返还”，或至少退还多收部分的费用。

1. 该情景刚出现的那一刻，您内心的真实感受是（请在您所选择答案的编号前打勾“√”）：

7	6	5	4	4	3	1
完全满意	满意	有点满意	不确定	有点不满意	不满意	完全不满意

2. 您是否亲身经历过类似的情景（请在您所选择答案的编号前打勾“√”）：

① 有过　　　　② 没有

3. 您目前选用下面哪一家移动通信服务商提供的服务，请在您所选择答案的编号前打勾“√”。(如有多种选择，请您选最常用的一家)。

① 中国移动　② 中国联通　③ 小灵通　④ 其他

第一种补救措施：如果服务人员马上对该失误向您真诚道歉并积极了解该失误给您造成的不便，但不退还多收部分的费用。请仔细阅读每一个句子，并在相应的数字上画一个圈。

7	6	5	4	4	3	1
完全同意	同意	有点同意	不确定	有点不同意	不同意	完全不同意

例题：我自信有能力完成各项工作任务。	7	6	5	4	3	2	①
请细心回答以下每一个问题，不要遗漏。							
1.　该公司管理制度处理服务失误有效率。	7	6	5	4	3	2	1

续表

2. 我相信该公司有一系列公正的管理政策。	7	6	5	4	3	2	1
3. 工作人员服的态度很谦逊。	7	6	5	4	3	2	1
4. 我会向他人说该公司的不是。	7	6	5	4	3	2	1
5. 该公司很在意没有为我准备我所需要的服务。	7	6	5	4	3	2	1
6. 这一补救结果是公平的。	7	6	5	4	3	2	1
7. 如果有人提起该公司，我会推荐。	7	6	5	4	3	2	1
8.. 该公司的管理机制对于自己失误反应很迅速。	7	6	5	4	3	2	1
9. 该失误给我造成了不便，但该公司弥补了我的损失。	7	6	5	4	3	2	1
10. 工作人员与我沟通得很好。	7	6	5	4	3	2	1
11. 尽管出现这种失误，但该公司响应迅速。	7	6	5	4	3	2	1
12.. 该公司给我弥补的结果超过了我所失去的。	7	6	5	4	3	2	1
13. 工作人员恰当地体谅我的难处。	7	6	5	4	3	2	1
14. 我以后会增加购买该公司产品的次数。	7	6	5	4	3	2	1
15. 工作人员并不努力帮我解决麻烦。	7	6	5	4	3	2	1
16. 补救结果并不能弥补它给我造成的损失。	7	6	5	4	3	2	1
17. 我认为接受这样的补救结果是不正确的。	7	6	5	4	3	2	1
18. 如果有别的选择，我也不会选择其他公司的产品。	7	6	5	4	3	2	1

下列表中的内容是针对服务商给您提供了第一种服务补救措施之后，您对该移动通信服务商的评价，请仔细阅读每一个句子，并在相应的数字上画一个圈。

7	6	5	4	4	3	1
完全同意	同意	有点同意	不确定	有点不同意	不同意	完全不同意

例题：我自信有能力完成各项工作任务。	7	6	5	4	3	2	①
请细心回答以下每一个问题，不要遗漏。							
1. 对于该公司的服务，我感到很满意。	7	6	5	4	3	2	1
2. 这家公司很值得我和她保持关系。	7	6	5	4	3	2	1
3. 我很高兴选择了他们的产品。	7	6	5	4	3	2	1
4. 我会一直购买这家公司的产品。	7	6	5	4	3	2	1

续表

5. 这家公司很值得信赖。	7	6	5	4	3	2	1
6. 我很喜欢他们。	7	6	5	4	3	2	1
7. 我会很积极维持与这家公司的关系。	7	6	5	4	3	2	1
8. 这家公司会真诚关注我的需要。	7	6	5	4	3	2	1
9. 使用他们的产品总是很愉快。	7	6	5	4	3	2	1
10. 这家公司不会隐瞒我应该知道的信息。	7	6	5	4	3	2	1
11. 即使有其他的选择，我也不会选择其他公司。	7	6	5	4	3	2	1
12. 我认为该公司总能给我详尽的咨询。	7	6	5	4	3	2	1
13. 要是其他产品都像这公司的产品就好了。	7	6	5	4	3	2	1
14. 我会努力支持这家公司。	7	6	5	4	3	2	1
15. 我觉得这家公司很诚实、很实在。	7	6	5	4	3	2	1
16. 我想继续与这家公司保持关系。	7	6	5	4	3	2	1
17. 我相信这家公司会遵守对顾客的承诺。	7	6	5	4	3	2	1
18. 我是这家公司的忠实顾客。	7	6	5	4	3	2	1
19. 跟其他产品供应商比起来，我很满意我所选择的服供应商。	7	6	5	4	3	2	1
20. 我对这家公司很有信心。	7	6	5	4	3	2	1
21. 这家公司总会优先考虑顾客的利益。	7	6	5	4	3	2	1
22. 我相信这家公司总会考虑顾客最佳利益。	7	6	5	4	3	2	1

第二种补救措施：如果该服务人员过了很久才对此失误向您稍示歉意，且不退还多收部分的费用，那么请您根据这种情景给下列内容打分。

7	6	5	4	4	3	1
完全同意	同意	有点同意	不确定	有点不同意	不同意	完全不同意

例题：我自信有能力完成各项工作任务。	7	6	5	4	3	2	①
请细心回答以下每一个问题，不要遗漏。							
1. 该公司管理制度处理服务失误有效率。	7	6	5	4	3	2	1
2. 我相信该公司有一系列公正的管理政策。	7	6	5	4	3	2	1

续表

3. 工作人员服的态度很谦逊。	7	6	5	4	3	2	1
4. 我会向他人说该公司的不是。	7	6	5	4	3	2	1
5. 该公司很在意没有为我准备我所需要的服务。	7	6	5	4	3	2	1
6. 这一补救结果是公平的。	7	6	5	4	3	2	1
7. 如果有人提起该公司，我会推荐。	7	6	5	4	3	2	1
8. 该公司的管理机制对于自己失误反应很迅速。	7	6	5	4	3	2	1
9. 该失误给我造成了不便，但该公司弥补了我的损失。	7	6	5	4	3	2	1
10. 工作人员与我沟通得很好。	7	6	5	4	3	2	1
11. 尽管出现这种失误，但该公司响应迅速。	7	6	5	4	3	2	1
12. 该公司给我弥补的结果超过了我所失去的。	7	6	5	4	3	2	1
13. 工作人员恰当地体谅我的难处。	7	6	5	4	3	2	1
14. 我以后会增加购买该公司产品的次数。	7	6	5	4	3	2	1
15. 工作人员并不努力帮我解决麻烦。	7	6	5	4	3	2	1
16. 补救结果并不能弥补它给我造成的损失。	7	6	5	4	3	2	1
17. 我认为接受这样的补救结果是不正确的。	7	6	5	4	3	2	1
18. 如果有别的选择，我也不会选择其他公司的产品。	7	6	5	4	3	2	1

下列表中的内容是服务商给您提供了第二种服务补救措施之后，您对该移动通信服务商的评价，请仔细阅读每一个句子，并在相应的数字上画一个圈。

7	6	5	4	4	3	1
完全同意	同意	有点同意	不确定	有点不同意	不同意	完全不同意

例题：我自信有能力完成各项工作任务。	7	6	5	4	3	2	①
请细心回答以下每一个问题，不要遗漏。							
1. 对于该公司的服务，我感到很满意。	7	6	5	4	3	2	1
2. 这家公司很值得我和她保持关系。	7	6	5	4	3	2	1
3. 我很高兴选择了他们的产品。	7	6	5	4	3	2	1
4. 我会一直购买这家公司的产品。	7	6	5	4	3	2	1
5. 这家公司很值得信赖。	7	6	5	4	3	2	1

续表

6. 我很喜欢他们。	7	6	5	4	3	2	1
7. 我会很积极维持与这家公司的关系。	7	6	5	4	3	2	1
8. 这家公司会真诚关注我的需要。	7	6	5	4	3	2	1
9. 使用他们的产品总是很愉快。	7	6	5	4	3	2	1
10. 这家公司不会隐瞒我应该知道的信息。	7	6	5	4	3	2	1
11. 即使有其他的选择，我也不会选择其他公司。	7	6	5	4	3	2	1
12. 我认为该公司总能给我详尽的咨询。	7	6	5	4	3	2	1
13. 要是其他产品都像这公司的产品就好了。	7	6	5	4	3	2	1
14. 我会努力支持这家公司。	7	6	5	4	3	2	1
15. 我觉得这家公司很诚实、很实在。	7	6	5	4	3	2	1
16. 我想继续与这家公司保持关系。	7	6	5	4	3	2	1
17. 我相信这家公司会遵守对顾客的承诺。	7	6	5	4	3	2	1
18. 我是这家公司的忠实顾客。	7	6	5	4	3	2	1
19. 跟其他产品供应商比起来，我很满意我所选择的服务供应商。	7	6	5	4	3	2	1
20. 我对这家公司很有信心。	7	6	5	4	3	2	1
21. 这家公司总会优先考虑顾客的利益。	7	6	5	4	3	2	1
22. 我相信这家公司总会考虑顾客最佳利益。	7	6	5	4	3	2	1

1. 请问您的性别：①男性　②女性

2. 请问您的年龄：① 18–25 岁　② 26–35 岁　③ 36–45 岁　④ 46–55 岁　⑤ 60 岁以上

3. 请问您的学历：①初中　②高中　③高职（中专）④大学（包括大专）⑤研究生及以上

4. 请问您的收入水平（年收入）：① 1 万元以下　② 1 万 –3 万元　③ 4 万 –6 万　④ 7 万 –9 万元　⑤ 10 万元以上

香港理工大学市场营销项目

调查问卷 D

您好！首先，衷心感谢您参与此项目研究。这份调查问卷由香港理工大学管理及市场学系设计，旨在研究中国移动通信服务消费者在运营商失误情况下对其补救措施的感受及行为倾向，同时也为中国移动通信行业管理层就管理提出建议。所有资料只作科学研究，调查资料将会保密，研究结果只展现组织状态，不涉及任何个人信息。

研究结果的可信赖度取决于阁下对问题认真和客观的回答，请您填写此问卷时，细心阅读各项问题，真实地表达您的感受。您所提供的资料对我们的研究会有很大的帮助，同时也会对中国移动通信服务商工作改进提供依据。

最后，再次对您的参与及帮助表示衷心的感谢！

李 瑾

香港理工大学管理及市场学系

下面的情景是您在接受移动通信服务时经常遇到的一个服务失误场景。如果您经历过与此相似的情景，请您按照您的真实体验来填答后面的表格，如果您没有经历与此相似的情景，请您把自己假想成该情景的经历者，并按照自己内心的体会来填答。

情景：

某移动公司推出“虚拟网”服务，即如果成员加入这个“虚拟网”，可享受“虚拟网”内部成员通话每分钟 1 角钱的优惠 (否则通话费为 2 角)。因为你觉得你有非常固定的通话对象群体，无形中就可以减少一笔开销，而平时通话频率最高的就是本群体内部成员之间的通话，于是你将群体内 20 余人的移动号码登记了下来，报送给了移动公司，并与对方签订了“虚拟网”协议书。可是好景不长，自从你加入了这个“虚拟网”，就有很多朋友抱怨，现在的每个月的话费比以前多了不少。你在想，不会吧，可能是因为降价而使得通话次数增多和通话时间加长了，才导致话费的增加。可是，没有过多久，又有很多朋友抱怨，现在的话费就是比以前增加了不少。

你终于来到了移动公司的营业大厅，将你加入“虚拟网”后 3 个月的话费详单打印了出来，仔细地核对详单上的电话号码，发现详单上的与“虚拟网”朋友中的通话，计费标准都是按每分钟 2 角收费的，你又仔细核对当时报送给移动公司的名单，发现这些号码全都准确地抄送给了移动公司。事实上，要是按“虚拟网”收费标准收费，移动公司整整多收了你一倍的费用。

实际情况是，由于移动公司后台工作人员的失误，未将你和你部分朋友的号码完全输入到“虚拟网”中，造成部分人员（大约一半）未正式加入“虚拟网”，于是造成了仍按每分钟 2 角钱收费的情况。于是你当即要求移动公司按照承诺的“话费误差，双倍返还”，或至少退还多收部分的费用。

1. 该情景刚出现的那一刻，您内心的真实感受是（请在您所选择答案的编号前打勾“√”）：

7	6	5	4	4	3	1
完全满意	满意	有点满意	不确定	有点不满意	不满意	完全不满意

2. 您是否亲身经历过类似的情景（请在您所选择答案的编号前打勾“√”）：

① 有过 ② 没有

3. 您目前选用下面哪一家移动通信服务商提供的服务，请在您所选择答案的编号前打勾“√”。(如有多种选择，请您选最常用的一家)。

① 中国移动 ② 中国联通 ③ 小灵通 ④ 其他

第一种补救措施：如果服务人员马上对该失误向您稍示歉意，且不退还多收部分的费用。请仔细阅读每一个句子，并在相应的数字上画一个圈。

7	6	5	4	4	3	1
完全同意	同意	有点同意	不确定	有点不同意	不同意	完全不同意

例题：我自信有能力完成各项工作任务。	7	6	5	4	3	2	①
请细心回答以下每一个问题，不要遗漏。							
1. 该公司管理制度处理服务失误有效率。	7	6	5	4	3	2	1
2. 我相信该公司有一系列公正的管理政策。	7	6	5	4	3	2	1

续表

3. 工作人员服的态度很谦逊。	7	6	5	4	3	2	1
4. 我会向他人说该公司的不是。	7	6	5	4	3	2	1
5. 该公司很在意没有为我准备我所需要的服务。	7	6	5	4	3	2	1
6. 这一补救结果是公平的。	7	6	5	4	3	2	1
7. 如果有人提起该公司，我会推荐。	7	6	5	4	3	2	1
8. 该公司的管理机制对于自己失误反应很迅速。	7	6	5	4	3	2	1
9. 该失误给我造成了不便，但该公司弥补了我的损失。	7	6	5	4	3	2	1
10. 工作人员与我沟通得很好。	7	6	5	4	3	2	1
11. 尽管出现这种失误，但该公司响应迅速。	7	6	5	4	3	2	1
12. 该公司给我弥补的结果超过了我所失去的。	7	6	5	4	3	2	1
13. 工作人员恰当地体谅我的难处。	7	6	5	4	3	2	1
14. 我以后会增加购买该公司产品的次数。	7	6	5	4	3	2	1
15. 工作人员并不努力帮我解决麻烦。	7	6	5	4	3	2	1
16. 补救结果并不能弥补它给我造成的损失。	7	6	5	4	3	2	1
17. 我认为接受这样的补救结果是不正确的。	7	6	5	4	3	2	1
18. 如果有别的选择，我也不会选择其他公司的产品。	7	6	5	4	3	2	1

下列表中的内容是针对服务商给您提供了第一种服务补救措施之后，您对该移动通信服务商的评价，请仔细阅读每一个句子，并在相应的数字上画一个圈

7	6	5	4	4	3	1
完全同意	同意	有点同意	不确定	有点不同意	不同意	完全不同意

例题：我自信有能力完成各项工作任务。	7	6	5	4	3	2	①
请细心回答以下每一个问题，不要遗漏。							
1. 对于该公司的服务，我感到很满意。	7	6	5	4	3	2	1
2. 这家公司很值得我和她保持关系。	7	6	5	4	3	2	1
3. 我很高兴选择了他们的产品。	7	6	5	4	3	2	1
4. 我会一直购买这家公司的产品。	7	6	5	4	3	2	1
5. 这家公司很值得信赖。	7	6	5	4	3	2	1

续表

6. 我很喜欢他们。	7	6	5	4	3	2	1
7. 我会很积极维持与这家公司的关系。	7	6	5	4	3	2	1
8. 这家公司会真诚关注我的需要。	7	6	5	4	3	2	1
9. 使用他们的产品总是很愉快。	7	6	5	4	3	2	1
10. 这家公司不会隐瞒我应该知道的信息。	7	6	5	4	3	2	1
11. 即使有其他的选择，我也不会选择其他公司。	7	6	5	4	3	2	1
12. 我认为该公司总能给我详尽的咨询。	7	6	5	4	3	2	1
13. 要是其他产品都像这公司的产品就好了。	7	6	5	4	3	2	1
14. 我会努力支持这家公司。	7	6	5	4	3	2	1
15. 我觉得这家公司很诚实、很实在。	7	6	5	4	3	2	1
16. 我想继续与这家公司保持关系。	7	6	5	4	3	2	1
17. 我相信这家公司会遵守对顾客的承诺。	7	6	5	4	3	2	1
18. 我是这家公司的忠实顾客。	7	6	5	4	3	2	1
19. 跟其他产品供应商比起来，我很满意我所选择的服务供应商。	7	6	5	4	3	2	1
20. 我对这家公司很有信心。	7	6	5	4	3	2	1
21. 这家公司总会优先考虑顾客的利益。	7	6	5	4	3	2	1
22. 我相信这家公司总会考虑顾客最佳利益。	7	6	5	4	3	2	1

第二种补救措施：如果该服务人员过了很久才对此失误向您稍示歉异，此外，同意双倍返还多收部分的费用，那么请您根据这种情景给下列内容打分。

7	6	5	4	4	3	1
完全同意	同意	有点同意	不确定	有点不同意	不同意	完全不同意

例题：我自信有能力完成各项工作任务。	7	6	5	4	3	2	①
请细心回答以下每一个问题，不要遗漏。							
1. 该公司管理制度处理服务失误有效率。	7	6	5	4	3	2	1
2. 我相信该公司有一系列公正的管理政策。	7	6	5	4	3	2	1
3. 工作人员服的态度很谦逊。	7	6	5	4	3	2	1

续表

4. 我会向他人说该公司的不是。	7	6	5	4	3	2	1
5. 该公司很在意没有为我准备我所需要的服务。	7	6	5	4	3	2	1
6. 这一补救结果是公平的。	7	6	5	4	3	2	1
7. 如果有人提起该公司，我会推荐。	7	6	5	4	3	2	1
8. 该公司的管理机制对于自己失误反应很迅速。	7	6	5	4	3	2	1
9. 该失误给我造成了不便，但该公司弥补了我的损失。	7	6	5	4	3	2	1
10. 工作人员与我沟通得很好。	7	6	5	4	3	2	1
11. 尽管出现这种失误，但该公司响应迅速。	7	6	5	4	3	2	1
12. 该公司给我弥补的结果超过了我所失去的。	7	6	5	4	3	2	1
13. 工作人员恰当地体谅我的难处。	7	6	5	4	3	2	1
14. 我以后会增加购买该公司产品的次数。	7	6	5	4	3	2	1
15. 工作人员并不努力帮我解决麻烦。	7	6	5	4	3	2	1
16. 补救结果并不能弥补它给我造成的损失。	7	6	5	4	3	2	1
17. 我认为接受这样的补救结果是不正确的。	7	6	5	4	3	2	1
18. 如果有别的选择，我也不会选择其他公司的产品。	7	6	5	4	3	2	1

下列表中的内容是服务商给您提供了第二种服务补救措施之后，您对该移动通信服务商的评价，请仔细阅读每一个句子，并在相应的数字上画一个圈。

7	6	5	4	4	3	1
完全同意	同意	有点同意	不确定	有点不同意	不同意	完全不同意

例题：我自信有能力完成各项工作任务。	7	6	5	4	3	2	①
请细心回答以下每一个问题，不要遗漏。							
1. 对于该公司的服务，我感到很满意。	7	6	5	4	3	2	1
2. 这家公司很值得我和她保持关系。	7	6	5	4	3	2	1
3. 我很高兴选择了他们的产品。	7	6	5	4	3	2	1
4. 我会一直购买这家公司的产品。	7	6	5	4	3	2	1
5. 这家公司很值得信赖。	7	6	5	4	3	2	1
6. 我很喜欢他们。	7	6	5	4	3	2	1

续表

7. 我会很积极维持与这家公司的关系。	7	6	5	4	3	2	1
8. 这家公司会真诚关注我的需要。	7	6	5	4	3	2	1
9. 使用他们的产品总是很愉快。	7	6	5	4	3	2	1
10. 这家公司不会隐瞒我应该知道的信息。	7	6	5	4	3	2	1
11. 即使有其他的选择，我也不会选择其他公司。	7	6	5	4	3	2	1
12. 我认为该公司总能给我详尽的咨询。	7	6	5	4	3	2	1
13. 要是其他产品都像这公司的产品就好了。	7	6	5	4	3	2	1
14. 我会努力支持这家公司。	7	6	5	4	3	2	1
15. 我觉得这家公司很诚实、很实在。	7	6	5	4	3	2	1
16. 我想继续与这家公司保持关系。	7	6	5	4	3	2	1
17. 我相信这家公司会遵守对顾客的承诺。	7	6	5	4	3	2	1
18. 我是这家公司的忠实顾客。	7	6	5	4	3	2	1
19. 跟其他产品供应商比起来，我很满意我所选择的服务供应商。	7	6	5	4	3	2	1
20. 我对这家公司很有信心。	7	6	5	4	3	2	1
21. 这家公司总会优先考虑顾客的利益。	7	6	5	4	3	2	1
22. 我相信这家公司总会考虑顾客最佳利益。	7	6	5	4	3	2	1

1. 请问您的性别：①男性　②女性

2. 请问您的年龄：① 18–25 岁　② 26–35 岁　③ 36–45 岁　④ 46–55 岁　⑤ 60 岁以上

3. 请问您的学历：①初中　②高中　③高职（中专）④大学（包括大专）⑤研究生及以上

4. 请问您的收入水平（年收入）：① 1 万元以下　② 1 万 –3 万元　③ 4 万 –6 万　④ 7 万 –9 万元　⑤ 10 万元以上